The Inner-Impulses and Gestures of Orchestral Conducting

The Psycho-Physical Function of Musical Leadership

THE INNER-IMPULSES AND GESTURES OF ORCHESTRAL CONDUCTING

The Psycho-Physical Function of Musical Leadership

Oleg Proskurnya

With Forewords by
Heather Buchman
and
Robert Tomaro

The Edwin Mellen Press
Lewiston•Queenston•Lampeter

Library of Congress Cataloging-in-Publication Data

Proskurnya, Oleg.
 The inner-impulses and gestures of orchestral conducting : the psycho-physical function of musical leadership / Oleg Proskurnya ; with forewords by Heather Buchman and Robert Tomaro.
    p. cm.
 Includes bibliographical references and index.
 ISBN-13: 978-0-7734-1509-6
 ISBN-10: 0-7734-1509-2
 1. Conducting. I. Title.
 MT85.P78 2011
 781.45--dc22
                         2011003964

hors série.

A CIP catalog record for this book is available from the British Library.

Front cover design by Алексей Бякин (Alexei Byakin)

Copyright © 2011 Oleg Proskurnya

All rights reserved. For information contact

<table><tr><td>The Edwin Mellen Press
Box 450
Lewiston, New York
USA 14092-0450</td><td>The Edwin Mellen Press
Box 67
Queenston, Ontario
CANADA L0S 1L0</td></tr></table>

The Edwin Mellen Press, Ltd.
Lampeter, Ceredigion, Wales
UNITED KINGDOM SA48 8LT

Printed in the United States of America

TABLE OF CONTENTS

Foreword I by Heather Buchman   i

Foreword II by Dr. Robert Tomaro   v

Preface   ix

Acknowledgements   xiii

Introduction   1

PART I. FROM ICTUS TO CONCEPTUAL MOTION

Chapter 1: Evolution   13

    Forming a Sovereignty   21

Chapter 2: Anatomy of the Strike   33

    Instrumental Response   33

    Time-lag   41

    Ictus and Click   54

    Instrumental Reflexes and Conducting   61

Chapter 3: The Art of Spirit ... 73

    Clichés and Imagination ... 73

    Action and Concept ... 85

PART II. DIMENSIONS OF CONDUCTING

Chapter 4: The Syntax and Semantics of Conducting ... 95

    The Power of Sound Governance ... 102
        Contour of Sound ... 102

    Semantics of Gesture ... 119

Chapter 5: Inner Mechanisms ... 129

    Inner and Outer:
        Fundamental Methodological Predicaments ... 132

    Conceptual Motions ... 142

    Inner Will ... 152

Chapter 6: Interactive Techniques ... 159

    Relaxation ... 161

    Incorporating Relaxation ... 169

Chapter 7: Milieu of Communication ... 173

Modification of the Beat	173
Emancipation of Metrical Schemes	178
Rounded Motion	184

The Zone of Communication	191
The Technique of Attention Gathering	191

The Communicative Position of the Arm	196

The Cycle of Interactions	200

Dimensions of Perception	205

PART III. METHODOLOGY

Chapter 8: Development of the Apparatus — 213

External Features of the Apparatus	215
Body Posture	217
Primary Arm Position	223
Down-beat Position	225
The Plane of Conducting	229
Modification of the Wrist Strike	232

Chapter 9: The Preparatory Motion-Impulse — 235

The Preparatory Upbeat-Impulse	237
Double- and Triple-Meter	
Preparatory Motions/Upbeats	239
Double-Meter Motion	240
One-Pattern Triple-Meter Motion	243
Combination of Double- and Triple-Meter Motions	249
Beat Connection (Intermediary Upbeat)	252
Beats' Connection throughout Schemes in	
Various Dimensions	261

Chapter 10: The Upbeat as a Conceptual Action — 269

Establishing a Sense of the
  Vicinity (Contour) of Sound — 270
Fusing the Upbeat and the Contour of Sound — 274
Intermediary Upbeats and the Contour of Sound — 275

Chapter 11: Types of Upbeats — 279

Suspended Mode — 279
Converted Mode — 286
Converted Suspended Mode — 288

Rebound — 296

Pendulum — 305

Chapter 12: Active Muscular Relaxation — 311

Breath Control, Active Muscular
  Relaxation and the Contour of Sound — 317

Chapter 13: Inner Techniques — 325

Inner Impulse — 326
Inner Vocalization (Auditory Differentiation) — 331
Anticipation of Musical Texture — 332

Multi-leveled Manifestation of the Arms — 336

The Method of Juxtaposition and Comparison — 338

Chapter 14: Baton — 343

Afterword	355
Translated Excerpts	361
Bibliography	371
Index	389

FOREWORD   I

I was first drawn to explore the St. Petersburg style of conducting in 2007 by the suggestions of three emerging conductors I met whose technique and musicianship I admired. Remarkably, all of them had taken conducting workshops with Dr. Proskurnya and his colleagues, former students of Ilya Musin. I was frustrated by the difficulty of finding the same level of musicality and mastery in conducting that had come relatively easily to me as an instrumentalist. From the start of this new chapter in my conducting studies it was clear that this approach had much to offer – a more subtle and refined approach to being expressive and clear in my conducting. It also posed a choice to me, as it does to everyone who encounters it having previously learned a different conducting style, whether I was willing to reconsider some basic ideas about how orchestral conducting is done, and to accept the implications of new ideas.

A conductor's basic understanding of the dynamics behind conducting, of how conductors and orchestral players communicate, will influence every gesture that you make on the podium. It is at this level that Dr. Proskurnya's analysis of the task of conducting begins. From a sophisticated understanding of these dynamics an entire technical approach emerges organically and logically.

With respect to Russian traditions of musical training in general, one thing that strikes a musician not raised in this tradition is that the Russian approach to musical training (whether in conducting, violin playing, or even for that matter ballet) is intensely rigorous and demanding, both physically and mentally. It draws on a highly sophisticated understanding of muscular anatomy and demands an extremely highly developed level of body awareness. It's also grounded in the understanding that musical sound originates in the mind, and that the gestural vocabulary and grammar of conducting flow directly from one's mental conception of the sound.

What distinguishes Dr. Proskurnya's description of conducting methodology is his immersion in the principles of physiology and psychology as they pertain to conducting, as well as his skill in bridging the gap between simply telling the student what to do and being able to explain exactly how to go about doing it, which is much harder. Addressing muscular structure and function and describing how these work in conducting technique is for many conductors a most direct and effective path to take one's conducting to a new musical level.

As reflected in this book, Dr. Proskurnya's teaching is especially resourceful in helping students experience certain physical sensations which are essential to this approach to conducting: "touching the sound," "taking the sound from below," and controlling the rebound motion which causes problems for so many conductors. He describes a wide range of gestural vocabulary to *evoke* or pull sound from the musicians – leading them, rather than playing the orchestra like a huge impersonal instrument. And it is vital to understand the psychological-physical theoretical framework in which Dr. Proskurnya positions the technique. This way of leading (being ahead of) the orchestra is like continually swimming upstream; to stay in front you must apply a continuous effort of proactive musical will against the current, so to speak.

This approach expands the physical space in which we conduct to three dimensions, rather than a flat two-dimensional plane. In this space the conductor can make contact with and "sculpt" the sound, initially with just hands and eventually adding the stick. This has greatly helped me, a wind player, to connect more effectively and expressively with the horizontal bowing of the string sections. It has also added greatly to my understanding of how to be simultaneously clear and expressive in initiating the sound for wind players by guiding the dynamic flow of their breath. Another revelation (particularly for someone coming from a wind instrument background) is that breathing in conducting is not literal, but energetic. It does take some time for orchestral musicians unaccustomed to playing behind the beat to adapt to this technique. But once they do adjust, the leading relationship between conductor and musicians becomes infinitely more comfortable.

Fundamentally this approach to conducting traces a path around and beyond certain technical barriers to the free expression of musical ideas. In outlining an approach which evokes sound and dynamic energy in a natural, unforced manner, Dr. Proskurnya points toward a higher level of gestural communication and of continuous feedback and adjustment which, together with refining one's musical concept to the highest degree, constitute great musical leadership.

Heather R. Buchman

Associate Professor,

Director of Hamilton College Orchestra

Clinton, NY

FOREWORD II

It is rare, in the world of classical music performance practice, for an entirely new approach to appear, one that posits a solution to a problem that has plagued a particular discipline since its inception two hundred years ago. It would be as if one claims to have invented a way of playing the violin with a bow that never required the player to shift from down to up, or the revelation of a vocal technique that expanded the soprano range by an additional octave. Are these analogies outrageous, reckless? Are we about to be assaulted by an unsupportable theory? This writer thinks not. We have something genuinely new here, something worth looking into.

In *The Inner-Impulses and Gestures of Orchestral Conducting*, Conductor, Violinist, and Professor Oleg A. Proskurnya codifies not only a new technique of the conductor's art, but an entirely new system that seeks to supplant the current approach to the art of the podium.

First, he identifies the problem inherent in the accepted technique: It is a remnant of the "battuta" approach from the eighteenth century, handed down from a time when ensembles grew so large and scores so complex that leading the orchestra from the keyboard or the concertmaster's desk became first unwieldy, then impossible, so the marking of passing time in tempo began to be beaten out, physically, in performance.

The current down-up striking motion of the conductor with his/her baton evolved from early practitioners like Lully, pounding out quarter notes on the stage floor with staves, evoking scenes echoing back to the rowing decks of Roman Triremes, with oar strokes beaten out upon drums, replete, as you may imagine, with the unfortunate eventual psychological consequences on all assembled under such tutelage. Years later, it was discovered that the beating of time, the "battuta," could be mimed silently in the air by waving some kind of stick and then, at last, the pounding stopped at symphonic performances. But the legacy of the pounding remains in a vestigial, flawed idea. It is this: directing a large group of musicians to play simultaneously at a moving point in time by describing a downbeat in that time as it passes ignores the physical fact that, after the conductor has given the beat, the moment he/she wishes to evoke is in the past and the group is always going to be "late", that is, struggling to catch up to a point in time that is gone before their instruments can speak.

The inherent failing embedded in this system has, heretofore, been compensated for and glossed over by a hash of conducting tips, addendums and theories or, more commonly, just simply ignored. "Just do what you need to do to play on my beat!" became the battle cry of the irate conductor, and orchestras ever since have been huffing and puffing to accommodate the maestro as he/she revs up the musical apparatus to ramming speed!

Maestro Proskurnya's book posits a world of thought that examines the problem of directing musicians in time and brings to bear solutions born of new advances in science and art that combine to form an amalgam, a solution that addresses what actually occurs when the musician attempts to perform in a large ensemble. It incorporates disciplines such as biomechanics, kinetics, physics, and psycholinguistics in the creation of a new technique culled and distilled, primarily, from the work of the great Russian conducting pedagogues Ilya Musin and Nicolai Malko.

It supplants "beating" with an elegant system of motion arising from the conductor's understanding of his own psyche and spiritual inspiration as it naturally relates to the music and to the musicians, thus eliciting an instinctive and authentic response from the ensemble. The Proskurnya approach describes a system of conductor's motions that represent to the musician both the character of the music and the technical requirements needed to produce it a moment <u>before</u> it is meant to sound in the air. Instead of pounding the players over the head with the temporal demands of a "traffic cop", his approach has the salutary effect of drawing the music out of the group from the reservoir of its own collective intuition.

The Inner-Impulses and Gestures of Orchestral Conducting is fresh and free of the encrusted dogma from the past. Instead of adding band-aids to an essentially flawed premise, it suggests a new start, supported by up-to-date advances in important and analogous fields of study in the area of motion connected to emotion.

Robert Tomaro, Ph. D.

Music Director and Conductor,

Beloit Janesville Symphony Orchestra

Professor of Music, Beloit College

PREFACE

My personal experiences as an orchestral musician and conductor stimulated my interest in advanced conducting techniques. While analyzing observations being made during my own teaching and performing, I noticed that current instrumental methods are mainly reliable practical guides to performing techniques. However, there are a limited number of acceptable methods available for conducting students. While the instrumental performance methods have been supported and sustained by successful practice, the most widespread conducting methods only illustrate schematically the external (visual) tools of conducting without exploring the inner psycho-physical functions of musical leadership (this imbalance was also mentioned by Nikolai Malko in *Osnovi Techniki Dirijirovaniya* [The Fundamental Techniques of Conducting], 12, and George Erzhemsky in *Psychological Paradoxes of Conducting, Theory and Practice of the Profession*, 9-17).

Throughout various professional engagements (workshops,

conferences or personal acquaintance) I have had numerous conversations with colleagues who have established their careers by practicing the generally accepted 'traditional' conducting methods, and I found that mostly they defend their conducting techniques with such 'valuable' arguments as: "it should be done this way because I believe that is the only way it should be done," or, "I am doing this because I've been taught this way by ..." - and then the name of a renowned artist follows.

The idea for the title of this manuscript came after an emotional discussion with an older colleague (a professor of conducting at a major university) who wondered why I was trying to "destroy the whole well-established system." He suggested that in modern times "everything is known about conducting."

This book is not for those who seek another set of numerous graphics and schemes or detailed instruction of score study and analysis. Nor is it for those who are in favor of a pictorial (to impress the audience) or "traffic-control" style of conducting. The principal goal of this book is to trace the history of the conductor's professional communicative tool - explicit (gestures) and implicit (inner impulses) - through major transformations as shaped by discoveries in psychology, psychophysiology, neuroscience, psycholinguistics, and biomechanics.

The book does not intend to outline or resolve all methodological or ideological conflicts present in modern conducting. Rather it will strive to acknowledge the principal existing predicaments through the recognition of the inner (mental) aspects of conducting as a specific form of non-verbal intercommunication (the terminology is suggested by Professor George Erzhemsky) and the intrusion of primary reflexes into conducting as a professional practice. This book seeks to oppose the artificial approaches in modern conducting methodologies: "against this inhuman use of human beings" (Norbert Wiener, *The Human Use of Human Beings*, 16).

In this book one can find a method for obtaining a reliable and flexible conducting technique (in the *Methodology* part, which includes exercises on inner and external features of the conducting apparatus). This apparatus incorporates techniques that are based upon the principals of communication and have a firmly established sense of connection with the orchestral sound.

The many quotes in this book come from the methodological texts of Professor Ilia Musin and Professor George Erzhemsky. Access to these texts is limited, especially in English-speaking countries; therefore I am presenting some of them here, for the first time.

ACKNOWLEDGEMENTS

I would like to express my great appreciation to my teachers, Professor Ilia Alexandrovich Musin and Professor George L'vovich Erzhemsky. I have been blessed by many in my life. There are a few people, though, to whom I would like to express my special appreciation for their help working on this book: Leah Abel; Teresa Colyer; Michael Hemphill, MD; Ian Nie, PhD; Jennifer Ottervik; and Scott Woodard.

INTRODUCTION

The art of orchestral conducting has always been accompanied by practical uncertainties and artistic controversies. Despite these conflicts, symphonic conducting remains one of the most distinguished achievements of humankind. As Nikolai Malko[1] has stated in his book *The Conductor and His Baton, The Fundamentals of the Techniques of Conducting*:

---

[1] Malko, Nikolai (Nicolai) Andreyevich (1883-1961). American conductor of Russian birth. A pupil of Rimsky-Korsakov, Lyadov, Glazunov and Nikolay Tcherepnin at the St. Petersburg Conservatory, he also studied with Felix Mottl in Munich. Beginning as a conductor of ballet and opera at St. Petersburg in 1908, he became a leading musical figure of the early Soviet regime, conducting extensively and holding a professorship at the Moscow Conservatory (1918-25) and at the Leningrad Conservatory (1925-9). Stanley Sadie, ed. *New Grove Dictionary of Music and Musicians*, 2nd ed. (London: Macmillan Publishers Limited, 2001), vol. 15, 705-6.

> *Conducting is the most complicated and the most difficult form of musical performance. One psychologist has in his lectures referred to conducting as the most complicated of psycho-physical activities, not only in music but in life in general. Be that as it may, conducting has been formulated upon a basis of theoretical analysis less than any other musical activity.*[2]

The craft of conducting, more than other performing activities, suffers from serious discrepancies between theory and practice.

> *Still, despite the rapt and constant attention, the process of mutual interaction of conductor and orchestra has, up to present, continued to remain "one of the vaguest and least understood fields of the musical art." . . . It is no secret that the basic mechanisms of conducting have up to present, been defined by many pedagogues and practical experience in form of a kind of "black box," that cybernetic analogue of the Kantian "Ding an sich."*[3]

The difficulties in conducting are rooted in the differences - one might say dissimilarities - between the visible, evident, physical action and the subconscious activating thought processes behind the action. Likewise, difficulties arise

---

[2] Nicolai Malko, *The Conductor and His Baton: The Fundamentals of the Technic of Conducting* (Copenhagen: Wilhelm Hansen, 1950), 11.

[3] George L. Erzhemsky, *Psychological Paradoxes of Conducting, Theory and Practice of the Profession*, trans. Jeffrey Skinner (St.Petersburg: Publishing House Dean+Adia-M, 1998), 9-10.

between the observer's individual musical experiences and the conductor's physical expression of them.

This book will analyze the phenomenon of the temporal interval (or time-lag) between a conductor's action and appearance of the sound, which, surprisingly, is either ignored or only vaguely recognized by the generally accepted conducting methods, and which in fact should be a cornerstone of the modern conducting routine.

The conductor's craft is one of communication and human interaction. However, in modern times the widely accepted methodological and pedagogical formulas are based on artificial and enforced notions of "beating time" – executing a musical passage "on the beat" – that were acquired and preserved as a part of the standard orchestral aesthetic; e.g., conducting "on the beat" or "on the strike" (as an inherited silent rudiment of the audible time-beating). Two centuries of conducting revealed that this style is subject to a variety of significant practical and artistic shortcomings.[4]

During rehearsal, the insistent demand to match the occurrence of the sound with the lowest point of the beat-strike (or ictus) is still common for conductors in our time.

---

[4] These become particularly obvious throughout the twentieth century with the increasing quality of symphony orchestras, which is facilitated by the musicians' early acquaintance with the orchestral repertoire since youth. This is made possible through professional academic training in ensemble and orchestral performing techniques - in contrast with sporadic or even nonexistent specific practical orchestral training in previous centuries.

However, in reality this may or may not occur even at the start of play, considering the mode of the orchestra's anticipation of the strike and denoting that the orchestra performs ahead of the conductor's actions. This defeats the purpose of the conductor! This reality creates a permanent inner discomfort and obliges musicians to switch their attentions to the orchestra's hidden leaders – the concertmaster, section principal or soloist(s). As a result, the *real* outcome of the musician's inner discomfort and stress is heard in a rigid, harsh and unbalanced sound.

Some conductors of the past intuitively noted such shortcomings in an attempt to overcome the limitations of striking "on the beat":

> *Arthur Nikish*[5] *... was conducting always before the time. That was the first example of what happened later with Furtwängler, who gave the beat and the moment after came the playing.*[6]

Through the history and up to the modern times, many conductors and musicians alike have felt tension between what the conductor wants to hear, and what the musicians actually generate. This tension indicates the inner fundamental

---

[5] Arthur Nikish (1855-1922). Famous Austrian conductor of Moravian and Hungarian descent. Nicolas Slonimsky, ed. *Baker's Biographical Dictionary of Musicians*, 8th ed. (New York: Schirmer Books, 1992), 1308.

[6] Robert Chesterman,, ed. *Conversations with conductors. Ernest Ansermet* (London: Robson Ltd., 1977), 78.

controversy and contradiction between conducting and music making. Today, all manually guided ensembles (professional, semi-professional, and even non-professional) perform more or less after the beat-strike in order to synchronize and follow the conductor's motions.[7]

The phenomenon of the temporal interval (time-lag) between the conductor's action and the occurrence of sound is due to the existence of the period of innate human reaction to visual and audible stimuli.[8] This reaction is required for the assessment of the motion originated, in this case, by the conductor, which leads to the collective execution of an ensemble's response. The presence of the temporal interval suggests the necessity of adjusting the conducting methodology and reveals conducting as a specific conceptual *quasi-linguistic*[9] action, rather than as a predominantly physical act.

> ***Physical energy is anti-musical:*** *music, the art of the spirit and spiritual tensions, cannot endure physical energy as an end in itself.*[10]

---

[7] Some well-known orchestras have a long tradition of considerable time-lag before the sound appears (e.g., the Berlin Philharmonic and St. Petersburg Philharmonic Symphony Orchestras).

[8] *Stimulus*, pl. *stimuli*: 1. A stimulant. 2. That which can elicit or evoke action (response) in a muscle, nerve, gland or other excitable tissue ... *Stedman's Medical Dictionary*, 28th edition, Illustrated in Color (Baltimore: Lippincott Williams & Wilkins, 2006), 1838.

[9] This term suggested by George Erzhemsky.

[10] Hermann Scherchen, *Handbook of Conducting* (London: Oxford University Press, 1935), 24. (Emphasis added)

Nevertheless, the existence of such a seemingly obvious phenomenon as a time interval (or temporal lag) is still widely unacknowledged by the adherents of the enforced tradition. Such controversies have arisen due to a lack of comprehension of the nature of the conducting practice as an interactive process.

Following the temporal, the inseparable nature of the conductor's internal and external techniques will be discussed. This book will also examine the interference of *conditioned*[11] *reflexes*[12] on the practice of orchestral conducting while seeking to discover hidden opportunities in the relationships of gesture and sound.

> *Scientists now avidly pursue ties between brain activity and physical manifestations. ... My colleagues thought I was bizarre for suggesting such a thing because we had been taught that the mind and the body were inexorably separate, as had been postulated by Rene Descartes, the seventeenth-century mathematician. Following Cartesian thinking, Western science never*

---

[11] Condition: To train a person or animal to respond in a predictable way to a stimulus. *Taber's Medical Dictionary*, Thomas L. Clayton, ed. (Philadelphia: Davis Company, 1989), 400.

[12] Reflex: [L. *reflexus*, bend back] an involuntary response to a stimulus; a reflex action. Reflexes are specific and predictable and are usually purposeful and adaptive. They depend upon an intact neural pathway between point of stimulation and responding organ (muscle or gland). Ibid, 1572.

questioned this model.[13]

The traditional (generally accepted) methodology of conducting, centered on the mechanical principles and fragmented theories that prevailed during the nineteenth and twentieth centuries, is currently in an unsatisfactory stance, largely due to long-standing systematic predicaments fueled by an incomprehension of the intangible mechanisms of conducting, as well as stagnation in the development of new communicative tools. This crisis[14] has revealed the urgent necessity of building new principles that will provide a framework for designing innovative approaches to practical conducting methods. Such a large-scale philosophical shift will require a reconsideration of the most basic aspects of the conductor's art, an analysis of its psychosomatic contents, and a critical development of accumulated practical experience. It will further require "the simultaneous usage of theoretical data obtained in related fields of modern science."[15]

---

[13] Herbert Benson, *The Relaxation Response*, x-xiv.

[14] It is important to mention here that in the modern times, there are many factors which were not issues over a hundred or even fifty years ago. Among them are burdensome economic pressures on the orchestral business (which is dictated by a high minimal hourly pay for musicians, monitored by the musicians' union), the resultant decreased number of rehearsals, and limited podium time (10-15 minutes at the most) for a conductor's appearance as a candidate during professional auditions.

[15] Erzhemsky, 9.

Music-making requires expression, not pressure.[16]

This suggests that one must develop a communicative (non-forcible) technique in the art of conducting. However, it is necessary to be aware that recommended technical approaches are not intended to be tied only to certain musical material. As was noted by Nikolai Malko, "a conductor's gestures, even the most 'masterly' ones, taken separately have no practical significance."[17]

In conducting, no techniques, approaches or modes taken individually without reference to the musical context have meaning. The direct connection between illustrative demonstrations of arm movements and manifestations of the conductor's expressive inner artistic intentions is rather uncertain. What is important is the interconnection of all the expressive elements possessed by the conductor, as well as of certain musical occurrences which will condition one's "gesture perception in certain ways or meanings."[18]

---

[16] Bruno Walter, *Of Music and Music-Making* (New York: W. W. Norton & Company Inc., 1961), 128. (Emphasis added)

[17] Nikolai Malko, *Osnovy Tekhniki Dirijirovaniya* [Fundamentals of the Techniques of Conducting], quoted in Erzemsky, *Psychological Paradoxes of Conducting*, 117.

[18] Ilia Musin, *Tehnika Dirijirovaniya* [The Technique of Conducting] (St. Petersburg: Dean-Adia-M, 1995), 210.

This manuscript is meant to provide general information on the interactive methodology of conducting. For further assistance in obtaining the practical knowledge of such techniques, interested colleagues are invited to participate in workshops taught by Professor Musin's[19] former students. Information on events and faculty members can be found at: www.musinconducting.org and www.advancedconducting.spb.ru.

---

[19] Musin, Ilya [Ilia] (Aleksandrovich) (1903-1999). Russian conductor and pedagogue ... tutored by Nicolai Malko. ... Although praised for innovations in conducting technique, Musin considered himself tied to 19th-century Russian musical principles. By all account, he was a rigorous but beloved teacher with enormous respect for music and its inherent integrity. Sadie, *New Grove*, 2nd ed., (2001), vol. 17, 541.

PART I

FROM ICTUS

TO

CONCEPTUAL MOTION

1

EVOLUTION

Modern conducting as an independent discipline evolved from relationships within instrumental ensembles, a process that began with the earliest known musical cultures.

Musical instruments have been around ever since man walked out of cave and blew down an animal bone. Since then literally thousands have been created.[20]

Musical instruments served human emotional, cultural, and

---

[20] Jan Younghusband, *Orchestra! Foreword by Sir Georg Solti and Dudley Moore* (North Pomfret, Vermont: Trafalgar Square Publishing, 1991), 3.

social needs in primeval societies, and despite being created as an imitation of natural sounds. Musical instruments began to be developed with complex nuances and different "voices." With the establishment of musical ensembles, instrumental virtuosity began to enrich the art of musical performance. Documentation of virtuosic instrumentalists and singers may be found in the earliest sacred and secular documents. Iconographic evidence testifies amply to the importance of skillful players, vocalists, and ensembles in the cultural life of the Ancient World.[21]

> *Instrumental ensemble's concerts date back to 6 BC in Babylon, when Nebuchadnezzar's orchestra was made up of horns, trumpets, pipes, lyres, harps and percussion.*[22]

In comparison with the long history of instrumental performance practice, the existence of ensemble or orchestral conducting as an independent professional activity is a much more recent phenomenon. Since the time of its earliest iconographic documentation (c. 1500 B.C.), the characteristics of musical leadership have been influenced by the evolution of rhythm and improvements in instrumental manufacturing (with consequent advancements in skills of performance).[23] Orchestral conducting as a modern independent discipline has existed for fewer than two hundred years: "Conducting, as we

---

[21] Sadie, *New Grove* (1980), vol. 13, s. v. "Orchestra," by Jack Westrup and Neal Zaslaw, 679.

[22] Younghusband, 38.

[23] Elliot W. Galkin, *A History of Orchestral Conducting in Theory and Practice* (New York: Pendragon Press Stuyvesant, 1988), 3.

understand it in our days, is a relatively young phenomenon. It still has many unstable and indefinite notions."[24]

The symphony orchestra is certainly one of the noblest creations of Western civilization. The term "symphony" comes from the Ancient Greek word meaning "sounding together." The word "orchestra" has origins in the theatrical language of ancient Greece, and this term was used to designate the semicircular space in front of the stage where the chorus sang and danced. In Roman theaters, this place was reserved for the seats of senators. Later, the word was applied to the stage itself. From the ancient theaters of Greece and Rome, we can find the earliest evidence of the leading of musical ensembles in ancient theatrical performances: "In ancient Greece the rhythm both of choral and of instrumental music was marked by stamping on the ground with the right foot, to which was attached a piece of iron."[25]

By the end of the Renaissance, the term "orchestra" was used to describe a wide variety of instrumental ensembles, ranging from musical groups associated with non-Western musical cultures to those identified with the noble courts of Europe (the West in particular). In any event, definitions of the term "orchestra" from this time forward generally began with a musical ensemble based around an organized body of bowed strings, to which a certain number of wind and percussion instruments may have been added.

---

[24] Malko, *Osnovi Tehniki Dirijirovaniya* [The Fundamentals of the Technic of Conducting] (Moscow: Muzgiz, 1965), 19.

[25] Sadie, *New Grove* (1980), s.v. "Conducting," by Jack Westrup, 641.

This confluence of developments is particularly relevant to the history of orchestral conducting. Consequent advancements of skills in instrumental performance, especially during the early Baroque era when the first scores with specific instrumentation were published, increased the demands placed on the musical leader. Before the Classical period, the role of the conductor, as an artistic orchestral leader as we know it today, was not necessary. Music was scored for a small number of players, and the simplicity of the orchestration allowed musicians to hear one another easily.

During the latter part of the seventeenth and the first years of the eighteenth centuries, many European countries maintained ensembles that consisted of strings, oboes, bassoons, and continuo. Some ensembles also included a variety of wind instruments and were often associated with court military regiments that featured a large number of trumpets and timpani. Throughout the eighteenth century, flutes, horns, and clarinets were added to the ensemble of four-part strings, oboes, and bassoons. Harmonic support for the orchestra was provided by harpsichord or harp (or organ in church). Despite the orchestra's development during this time, conducting technique was based upon audible beating to indicate rhythms and tempos were in wide practice. "Beating time with the hand, with a rolled-up scroll of music paper, or with a short, thick baton"[26] were common methods not only for performances of military music played by marching bands but also in the opera houses and churches of Europe:

---

[26] John Spitzer and Neal Zaslaw, *The Birth of the Orchestra* (New York: Oxford University Press, 2004), 387.

> *A later example of audible time-beating is the practice at the Paris Opera in the 17th and 18th centuries . . . the conductor originally sat on the stage and beat time on a table. Later he moved to the orchestra and hit the floor with a long stick, which made just as much noise . . . this was also the practice in London six or seven years ago . . . This practice was unknown in Italy; but it was not uncommon there, even in the early years of the 19th century, for the principal violinist to stamp his feet on the ground or strike his music-stand with his bow. Foot-stamping was still practiced in German churches at the end of the 17th century . . . None of these methods can properly be called conducting.*[27]

Conducting from the continuo, where the figured bass was realized, was often done with the composer at the keyboard.

> *In Italian opera, the composer was expected to preside over the first three performances from the first harpsichord, after which the principal first violinist was in charge. In concerts, the keyboard player was customarily subordinate to the principal first violin.*[28]

When the practice of writing figured bass began to decline, the role of orchestra leader was transferred to the first violinist, or *Konzertmeister*:

---

[27] *New Grove* (1980), vol. 4, s. v. "Conducting," by Jack Westrup, 641.

[28] Ibid, vol. 13, s. v. "Orchestra," 681.

> *Handel directed his oratorios from the harpsichord or organ . . . Haydn 'presided at the pianoforte' when his symphonies were performed in London.*[29]

> *Haydn would sit at the piano to conduct his London Symphonies (1794) – in the same position in front of the orchestra as the musical director using a harpsichord had occupied. ... Haydn ... shared the responsibility for direction with Salomon,*[30] *who also 'led' from the first violin. Mozart also conducted some of his operas seated at a keyboard. Johann Stamitz*[31] *in Mannheim,*[32] *on the other hand, led from the violin, and is reported to have controlled his orchestra with 'no more than a nod of his head and the movement of his*

---

[29] *New Grove* (1980), s. v. "Orchestra," 681.

[30] Salomon, Johann Peter (1745-1815). German violinist, impresario and composer, later resident of England. *New Grove Dictionary*, 2nd. ed. (2001), vol. 22, 172-3.

[31] Stamitz, Johann (Wenzel Anton) (1717- 1757). Composer, violinist and teacher. He ranks among the most important early Classical symphonists and was influential in making court of the Elector Palatine at Mannheim a leading centre of orchestral performance and composition. *New Grove* (2001), vol. 24, 264-8.

[32] Mannheim, a town in Western Germany, famous in the mid of 18th century for its orchestra. The reputation of this ensemble was due to its excellent discipline, the individual skill of its players and lively style of performance which included boldly contracted dynamics, a calculated use of crescendo and diminuendo, and early use of the clarinet as an orchestral instrument. *Collins Encyclopedia of Music*, s. v. "Mannheim," by Sir Jack Westrup and F. Ll. Harrison (London: Chancellor Press, 1984), 340.

bow.'[33]

Conducting (without playing an instrument) was considered necessary only in choral music (*chironomy*[34]), particularly if the performers were widely dispersed. The time-beating, which had a leading significance in the "bandmaster" system of managing an orchestra, lost its original dominant position and turned into a background activity. The increased freedom of interpretation was added to the responsibilities of the orchestral leader and required far more adequate direction.

During the second half of the eighteenth and early part of the nineteenth centuries, the leading tasks were dispersed among the most respected and experienced orchestral musicians. The managerial duties were divided between *Kapellmeister* (usually a harpsichord player) and an orchestra's first violinist, the *Konzertmeister*. Throughout performances, these two musicians transferred their leading functions from one to another: "In this period the orchestra was not yet the conductor's partner in the creative act. For the most part it was defined as, so to say, a "'living instrument' on which, in analogy with the usual instrument, the conductor 'played,' beating time."[35] All preparations for a performance—the arrangement of rehearsals, the choice of the compositions for the performance, the seating arrangement of the orchestra, and the placement and number of

---

[33] Younghusband, 172.

[34] James Jordan, *Evoking Sound. Fundamentals of Choral Conducting and Rehearsing* (Chicago: GIA Publications: Inc., 1996), 17.

[35] Erzhemsky, 160.

performers for the parts were the duties of the *Musikdirektor*.[36] In the current age, such a position would combine the duties of the orchestra's general manager, operational manager, personnel manager, and the modern music director.

Rapid developments brought on by the French Revolution and the subsequent Napoleonic Wars brought about significant changes to the social and cultural landscapes of Europe. The swift democratization of public access to musical events in general and orchestral performances in particular allowed further development of the orchestra as an autonomous public and communal institution.

> *As entertainment became public, composers became entrepreneurs, presenting public concerts for financial gain. Professional concerts took hold very swiftly from 1750 and the following 150 years saw the birth of many of the leading orchestras of today.*[37]

The profound social transformations during the eighteenth century, combined with contemporary musical developments, provided a foundation for the evolution of the orchestral leader as an independent artistic and social figure.

---

[36] Galkin, 209-213.

[37] Younghusband, 39-40.

FORMING A SOVEREIGNTY

By the end of the eighteenth century, large European instrumental ensembles depended upon a tripartite hierarchy for the supervision of musical and administrative orchestral activities (*Kapellmeister*, *Konzertmeister* and *Musikdirektor*). Originally, the *Kapellmeister*'s and *Konzertmeister*'s responsibilities included providing cues at the beginning of the piece with indications for the correct tempo, meter, and dynamics. Gradually this list of duties was expanded to include correcting mistakes in pitch and intonation, consistency of phrasing, and orchestral balance. Eventually the growing complexity of the orchestra's artistic tasks consolidated the spread-out duties of the orchestra leaders to a one-person competency:

> *From the Classical period on, there was a rapid growth and expansion of the orchestra. First auxiliary instruments were added to increase the range of the wind choir (such as piccolo, contrabassoon, and English horn) and other instruments were brought into the symphony orchestra from the opera orchestra*

(trombones, harps, and the larger percussion battery).[38]

The size of the orchestras grew, due to the work of composers in Mannheim, Paris and Vienna.

> *From the time of Mozart onwards, music took on more complex construction, requiring careful interpretation of dynamic markings, with each instrumental section having more solo music to play. The necessitated guidance from someone standing independently of the orchestra to achieve and keep the correct balance. As the size of the orchestra increased it became unrealistic to try to play an instrument and control up to seventy people at the same time.*[39]

By the end of the eighteenth century, new orchestral instruments (clarinet, tuba, percussion: triangle, side drum, bass drum, and piano [instead of harpsichord]) and new designs for old ones (flute, oboe, bassoon, horn, Tourte-style[40] bow for violin and viola, etc.) were introduced, and the balances among instruments changed.[41] The new rhythmic patterns and the

---

[38] Samuel Adler, *The Study of Orchestration*, 2nd ed. (New York: W. W. Norton and Company, 1989), 5.

[39] Younghusband, 192.

[40] François Xavier Tourte (1747-1835). French bow-maker, in cooperation with Italian violinist Giovanni Battista Viotti made a significant contribution to the development of the modern bow for string instruments. *New Grove*, 101-2.

[41] Spitzer and Zaslaw, 309-337.

complex harmonic innovations that characterized the orchestral compositions of Mozart, Beethoven, and composers of the early Romantic period, as well as the increased number and diversity of the instruments in the orchestra, made directing from the first violin desk or from behind a keyboard an unsatisfactory solution.

> *It became fashionable to give concerts with huge orchestras. In 1800 an orchestra totaling forty players would have been normal. But, the string alone would number that, having become more numerous to keep pace with the burgeoning woodwind and brass. These changes meant that the orchestra could regularly number a hundred players, although the concept of the four basic sections continued – strings, woodwind, brass and percussion.[42]*

At the beginning of the nineteenth century, Louis (Ludwig) Spohr was among those musical leaders who revolutionized the practice of conducting.

> *Louis Spohr, the German violinist-conductor came to London to play with the Philharmonic Orchestra. The regular pianist-conductor offered Spohr his place at the keyboard, but Spohr declined, and instead stood in front of the orchestra as conductors do*

---

[42] Younghusband, 84.

now.[43]

There is evidence that Spohr introduced the baton during a concert at Hamburg in 1817 (as did Carl Maria von Weber elsewhere[44]). In his autobiography he paid a tribute to the baton as a perfect "time-giver."[45] Strongly opposed to audible time-beating with a stick against a conductor's stand, Spohr instead suggested a manner of "silent" striking along an imaginary plane and reorganized the orchestra seating in a manner that allowed string players to have a better ensemble connection with the woodwinds and brass:

> *Spohr was influential in introducing the baton all over Europe. . . . One of the major things noticed about this new method was that it seemed to make conducting easier; and another aspect, about which contemporaries marveled, was that it was silent. Conducting without noise! No rapping, stamping, clapping!*[46]

Spohr's innovative silent manner, however, aroused antagonism at first from some orchestral players, who preferred to be led by the concertmaster. Others favored his manner because it was

---

[43] Ibid, 192.

[44] Younghusband, 192.

[45] Louis Spohr, *Autobiography*, 2 vols. (New York: DaCapo Press, 1969), 2: 81-2.

[46] Harold C. Schonberg, *The Great Conductor* (New York: Simon and Schuster, 1967), 84.

silent, unlike that of the stick-wielding conductors, who accompanied the music with thumping on the floor. It is difficult to overestimate the significance of such silent changes for the evolution of modern conducting. Spohr's victory over the old chopping (stomping) tradition opened new horizons for the further development of the profession and provided the basis for new progressive principles of conducting. Thus Spohr, having eliminated audible beating, preserved its mechanical function and the striking character of time-beating practice. This combination allowed the standard rhythmic schemes to remain tightly connected to the manual management of the orchestra, and the consolidation of duties led to a sharp contradiction between the external traditional system of gestures and the internal, non-formal, and expressive content of the music. This basic internal conflict carried on through the nineteenth and twentieth centuries in the form of contradictory practical approaches and methodological formulas.

Orchestral conducting, as an independent art, entered a new phase with Hector Berlioz and Richard Wagner. In 1856, Berlioz published the first theoretical opus on modern conducting, *Le Chef d'Orchestre: Theorie de Son Art* [Theory of The Conductor's Art],[47] in which he made a clear distinction between time-giving and the genuine art of the conductor as an interpreter of the musical piece. The true conductor applies a majestic power; without that, he is merely a time-beater. The important innovations for orchestration in his theoretical work,

---

[47] Hector Berlioz, *Grand Traite: d'Instrumentation et d'Orchestration Modernes Contenant* [Grand Treatise: About Modern Instrumentation and Orchestration] (Paris, 1856; English translation, 1917).

Grand Traite: d'Instrumentation et d'Orchestration Modernes Contenant [Grand Treatise: About Modern Instrumentation and Orchestration], and his ideas on expanding the size of the orchestra help identify Berlioz as the creator of the modern symphony:

> *Huge orchestras were assembled by Berlioz for specific occasions in which the wind, brass, and percussion sections were more than doubled and [the] string choir was greatly enlarged.*[48]

> *Throughout his life* [Berlioz] *dreamt of one chance to use his ideal orchestra of 465 players, including 30 pianos and 30 harps.*[49]

Along with Berlioz, Richard Wagner exerted the greatest influence on conducting approaches during the second half of the nineteenth century. In his work *Über das Dirigieren* [On Conducting],[50] Wagner insisted that the conductor should be obsessed by an observation of the inner spirit of music as revealed by the unfolding of its narrative and poetic meaning:

> *He sought for the unifying thread, the psychological line, the revelation of which suddenly*

---

[48] Adler, 7.

[49] Younghusband, 88.

[50] Richard Wagner, *Über das Dirigiren* [On Conducting], Published in 1896.

transforms, as if by magic, a more or less indefinite sound-picture into a beautifully shaped, heart-moving vision.[51]

Nikisch argued that Wagner was not a routine Kapellmeister, and that his stick technique was not that of dry 'Taktschlaeger' but, rather, of a musician who spoke from the soul, lifting the listener to a higher artistic plane through gestures that were pure music.[52]

It was Wagner who, "finding in himself the courage to break the canonical laws of courteous behavior, turned his face to the performer-instrumentalist, thereby laying the foundation for the principally new system of conducting, based on the communication and interaction of creative partners."[53]

Franz Liszt contributed to the evolution of conducting with his efforts to emphasize the expressive content of the music through the new style of leading. The specific communicative approach to conducting, in relation to contemporary scientific notions (such as about human communication), was also first articulated by Liszt in his "Letter on Conducting:"

---

[51] Felix Weingartner, *Three Essays by Felix Weingartner* (New York: Dover Publication Inc., 1969), 7.

[52] Raymond Holden, *The Virtuoso Conductors. The Central European Tradition from Wagner to Karajan* (New York and London: Yale University Press, 2005), 39.

[53] Erzhemsky, 161.

> *He defined his attitude to the . . . conductor's activity with sufficient precision, declaring: 'We are helmsmen, but not oarsmen'...*[54]

Alexander Ziloti,[55] one of Liszt's prominent students and contemporaries, spoke of Liszt's approach to conducting:

> *Liszt did not conduct a large part of the play at all. . . . While the music was more or less peaceful, he barely noticeably (and often not doing it at all) marked the beat. But when it was necessary to perform a big crescendo, he suddenly spread his long arms, like an eagle spreads his wings, and you felt along with the musicians such an upsurge that you felt like rising from your place.*[56]

Despite the importance of Liszt's innovations, they were not very influential during his lifetime. The players were not ready for them, and collective self-organization was at an unsatisfactory level. Only a few full-time orchestras with significant numbers (up to 45 core musicians) existed in Europe at the middle of the nineteenth century. The search for an

---

[54] Leo M. Ginzburg, ed., *Dirijerskoe Ispolnitel'stvo, Practika, Istoria. Estetica*, [The Performance of Conducting Practice, History, Aesthetic.], 142, quoted in Erzemsky, *Psychological Paradoxes of Conducting*, 213.

[55] Ziloti [Siloti], Aleksandr Il'yich (1863-1945). Ukranian pianist and conductor. *New Grove Dictionary*, 2nd. ed. (2001), vol. 27, 830.

[56] Alexander I. Ziloti, *Vospominaniya I Pis'ma* [Memoirs and Letters] (Leningrad: Muzgiz, 1963), 58-9.

expressive manual technique would continue with Gustav Mahler. As did Wagner and Liszt, Mahler insisted on a subtlety of accent that often involved a complete disregard of the bar line. Mahler was among the first to instinctively feel the artistic limitations of the schematic manual technique, and he insisted that the conductor's most important task was to disguise the regularity of measures behind the melody and rhythms.

Mahler's contemporary and another important innovator was the Austro-Hungarian conductor, Arthur Nikisch. His conducting style was distinguished by extreme expressiveness and clarity. Niksich's contemporaries noted that he was a romantic conductor, in the truest sense of the word. Under his direction, even semi-professional orchestras sounded much better than their usual performing level. As one of Nikish's contemporaries, the famous German violinist Carl Flesch[57] stated:

> *Nikish impressionistically described in the air not simply the bare metrical structure, but above all the dynamic and agogical nuances as well as the mysterious feeling that lies between the notes; his beat was utterly personal and original. With Nikisch began a new era in the art of conducting.*[58]

---

[57] Flesch, Carl (1873-1944). Celebrated Hungarian violinist and pedagogue. *Baker's Biographical Dictionary of Musicians*, 550.

[58] Shonberg, 214.

One of the most important of Nikisch's innovations was the concept of anticipation of the conductor's action.[59] This new approach, which allowed the conductor to forward an artistic message a fraction before the actual occurrence of sound, revolutionized the discipline and opened new horizons for creativity. Such an innovation is hard to underestimate – even over a hundred years after Nikisch's death, conducting methodologies are still polarized by differing opinions as to whether the conductor's intentions should be manifested "on time" or in an anticipatory manner: "Among other innovations of Nikisch was the device of beating in advance, giving the note value a fraction of a second early. This was adopted by Furtwängler (as, indeed, he adopted many things from Nikisch)."[60] It would be appropriate to assume that Nikisch's creative innovations (as well as Malko's, Furtwängler's and those of their other contemporary colleagues who succeeded with Nikisch's practical innovations) were disseminated because of his ingenious talent, enormous practical experience, and artistic intuition, and without an apprehension of the mental and physical complexities of conducting.[61]

---

[59] Even though I could not find any written sources left by Nikish's contemporaries, which would include a description of the psychological peculiarities of his approach to the conducting process, the modern concept of the inner (psychological) mechanism of conducting supports the idea that Nikish's anticipatory manner was a visual element of his technique of psychological advancing.

[60] Schonberg, 212.

[61] Though the first theses which are relative to modern psychology were composed by French philosopher Rene Descartes in the seventeenth century, psychology as an independent science was established in 1879 in Leipzig by German physician Wilhelm Wundt. Dennis Coon, *Essential of Psychology, Exploration and Application*, (St. Paul: West Publishing Company, 1988), 9.

From the middle of the nineteenth century forward, the complicated pattern of meters, abrupt tempo changes, and high expressive content of the music created in works of Berlioz, Brahms, and Wagner, mandated a revision of older approaches to conducting. This change in philosophy facilitated innovations in orchestration and instrumentation brought about by Gustav Mahler, Richard Strauss, and Arnold Schonberg, Igor Stravinsky, and Paul Hindemith.[62] The requirements of contemporary musical scores have demanded a further expansion of the conductor's duties to incorporate an even greater range of responsibilities and have ushered in a new era focused on the inner intercommunicative mechanism of conducting.

---

[62] Hermann Scherchen, *Handbook of Conducting*, 5.

2

THE ANATOMY OF THE STRIKE

INSTRUMENTAL RESPONSE

Despite the fact that for over two centuries the art of orchestral conducting has been an independent occupation, it is difficult to assume that any professional conductor has not had previous musical experience of any kind, particularly without mastering performance on one or more musical instruments.

When one is viewing instrumental and practical conducting reflexes, it is essential to consider them as somewhat correlated.

One of the principal implications is that conducting, as an independent artistic practice, requires an autonomous (as distinguished from instrumental) mental and physical setting. The most obvious aspect, which makes the conducting practice dissimilar from instrumental practices, is the absence of any direct physical application (similar to the natural merging with a musical instrument) that may generate the sound in response[63] to muscular contraction:

> *What is so difficult about conducting and what is so difficult about becoming a conductor? An instrumentalist must be able to play his instrument, and to have the physical power and manual skill to manage and control his instrument. But how to control an orchestra? . . .* **The manipulation of sound is very hard to learn**, *and particularly difficult for a conductor, who has no physical contact with the sound.*[64]

In his book, *The Fundamental Techniques of Conducting*, the prominent Russian conductor and teacher Nikolai Malko touches upon an important challenge with which conducting pedagogy often collides. From his experience as a conducting teacher, Malko asks: does the conductor have to unlearn "foolish habits" before starting with the fundamentals of the profession? But what kind of "habits" could a novice conductor

---

[63] Response [L. respondere, to reply]. A reaction, such as contraction of a muscle or secretion of a gland, resulting from a stimulus. *Taber's Medical Dictionary*, 1589.

[64] Daniel Barenboim, *A Life in Music* (New York: Charles Schribner's Sons, 1992), 131. (Emphasis added)

have and where did they come from, if, up until that moment, the student has conducted neither an orchestra nor the sound of the piano? In Malko's opinion, "the answer is quite simple:" those same trivial muscular anomalies that are found in students at their lesson on the piano or the violin, etc., are found in those who aspire to a conductor's career: e.g., "'clutched' fingers, a stiff 'numb' hand," and the absence of independence and freedom in the necessary movements, "unwanted motor-irradiation and habits."[65] Though Malko has stated that "the answer is quite simple," the existence of that common phenomenon "does not have a satisfactory interpretation in pedagogical literature."[66]

From the prenatal period to birth and beyond, the human body develops a repertoire of set responses to specific movements.

> *The way we walk, bend, sit, breathe, reach, speak, comb our hair, drive a car, and pick up a package is for the most part **unconsciously determined**. These are reflexive responses carried out **with little or no thought**.*[67]

Ivan Pavlov (1849-1936)[68] was the first scientist to introduce

---

[65] Malko, *The Conductor and His Baton*, 36.

[66] Erzhemsky, 91.

[67] Judith Leibowitz and Bill Connington, *The Alexander Technique.* New York: Harper and Row, Publishers, 1990, 36. (Emphasis added)

[68] Ivan Pavlov P., Russian physiologist and Nobel laureate,

the concept of dynamic stereotype's formation: "In examining the different aspects of [dynamic stereotype's] formation, [Pavlov] especially emphasized that, 'the formation, the setting of the dynamic stereotype is the work of nerves under extreme tension.'"[69]

It is known that physiologically, under the normal development of a fetus, the human body is born with a scale of unconditioned reflexes, which allow a child's body to function and survive in new, and, in many ways, aggressive physiological environments (especially in the first months of a child's life). From the very first inhalation, the human body as mental and physical responses to various stimuli is continuously developing conditioned reflexes. Unsurprisingly, from the very first moment of acquaintance with a musical instrument our bodies and minds also begin to develop the repertoire of responses to specific complex stimuli.

One of the professional musician's most subconscious stereotypes is an immediate contiguity of applied physical tension with the occurrence of sound. It is firm and fundamental because it is inherited by every musician from the **primary instrumental performance** as a *conditioned* response and is a result of the psycho-physical complex of straight-forward interactions between the player and the instrument. Such

---

1849-1936. *Stedman's Medical Dictionary*, 1042.

[69] Ivan P. Pavlov, *Polnoe Sobranie Sochinenii*, [Completed Collection of Works] (Moscow: Gosizdat, 2nd ed., 1951), quoted in Erzhemsky, *Psychological Paradoxes of Conducting*, 103.

conditioned responses can be denoted by this simple scheme: **sound always occurs as an instant result of the player's physical effort**:

> *If we would take a closer look at the way that musical instruments are played, we can find that instrumental techniques consist of a pattern of specific motions that have to be learned as thoroughly as possible. . . Later, when they are coupled with the sound, such motions psychologically are not taken by the instrumentalist into account as an independent motion.* ***The performer is thinking in musical images; his fingers humbly execute all motions needed for adequate personification of musical thoughts. The musician does not think about motions themselves; he operates mainly by the sense of the motions.*** *This allows him to pull the sound to a certain dynamic and color, and helps to connect sounds into phrases and so on.* ***The musician 'talks off' his musical thoughts by his hands. In a similar way, we could verbally state our thoughts without thinking about the motions of lips, tongue, and larynx that are needed for this action.***[70]

However, the complex of instrumental[71] reflexes as a tool of dynamic psycho-physical intercommunication cannot be simply

---

[70] Musin, 4-5. (Emphasis added)

[71] The meaning of the term *instrumental* in psychology and physiology is different than in this manuscript. For practical purposes I use this term to characterize responses gained during the practice and performance of musical instruments.

transferred to the conducting practice without essential adjustments because a conductor's creative realization requires non-instrumental (non-tense, non-dynamic) settings for realization of inner activity: "As conducting is a process of management, there is no place in its structure **for physical action as such**."[72]

Ironically, the instrumental dynamic (battuta) stereotype still prevails in generally accepted conducting methods as the oldest striking tradition, with psychological expectation of the occurrence of sound on the breaking point of the stressed motion, which some professional conductors and conducting scholars identify with simultaneous indication of the marking-point of the beat and occurrence of the sound:

The beat-strike in and of itself can by no means be called a proper musical action. It is a 'smudge' on the living body of the music. It is artistically introduced into the process of performance in the form of recurrence of the sadly famous "battuta-stick." Besides this, according to the law of dominant, the implementation of the beat-strike as an active, precisely psychical action . . . *to a greater or lesser degree "muffles" the actual sounding of music for the conductor and suppresses his intellectual functions.*[73]

The diagram on the following page schematically depicts the

---

[72] Erzhemsky, 152. (Emphasis added)

[73] Ibid, 212. (Emphasis added)

downward-upward motion with an indication of the psychological expectation of the beginning of the sound at the marking-point of the beat (such psychological [stereotypical] identification of the downward-upward motion's breaking point and occurrence of sound is characteristic for the prevalent forcible *beat-strike* style of conducting practice) and the actual occurrence of sound.

Dynamic (Striking) Motion*

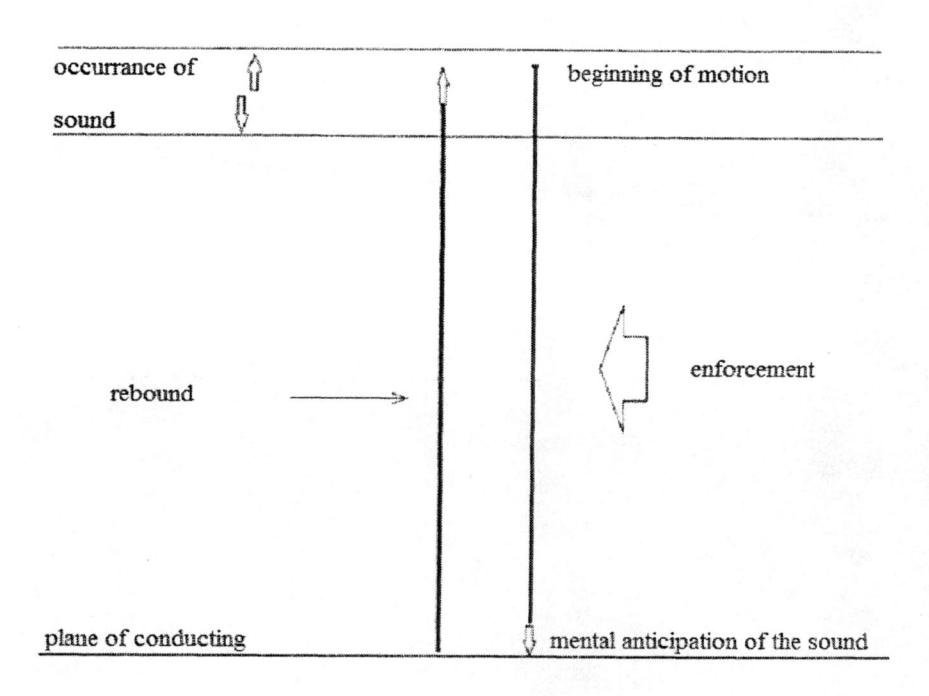

occurrance of sound	⇧⇩	↑	beginning of motion
rebound	→		enforcement
plane of conducting		⇩	mental anticipation of the sound

*This diagram is conditional and depicts a common performance of the force-overcoming beat.

TIME-LAG

To comprehend the phenomenon of a *time-lag*, we have to realize that the inner psycho-physical state and, consequently, the velocity of reactions (reflexes) to expected audible incidents are dissimilar for instrumental and conducting actions. A player's implementation of direct determinate physical action to the instrument causes the occurrence of the sound as an instant outcome of applied muscular contraction. On the contrary, the conductor's actions and subsequent reactions are also connected to the appearance of the sound, though indirectly.

The following description depicts the pattern of psycho-physical actions and the result of an instrumental performance:

Occurrence of Sound

Sound Production   **Occurrence**

Percussions   striking with mallets   relatively instant

Piano/Harp   pressing/plucking keys   relatively instant

Strings   bow and strings   relatively instant*

Winds   blowing air   various temporal delays**

Pipe-organ   pressing keys   delayed with constant lag**

Conductor   action (motion/upbeat)   delayed with various time-lags

* With temporal delay for double bass

**For some wind instruments and the pipe-organ, the existence of time-lag is constant and due to the nature of the instrument. This is not to mention the conducting of a choir, in which the occurrence of sound mostly appears with various temporal delays.

Thus, some instruments may generate sound with a natural time-gap (woodwind and brass instruments as well as the pipe organ). Such a delay is temporally steady and becomes a stable and eventually psychologically adjusted part of the terms necessary to originate a proven conditioned response.

The reference to the delay in the occurrence of sound is a fundamental aspect of the conducting technique (it appears as a necessary time-lag for musicians' psychological adaptation of a conductor's action) and presents one of the central psycho-physical dissimilarities between solo instrumental performance and conducting enactment. Though the existence of that phenomenon could be perceived as obvious and banal, it has to be taken into serious consideration for the implementation of artistically valuable conducting.

The predominance of primary instrumental (dynamic) reflexes often has a negative effect on the practical and creative sides of conducting. The modification of the conductor's primary musical (instrumental) reflexes becomes necessary because of the existence of a given functional factor, which is continuously present (such as the various intervals of time between the lower point of the motion [performed with either a forcible or non-forcible physical approach] or the visual indication of the desired beginning of the beat [and eventually sound] and the actual occurrence of sound). This factor is idiosyncratic[74] to the conductor's activity and partially reveals the orchestral musicians' mental reaction to a conductor's actions (*stimuli*). Because the definition of time could have a different extension, it seems appropriate to use "time-lag" as a term for the characterization of this phenomenon:

> *Here we again encounter the existence of a definite temporal interval between the action of the conductor and the response in sound from the orchestra (the so-called phenomenon of "time-lag") . . . Still, certain logic and practical expediency can be seen in it.* **After all, "time lag", as we have already noted, is the manifestation of the intuitive demand of the collective in the time required for the assessment of the signal emanating from the conductor and making a decision about the content of the joint response** ... *In the process of analyzing the internal organization of the actions of orchestras of the most varied professional levels a general tendency becomes apparent, constantly confirmed by the practice of performance activity: today all collectives, down to amateur ones, strive to play more or less later than the beat-strike in order to have the ability to somehow assemble and feel like a unified whole.* **Even where the strict set on playing "on the beat-strike" exists, it is carried out only at the beginning of the performance. By the middle of the**

---

[74] *Idiosyncrasy*: A particular mental, behavioral, or physical characteristic or peculiarity. *Stedman's Medical Dictionary*, 945.

work everything is standing in its own place.[75]

The constant presence of this time-interval scatters the complex of the conductor's dynamic responses that were gained through primary instrumental performance. It would be appropriate to assume that a conducting enactment with the expectation of the occurrence of orchestral sound as an instant outcome of the conductor's motions (muscular contractions) is a set-back of primary instrumental reflexes (or silent reoccurrence of the original battuta style); without adjustment to the existence of the time-lag, such a performance may face a variety of limitations. From the very first upbeat the conductor has to become accustomed to the time-lag throughout the process of conducting. As an alternative for the subconscious involvement of the primary instrumental recurrence in the mode of perpetual application of stressed striking motion, the embodiment and practical realization of the intercommunicative settings of conducting require different reflected settings as indicated in the following schematic explanation:

---

[75] Erzhemsky, 168, 215. (Emphasis added) The existence of a "delay-time-lag" also is noted in the works of the creators of St. Petersburg's school of conducting, Nicolai Malko and his pupil Ilia Musin. Malko, *Osnovi Techniki Dirijirovaniya* [The Fundamental Techniques of Conducting], 49; Musin, *Tehnika Dirijirovaniya* [Technique of Conducting], 56. It is important to emphasize that the existence of such a seemingly obvious phenomenon is still widely and negatively denied by many conductors (especially in countries with strong on-the-beat methodological traditions). Such controversies are due to the absence of a mutually accepted methodology, which would be based on the latest scientific developments in the comprehension of non-instrumental but inner, and intercommunicative (psycho-linguistic) principles of the conducting process.

The motion-impulse[76] (indication of the beginning of the sound) precedes time-lags of various durations (see table on page 42)

↓

Occurrence of sound as musicians' reactions to an action/stimulus[77]

The existence of the time-lag as one of the intercommunicative (psychological and quasi-lingual) characteristics of conducting requires (in contrast with instrumental performance) the manifestation of a *conceptual*[78] (informative) motion in the

---

[76] I use the term *impulse* instead of *upbeat* because of the complex innate (non-evident) characteristics of that action. The hidden communicative phenomenon of an upbeat will be discussed in Chapter 5, *Inner Mechanisms. Conceptual Motions*.

[77] Though the motions may have a variety of vectors (e.g., from upper point down to left or right sides of the metrical scheme), the occurrence of the sound would have a similar outcome since motion has a breaking lower point.

[78] *Conceptual*: Relating to the formation of idea, to mental conceptions. *Stedman's Medical Dictionary*, 338. A concept is considered both as a mental construct and as the socially accepted meaning of terms that represent the particular concept. Concepts are learned and change greatly from early childhood into late adolescence, whereas the socially accepted meanings are more stable. Corsini, Raymond J., ed. *Encyclopedia of Psychology*, 2nd ed. (New York: A Wiley-Interscience Publication, 1994), 1: 285. Here, the utilization of the term "conceptual" is probably not the best one. Therefore

mode of a preparatory upbeat (especially at the beginning). The presence of such a conceptually commissioned preparatory motion is imperative due to the task of setting a creatively productive communicative bond with the conductor's virtual instrument.[79] Conducting practice shows that the expressiveness (or informative fulfillment) of the preparatory motion at the beginning of the piece (or new phrase) may be sacrificed for reasons of improving the ensemble. Later, during a performance, the absence of the expressive and informative preparation motion, executed in the mode of an advanced *internal* upbeat (the continuous *intermediary* upbeat within the pattern of the conducting scheme) will keep the performance at an unsatisfactory artistic level:[80]

> *The orchestra **as a rule acts "on return,"** withholding [its] reaction-response to the conductor's motivating influence.* **This is not the special exception but a reality of modern orchestral play confirmed**

---

in contrast with terms describing the forcible (overcoming) manner of conducting such as "ictus," "click," "strike," "beat," etc., this one ("conceptual") describes the motions whose performance reveals the non-physical and communicative nature of conducting, and which are just a somewhat visual (physical) extension of the conductor's inner creative impulse.

[79] It is important to note the psychological (communicative, non-instrumental) origin of the preparation motion. It serves a variety of psychological tasks from gathering the musicians' attention to the formation of the quality and character of the orchestra's upcoming sound.

[80] A technical description and practical importance of the perpetual application of the *internal* (intermediate) upbeat (preparatory motion) as a tool of conceptual visualization of a conductor's creative intentions can be found in: Musin, *Technique of Conducting*, 80.

everywhere. . . . Such an initiative on [the] orchestra's part required from the leaders a certain reconstruction of the structure of their managing activities. As a consequence of this, a new system of conducting arose, based on the differentiation of the beat-strike from [the] impulse.[81]

As Isaac Stern stated in one of his interviews: "... it is a well-known fact that **psychological reaction accompanies the emotional and physical stress of performing**."[82]

Comprehension of the complex mechanisms that govern musicians' temperaments, emotional states, and different professional experiences during performance is crucially important, as is an appropriate knowledge of the character and content of the score's musical texture.

A magazine survey shows that an alarmingly large majority of orchestral musicians live in a state of constant apprehensive insecurity. ... most [musicians] complain of various illnesses seemingly related to work, including backaches, headaches, tendonitis, repetitive strain injuries, ulcers, and a plethora of mental conditions, including depression and plain unhappiness. ... The waste of talent, the shortened careers, the

---

[81] Erzhemsky, *Psihologiya Dirijirovaniya* [The Psychology of Conducting], 123. (Emphasis added)

[82] Samuel Applebaum and Henry Roth, *The Way They Play, Isaac Stern* (New York: Paganiniana Publications, Inc.: 1981), 116. (Emphasis added)

> *inadequate performances, the objectionable behavior, the frustration, suffering, and pain are the norm of the music profession.*[83]

Aside from the aforementioned physical side effects, there are a variety of other causes that delay the orchestra's sound. The duration of time taken by musicians for the generation of sound varies and may rely on a variety of factors.

> *Each orchestral musician will respond to the preparatory beat according to his or her individual technical proficiency and experience.* **Reaction time to the signals received varies considerably from one instrument or section to another; consequently, the instruments or combination of instruments making the entrance significantly influences the shape of the preparatory beat.** *...*

> *Lower-pitched instruments respond to signals more slowly than higher-pitched ones. In the string section, the heavier and thicker strings of the lower-pitched instruments require more physical effort to vibrate than the higher strings.*

> *As the conductor moves from the violins to the double basses, responses to signals become slower. Similarly, in*

---

[83] Pedro de Alcantara, *Indirect Procedures. A Mucisian's Guide to the Alexander Technique* (Clarendon Press, Oxford, 1997), 1.

the brass section, the lower-pitched instruments must set in motion a larger column of air than the higher-pitched ones.

*The situation is different in the woodwinds, where **variations in response** to the conductor's preparatory beat are based not on the instrument's volume of sound but rather on the means of tone production. The attacks of the double-reed instruments are generally more distinct than those of the single reeds. For example, the clarinets, owing to the particular way players produce a tone, have a tendency toward late entrances. The range of response to the conductor's signals, from the fastest to the slowest, is oboe, piccolo, flute, English horn, bassoon, contrabassoon, clarinet, and bass clarinet. ...*

*Another factor affecting the musician's response to the conductor's beat information is the physical distance separating the players from the conductor. A **delayed response** becomes more likely the farther a musician is seated from the podium.*[84]

Understanding the natural irregularity of the instruments of orchestral sections and the required method of performance, and the individual physical and psychological *status*[85] of orchestral musicians (such factors as age, gender, and health can affect

---

[84] Gustav Meier, *The Score, The Orchestra, and The Conductor* (New York: Oxford University Press, 2009), 9-10. (Emphasis added)

[85] *Status*: A state or condition. *Taber's Medical Dictionary*, 1744.

musicians' sensory reactions, especially auditory and visual) is vital for successfully managing conductor-orchestra communication:

> *Sound is an extremely complicated stimulus, ranging from the lowest notes of a tuba to the highest tones of a shrill whistle, changing in volume from the merest hint of a whisper to the most deafening clap of thunder, taking such diverse and varied forms as the click of two coins in a pocket, the human voice, and the blended richness of a hundred different instruments in a symphony orchestra. The receptors in the human ear have to be very sensitive indeed to respond to such a wide range of stimuli.*[86]

> *By using electrical recorders to measure the speed of nerve impulses, psychologists have found the top speed to be 120 meters per second. . . . That's fast but certainly not instantaneous.*[87]

Neuro-physiological research indicates that the human sensory system (visual and auditory) includes a natural muscular delay in reaction to a visual or audible signal (stimulus); "a special characteristic of all sensory receptors is that they *adapt* either partially or completely to their *stimuli* **after a period of**

---

[86] Jerome Kagan and Ernest Havemann, *Psychology: An Introduction*, 2nd ed. (New York: Harcourt Brace Jovanovich Inc., 1972), 203.

[87] Coon. 26.

time."[88] Various factors such as age, personal temperament, and psychological state, affect human reactions to stimuli. For an orchestra's musicians, other important (and specific) factors could be the distance between the musician's location and the conductor's podium, specifics of the performing techniques of his/her instrument, as well as the acoustical characteristics of the concert hall. In the modern age, successful conducting practice is impossible without a general knowledge of human reaction patterns and an awareness of the psychological adaptation of outer impulses:

> *It is proved that in psycho-physiology the effect of intensity is directed by the content of perceptible stimulation. . . .* ***The time of reaction on visual and audible stimuli [is] conditioned by the immediate emotional status of the recipient.***[89]

The musicians, on their part, can conceive only what they perceive. However, it is necessary to emphasize that orchestral musicians' performances are a complex action and cannot be described as simple *stimuli-responses* (a psycho-physical type

---

[88] Maurice Victor and Allan H. Ropper, *Principal of Neurology*, 7th ed. (New York: McGraw-Hill Medical Publishing Division, 2001), 498. (Emphasis added)

[89] M. J. Nissen, *Stimulus Intensity and Information Processing*, (Perception and Psychophysiology, 1977), vol. 2, 338; P. Niemi and E. Lehtonen, *Foreperiod and Visual Stimulus Intensity: A Reappraisal* (Acta Psychology, vol. 50, 1982), 73-82. (Emphasis added)

of activity in the form of conditioned behavior[90] analogous to Pavlov's dogs). It is more appropriate to refer to musicians' reactions (as a part of the conductor-orchestra communication) as an "anticipated reflection of reality,"[91] and as a psychophysical anticipatory adaptation of the forthcoming material.

> *Current neurobiological research argues that 'emotions and feelings are not, as poets and philosophers say, ephemeral reflections of the human soul', but rather 'the brain's interpretation of our visceral reaction to the world at large.*[92]

---

[90] *Behavior*: 1. Any response emitted by or elicited from an organism. 2. Any mental or motor act or activity. 3. Specifically, parts of a total response pattern. *Stedman's Medical Dictionary*, 211.

[91] Petr K. Anokhin, *Izbrannie Trudi. Filisofskie Aspekti Teorii Funkzional'noi Sistemi* [Selected Works. Philosophical Aspects of the Functional System], M., 1978, 41, quoted in A. A. Leontiev, *Deyatel'nii Um. Deyatel'nost'. Znak. Lichnost'* [The Active Mind. Activity. Sign. Personality], 122.

[92] Sandra Blakelee, *The Physical Roots of Emotion*, International Herald Tribune (8 Dec. 1994), 8, quoted in Alcantara, 261.

ICTUS AND CLICK

The practical tradition of psychological anticipation of orchestral sound at the breaking point of the stressed forward downward-upward motion (or on the beat-strike) is the oldest one and serves as "a rudiment of the battuta's type of audible measuring."[93] "Emphasizing the beat by 'clicking' . . . . This is sharp, quick wrist motion, which speeds up the movement of the baton just before reaching a count."[94]

The distinctive features of this traditional method are the stressed physical strike as an element of time-beating and the manifestation of a visual impulse, which some conductors and scholars also identify as the ictus:[95] "The precise moment when

---

[93] Erzhemsky, *Dirijirovanie kak Obschenie I Tvorchestvo* [Conducting as Communication and Creativity], 16.

[94] Max Rudolf, *The Grammar of Conducting* (New York: Schirmer Books, 1980), 12.

[95] *Ictus* (Lat.) A term which in prosody indicates the stress or accent schematically implied on a certain syllable of a foot or verse; hence in music, it is a comparable stress or accent schematically implied on a certain beat of a bar, in a certain metre, whether or not this implication coincides with stress or accent actually made. Stanley Sadie, ed., *New Grove Dictionary of Music and Musicians* (London: Macmillan Publishers Limited, 2001), 71.

the metric pulse is felt and the tone begins is called the ictus."[96]

> *What is a 'click?' A 'click' emphasizes and affirms the pulse point within strokes. The pulse points outline the beat. ... The up and down movements are called 'clicks.'*[97]

> *The point of change is known as the click of the beat; it indicates to the orchestra the precise moment at which to play. The terms beat point and ictus are also used by some authorities to denote the click of each beat. (The click can also be thought of as the moment of impact, as if you were to tap, or gently stroke, the top of an imaginary object.)*[98]

This method[99] was initially designed to establish the proper tempo, meter and dynamics as well as the transmission

---

[96] Donald Hunsberger and Roy E. Ernst, *The Art of Conducting*, 2nd ed. (New York, McGraw-Hill, Inc., 1983), 6.

[97] Farberman, *The Art of Conducting Technique: A New Perspective* (Warner Brothers Publications, 1997), 24.

[98] John Lumley and Nigel Springthorpe, *The Art of Conducting. A Guide to Essential Skills* (London: Rhinegold Publishing Limited, 1989), 17.

[99] Here I would like to emphasize again that there is a certain practical cause behind the concept of the manifestation of a visual stroke which apparently stays behind the striking motion, or the so-called "click." However in reality, for this reason, such a style works against the principal of intercommunication. The interactive transformation of the click (and the striking motion in general) into a communicative tool will be discussed later in Chapter 7 (*Milieu of Communication. Emancipation of Metrical Schemes*).

(supposedly) of the emotional content of music (or the conductor's creative intentions), and all of these elements were supposed to coincide in time.[100] For some modern scholars, this tradition has severe shortcomings:

> *[It] is in no way a 'marriage of love' but rather an unnatural symbiosis. Because of such undesirable (speaking frankly) unity, the impulse's natural activity is involuntarily transferred onto the function of the time-beating, increasing the 'striking' character of this function,* **which leads to the fragmentation of the unified musical form of the work into separate metrical pieces.**[101]

It is important, however, to separate the concept of the click as a vestige of the battuta style (as a minimized version of a striking motion), its performance, and the use of the wrist during conducting. The wrist technique is an important part of the conductor's apparatus (see Part III: *Methodology. Modification of the Wrist Strike*).

Although the forceful dynamic conducting practice inherited

---

[100] Though the term *ictus* is still in wide use among scholars (e.g., E. Green, E. Galkin, H. Farberman, M. Rudolf), although there is no agreeable methodological description of it.

[101] Erzhemsky, 211-212. (Emphasis added) Ilia Musin, in his book *Tehnika Dirijirovaniya* [Technique of Conducting], also strongly oppose the striking type of conducting. Ilia A. Musin, *Tehnika Dirijirovaniya* [Technique of Conducting], 2nd ed. (St.-Petersburg: Dean - Adia-M, 1995), 189.

traits from the old battuta-strike audible style, its method of musical leading has clear ties to the instrumental psycho-physical mindset. Most orchestral conductors have established their instrumental skills by the time they start their conducting careers. All musical performers have specific psycho-physical conditioned responses gained from experiences with their primary instruments, which naturally reflect the physical (forcible) part of instrumental performance.[102] Because these responses are developed as part of early musical experiences, such reflexes have well-established patterns of psychological reaction:

> *The elements of definite **physical work** connected with the necessity of sound production (the pressing of keys, the movement of the bow, the pressing of strings, the effect of an air column, etc.) give their activities an obvious material direction.*[103]

In light of this long history of various instrumental responses, it is highly likely that conductors would try to impose these previously-gained mental and physical stereotypes on their approach to orchestral conducting. Thus, the instrumental form of the implementation of physical tension has instinctive interferences with conducting, and at many occurrences such interferences have unproductive effects on the conductor's

---

[102] A conditioned response is defined as one that is "already in an individual's repertoire but which, through repeated pairings with its natural stimulus, has been acquired or conditioned anew to a previously neutral or conditioned stimulus." *Stedman's Medical Dictionary*, 1348.

[103] Erzhemsky, 92. (Emphasis added)

technique:

> *One of the most remarkable conductors of the recent past, Fritz Reiner[104], who very much practiced what he preached, once put it similarly in an interview: 'The best conducting technique is that which achieves the maximum musical result with a minimum of effort.'[105]*

There are numerous examples of great instrumentalists who were successful in their careers as solo performers but became helpless on the conductor's podium. Such cases could provide specific illustrations of the unproductive effect of the direct implementation of instrumental physical (forcible) mannerisms onto the conductor's technique:

> *The history of world musical culture has left us tremendous amounts of evidence of attempts by well-known performers to 'descend upon' and master the conductor's profession. In itself, this possibility might not arouse any objections, if it were not one circumstance: the results of such unprepared 'cross-training' very seldom corresponded to what was*

---

[104] Reiner, Fritz (1888-1963). American conductor of Hungarian birth. *New Grove Dictionary*, 2nd. ed., 2001, vol. 21, 159-60.

[105] *Etude*, October 1951, n. p, quoted in Gunther Schuller, *The Complete Conductor* (New York: Oxford University Press, 1997), 9.

expected.[106]

Technical problems generally begin to reveal themselves when solo performers attempt to directly incorporate instrumental dynamic stereotypes into the conductor's manual technique without realizing the basic psycho-physical differences between instrumental practice and the communicative principles of conducting as a non-verbal, manual form of expressive leading. Instrumental dynamic reflexes supplemented instinctively or deliberately usually produce poor practical and artistic results. Immediate supplements (without adjustments) to instrumental knowledge in the conducting practice bypass the main psycho-physical stages of development as well as the creative intentions of conducting as a form of artistic intercommunicative supervision: "Thus beginning conductors, proceeding from the logic of other musical professions, attempt to study the 'direct' sound production from the orchestra."[107]

This "direct" approach to sound is not only typical for beginners but very much depends on the type of professional guidance received during apprenticeships, as well as on the appropriate mental and physical coordination and subordination of the conductor's outer and inner professional activities:

> *"If teaching actually went, from the very beginning, from the internal to the external instead of*

---

[106] Erzhemsky, 21.

[107] Ibid, 92.

going from the external to the internal, and the will to sound creation was actually its foundation from the very beginning," then as a result . . . the beginning musician would . . . be able to discover the creative precepts within himself, and imaginary, artistic thought; this will unquestionably lead in the future to his formation and development as a creative personality in all his many-sided, potential diversities.[108]

The individual practice of musical performance, either instrumental or conducting, is a complex action and elaborates many sides of the musician's emotional, physical, and mental abilities. Nevertheless, an understanding of the mental and physical dissimilarities between an instrumentalist and a conductor's actions is essential not only for tutorial purposes but also for the practice of professional conducting. An apt apprehension of those dissimilarities can open new pathways in the development of the modern conducting style.

---

[108] Aleksei Losev, *Problema Simvola I Realisticheskoie Iskusstvo* [The Problem of Symbol and Realistic Art] (Moscow: Academy of Science, 1976), quoted in Erzhemsky, 93.

INSTRUMENTAL REFLEXES AND CONDUCTING

Most likely, all professional conductors have their first music leading experience after developing an acquaintance with musical instruments and/or choral practices. The realization of the character of these original musical experiences is crucial to comprehending the development of the dynamic artistic knowledge-stereotypes and the practical use of conditioned responses and biomechanics.[109] There are essential differences between the functions of the psycho-physical apparatus for instrumental and conducting performance (though original instrumental reflexes have a subliminal interference with the artistic tasks of orchestral leading).[110] During the execution of an instrumental performance, the sound occurs as an immediate result of muscular contraction – striking a drum with a mallet,

---

[109] *Biomechanics*: The science concerned with the action of forces, internal or external, on the living body. *Stedman's Medical Dictionary*, 187.

[110] It is important to mention that the original conducting method (time-beating) with the use of the battuta had a definite subliminal instrumental (dynamic) nature. It functioned as an auxiliary audible or rather as an additional (out-of-score) percussion type of instrument, which could be elaborated with lesser or greater success depending on the conductor's creativity within the flow of musical texture.

pressing the keys on the piano's keyboard, plucking or pressing a bow against strings, and blowing air through a woodwind or brass instrument.[111] This demonstrates that there is an instant mental and physical coupling between sound and muscular contraction:

> *There is one point I want to make which very rarely is considered by people who otherwise are at home in the world of music. This is the difference between the time of studying for the conductor and for the instrumentalist - the violin player or the cellist or the pianist. These three instrumentalists have their whole boyhood and their whole adolescence to study on their instrument, to perfect themselves in a technique. But the poor conductor, he cannot do the same.*[112]

Based on my own observations of conducting students in the class of Ilia Musin, I noticed that many students (including myself) who accepted the mannerisms and conducting principles of the famous professor (such as non-dynamic techniques of "picking," "taking" or "transferring" the orchestral sound), demonstrated, after being absent from class for some time, a noticeable shift towards the more forceful striking manner. In many instances their gestures lost their previous elasticity and instead their conducting began to

---

[111] Suggested exercises for modification and adjustment of non-practical instrumental primary responses can be found in the methodological part of this book.

[112] Chesterman, *Conversations With Conductors*, Bruno Walter, 96.

demonstrate stiffness and hardness in their strokes. Naturally, such changes evoked unpleasant comments from Professor Musin.[113] I've also noticed that students with different instrumental backgrounds (piano, strings, winds or percussion) obtained a sense of connection with orchestral sound in different manners. Those who had a primary training as pianists generally assimilated the technique of 'taking' the sound differently (due to "the **percussive** quality of the piano"[114]) than those who were trained as violinists or wind players.[115] The deepness of newly obtained reflexes was also varied. The answer may lie in the area of the development of primary musical reflexes that are conditioned by the specific nature of musical instruments.

Those conductors whose primary musical responses are conditioned by their acquaintance with string instruments may have to recondition reflexes ingrained by their primary instrumental experience. In reference to the specific nature of string instruments, a string player's physical musical reflexes are predominantly determined by monophonic perception. This may limit the development of a multilayered (stereoscopic) assessment of sound, which is valuable for the conducting practice but may also include a specific "non-striking" psycho-

---

[113] Also, it is important to mention that when practicing in class, the majority of students try to imitate Musin's conducting manner without understanding the psycho-physical aspects of his technical approach.

[114] Walter Piston, *Orchestration* (Ney York: W. W. Norton & Company Inc., 1955), 341. (Emphasis added)

[115] The phenomenon of the vicinity (contour) of sound will be discussed in Chapter 4.

physical pathway for interpreting the "continuity of sound."[116] Such conductors may instinctively employ the action that imitates the movement of the arm holding the bow. If applied properly (with the corresponding preparatory beat), such imitation may have a valuable and expressive musical impact, especially with reference to string sections: "The string body occupies a primary position in the constitution of the orchestra."[117]

The motion may evoke a psychological impression as an imitation of the subject lifting differing amounts of weight and may be useful to indicate the gradual growth of the dynamic through the musical line. However, the psychological efficiency of this visual imitation will only be valuable with its application to the well-established provisional *contour of sound*. Ignorance of the phenomenon of the contour of sound is a common error among novice and even experienced conductors.

There is a noticeable visual similarity between some of the conductor's gestures and the motions used by a timpani player. The complex motions used by percussionists while playing drums may resemble some of the most common gestures of the conductor. This motion may be divided in three parts: the preparatory motion, the hitting motion, and then the rebound motion:

---

[116] Musin, *Technique of Conducting*, 256.

[117] Norman Del Mar, *Anatomy of the Orchestra*. (Berkeley and Los Angeles: University of California Press, 1987), 29.

> *The essential element of the conducting technique ... is that motion which is used when you beat a drum with sticks or when you clap your hands in time to music. While watching someone beat a drum, you could clap your hands or vocalize precisely in time with the drum beat by simply following the up and down motion of the drum stick.*[118]

But with the apparent visual similarity between the motions of the drum player and the conductor, there are important issues concerning the actual origin of the sound that should be taken into consideration. The drum has always responded with the sound at the lowest point of the player's motion. And because this incident is conditioned by the nature of the instrument, it is inappropriate to transfer the visual similarity between the conductor's striking gesture and the timpanist's motion into the conducting practice (as suggested by Saito[119]) without of the recognition of communicative principles of the conducting process, such as the delayed occurrence of sound.

Despite the visual similarities between the motions of a drum player (or to some extent, the motions of a pianist) and the conductor's preparatory motions, the nature of the mental and physical expectations in conjunction with the sound is different. These differences become evident with the direct superimposition of the conditioned responses gained by the

---

[118] Hideo Saito. *The Saito Conducting Method by Hideo Saito* (Tokyo: Min-On Concert Association & Ongaku No Tomo Sha Corp., 1988), 8.

[119] Ibid, 9.

drum/piano player onto the conducting practice without adjustments (despite the apparent primitiveness of this type of orchestral leading, there are many professional conductors who implement intensive hitting as the predominant hammering visual stimulus for clarity of the beat). A similar conditioned response at the instant of the expectation of the sound at the breaking point of the hitting motion also exists in piano and percussion performing practices. This occurs due to the fact that sound is the immediate result of direct pressure (a strike) on the keys of the keyboard or on the surface of a drum. In both instances, drum and piano, the psychological expectation of the sound and the beginning point of the muscular relaxation stipulated by the physical characteristics of the instrument (timpani or piano) are kept firm as is the player's steady, conditioned response.[120]

An awareness of such psycho-physical dissimilarities is important for successful conducting and must be taken into account by professional conductors. It is especially important because playing the piano is one of the introductory instrumental experiences for the majority of conductors. It is true that conductors who have mastered their skills in piano performance may have advantages during the search for an expressive interpretation of the orchestral score. With better

---

[120] Here again, it is valuable to mention the unproductive outcome of the predominance of the striking or hitting approach. Professor Ilia Musin expressed the idea that "emphasized" beating eliminates the possibility of demonstrating a logically bonded musical structure (phrase). This approach continuously "partitions the musical texture" and finally finishes up "just to serve the utilization of metrical schemes by themselves." Musin, *Technique of Conducting*, 189. The interactive modification of metrical points (beats) will be discussed in Chapter 7.

comprehension of a score's polyphonic structure and experience with privileging one particular instrumental line (inner-voice) over another, a pianist-conductor also is generally more aware of specific harmonic sensations that could be decoded into expressive gestures.[121] As violinist Isaac Stern mentioned in one of his interviews: "A piano background, as I had, is most beneficial, because it develops the harmonic sense."[122]

An anticipated preparatory *impulse*-upbeat as an inseparable part of the effective concept-formative pattern of actions (not only as the preparatory but also within the pattern of schemes of conducting as a continuous *internal intermediate upbeat* [Ilia Musin]) is vital for successful conducting. The inner anticipated preparatory upbeat is one of the most important aspects of the conductor's practical approach that allows for performances which are lively and vibrant. This practice requires the abolition of the instrumental type of conditioned response. For example, there is not much need for the pianist, percussionist, or other instrumentalist to be preoccupied with the visually articulated and advanced preparation motions used to extract colorful sounds out of the instrument; however, some type of the preparatory body motion might be needed by the pianist, as well as by the other instrumentalists, performing in chamber ensembles. Despite this similarity with conducting, the use of any kind of bodily preparatory motion as a visual signal for small instrumental ensembles is limited because of the player's preoccupation with the instant physical contact of their

---

[121] Musin, 256.

[122] Applebaum and Roth, 113.

instruments and sound.

The nature of an instrument influences not only the artistic skills of musicians, such as phrasing and articulation, but also conditions their various perceptions of the sound. Also, each musical instrument gives the musician a different psycho-physical experience in coupling with the sound. Conductors with a primary background in strings probably have the most valuable conditioned reflexes related to the coherence of sound.

> *Very often baton strokes resemble bow strokes and can elicit **the same sounds from a string ensemble.***[123]

The different types of wind instruments have a different pathway for sound production that depends on the level of applied physical tension and the amount of time existing between the muscular tension and actual occurrence of the sound. The character of wind instruments establishes an important sensation of upbeats as a perpetual breathing pulsation, which is an essential vertical component of the conductor's apparatus (see Chapter 7, *Milieu of Communication*).

The pipe organ would be the instrument that has the greatest similarity with one particular phenomenon of conducting. The organist, as well as the conductor, has to count on the existence

---

[123] Farberman, 176. (Emphasis added)

of the time-lag during performance because of the distance between the player and keyboard on one side and the pipes generating the sound on the other. Such is the nature of the instrument - it takes a fraction of time for air to blow through the pipes and generate the sound, although the time-lag is stable and not varied.[124]

In the modern age, a profound emphasis on the conductor's creative purposefulness is moving to the fore. The historical development of conducting confirms that the most challenging component of the discipline is defining the roles of the internal (non-visual and psychological) settings of the conductor's activity. Modern conducting methodologies have to realize the informative (*quasi-linguistic* [G. Erzhemsky]) nature of such creative activity as a non-verbal (intercommunicative) process. It is appropriate to assume that the modern conducting methodology has to embrace the most general psychological and biomechanical regularities; these interactions provide the basis of the conductor's physical (motor) activity (referring to the natural tools of human physical motion - obtained biologically and socially as innate responses [through phylogenesis[125]]) and reinforce the importance of the correct coordination of all its aspects and functions as an amalgamated psycho-physical system, which assists in the projection of the conductor's creative intentions.

---

[124] The importance of a deep comprehension of the performing specifics of different groups of orchestral instruments will be discussed in Chapter 7.

[125] *Phylogenesis*: [Gr. *phyle*, trybe, + *genesis*, generation, birth] The evolutionary development of a group, race, or species. *Taber's Medical Dictionary*, 1396.

Updated methodological resources that include analyses of the influence of the original instrumental reflexes on the internal mechanisms of a conductor's performing activity will further expand the creative possibilities of contemporary approaches. The apprehension of instrumental reflexes and their influence on the development of the conducting apparatus should be taken in a broad context which includes profound knowledge of orchestral instruments and their specifics.

The uncontrollable influence of instrumental reflexes (or rather the various forms of involuntary tension which are non-communicative in nature) **simply serves as a fuse or a filter between the conductor's valuable mental and physical sensorial abilities and the perception of sound.** Overall, the dynamic (forceful) approach is a trivial transformation of such instrumental reflexes into conducting.

The preservation and artificial implementation of the practical forcible stigmata refer to original audible conducting (time-beating) with the battuta (which in reality was an imitation of an additional [auxiliary] percussive instrument - i.e., floor or stand 'drum'). In modern times this manner (and, consequently, methodological approach) eventually arrived into its final crisis. This type of conducting manifests itself as an inelegant clumsiness, resulting in a consequent stiffness of sound in orchestral response. A conductor with a forcible manner is similar to an instrumentalist who suffers from excessive tension because of an imbalanced apparatus - e.g., a permanent high right shoulder position for violinists or violists which causes the transfer of excessive tension to their backs and both arms, or an over-striking manner for a pianist, etc. Naturally, that talented musician (either instrumentalist or conductor) will find a way to overcome the technical shortcomings of his/her apparatus; thus any positive outcomes in the performance will be achieved not as benefits of his/her technical apparatus but, rather, in spite of it.

The individual musical performance practice, either instrumental or conducting, is a complex action and elaborates many sides of the musician's emotional, physical, and mental abilities. Nevertheless, an understanding of the mental and physiological dissimilarities between instrumental and conducting actions is essential not only for tutorial purposes but also for the practice of professional conducting, and this approach may open new pathways in the development of the modern conducting style.

3

THE ART OF SPIRIT

CLICHES AND IMAGINATION

Both a conductor's and an instrumentalist's creative processes reside in the inner psychological sphere. However, conducting (unlike playing an instrument) is part of a musical activity that is located mainly in a **non-physical (non-tense) sphere of practical realization**: "To acknowledge that the conductor's domain is largely spiritual is to realize the exceptional character of his art. ... The main defect in musical life today is lack of imagination on the part of artists. ... Music is the most spiritual of arts."[126] Nikolai Malko in his book *Fundamentals of the Technic of Conducting* stated: "For the conductor, the work of the imagination, (the comprehension of the music up to the point of its actual performance by the orchestra or chorus), has an exceptional significance."[127] As expressed by George Solti in an interview from the 1970s: "To be a conductor, one must have imagination. . . . I firmly believe that the essential quality of [a] conductor is first of all, to **project** your imagination to other people."[128]

Despite the absence of physical contact with the conductor's 'virtual instrument' (the orchestra), it is necessary to establish a productive visual and psychological correlation between the conductor and orchestral musicians and to find an appropriate and comprehensive mode of interaction that will establish a creative and productive **conceptual technique** of intercommunication: "There are fourteen, sixteen or eighteen people playing exactly the same notes at the same time. Imagine if those sixteen people sitting at a table were expected, at a sign from the head waiter, to lift a fork at exactly the same time, with the same speed and the same enthusiasm."[129]

---

[126] Scherchen, 1-2. It is also appropriate to mention one of Bruno Walter's famous apothegms, "I was touched through my heart by one known saying: 'The Art – it is something with absence of strain.'" Bruno Walter, *O Muzike I Muzizirovanii* [Of Music and Process of Music-Making] (Moscow: Gosizdat, 1962), 33.

[127] Malko, 23.

[128] Sir George Solti, interview for WFMT program, "Profiles of Greatness," 28 November 1974, as quoted in Galkin, *A History of Orchestral Conducting*, 767. (Emphasis added)

[129] Barenboim, 134.

> *It is commonly known that any action mutually performed by a number of persons could be started precisely together only by signal either audible (word, knock, singing etc. ...) or by the power of motion (by force of the moving arm). But none of any abrupt isolated sound or motion will serve as a sign. Any signal which pretends to be associated with its intention has to organize consciously all involved personalities and develop a similar rhythmic modification from them.*[130]

The modern conductor's principal role as a musical leader has constantly evolved to incorporate additional duties over the past centuries.

> *A century ago, in 1894, the great theorist Heinrich Scherchen (1868-1935) predicted (with characteristic pre-science) that the future would require a new kind of orchestra conductor, not the proverbial "time-beater" (the so called Kapellmeister) to which late nineteenth century concert audiences had become accustomed.*[131]

The ability to provide a clear concept of the conductor's own musical inspiration through the complexity of specific communicative actions (pro-linguistic in nature, which appears to be an external part of the conductor's psycho-physical

---

[130] Musin, 56.

[131] Leon Botstein, Introduction to *The Art of Conducting Technique: A New Perspective* by Harold Farberman, vii.

'instrument') has a different mission in comparison with the centuries-old *Kapellmeister* type of conducting by the manifestation of the metrical clichés: "Under present conditions a conductor is necessary not only for 'marking time' and showing the musicians where to enter. Any military bandmaster can handle this by proceeding from the requirements of the 'Rules of Garrison Service.'"[132]

Such practices framed basic descriptions of the conductor's duties. For example, gestures should be small when the orchestral dynamic is *piano* and large with *forte*: "Generally speaking, large movements represent *f* playing and small ones *p* playing."[133] In order to illustrate a *crescendo*, the conductor's gestures should grow larger, and they should get smaller for a *diminuendo:* "As the dynamics gradually increase or decrease, your gesture changes its size."[134]

Methods of expressive conducting, launched by the creative impulses of such exceptionally artistic personalities as Berlioz, Liszt, Wagner, and Mahler, are based upon the supremacy of musical content and its disclosure. At the execution of the performance, the modern orchestra leader has to indicate the expressive spots of the musical phrases and lines, and, most importantly, **actively disclose** the inner substance of music

---

[132] Erzhemsky, 98.

[133] Meier, 6.

[134] Rudolf, 58. Similar descriptions can also be found in: Hunsberger and Ernst, 22, or in Daniel L. Kohut and Joe W. Grant, *Learning to Conduct and Rehearse* (Englewood Cliffs, New Jersey: Prentice-Hall, Inc., 1990), 31-2.

(which should be jointly comprehended by the orchestral musicians who are preoccupied with performing a single instrumental line of the score).

In order to provide an expressive and artistically attractive performance, the modern conductor has to demonstrate a capacity for psychological anticipation (with subsequent visualization) of all of his/her intentions **before** they are embodied in sound (forming the musician's concept about the future [upcoming] character of the sound); the "conductor's hands, ideally, **always have to accomplish the outstripping function; i.e., to act exclusively and permanently before the orchestra**."[135] The acceptance of that description makes the modern definition of 'conducting' distinct from the undifferentiated measuring (or time-beating) that shows the right pattern of metrical schemes or different tempos and dynamics (and is still in wide practice). Thus, from the very first upbeat, the conductor has to provide clear indications of the upcoming tempo, dynamics, and character of the music. As soon as an orchestra begins to perform, the conductor's duty is to sustain the flow of musical texture with visual realizations of his/her **inner creative intentions**. Such tasks include preparation for alterations in tempo, dynamics, character of sound, and the structure of the musical phrases and lines, which refer to the composer's score and, more importantly, the conductor's "inner creative encounter activity"[136] as the conductor's personal interpretation of the piece.

---

[135] Erzhemsky, *Dirijirovanie kak Obschenie* [Conducting as Communication], 42. (Emphasis added)

[136] Dmitri A. Leontiev, *Vvedenie v Psihologiyu Iskusstva* [Introduction of the Psychology of Art] (Moscow: Moscow University Press, 1996), 7.

As Wilhelm Furtwängler stated: "Technique must make free regulation of the rhythm possible, and go beyond this to influence the **tone**."[137] Also it is valuable to mention Gunther Schuller's remark about metronome markings:

> *As much as I may plead – along with Beethoven and Berlioz and many other composer-conductors – for a basic respect for metronome markings, with all the attendant qualifications, I must make it very clear that I do not believe that an exacting adherence to metronomic indications will by itself guarantee a good, a great, or a 'correct,' performance.*[138]

Johann Sebastian Bach stated that the reason he "rarely marked *tempi* in his scores was because he said to himself, as it were: 'If anyone does not understand my theme and my figuration, has no feeling for their character and their expression, of what use will an Italian tempo-indication be to him?'"[139] Ivan Galamian[140] considered the music of J. S. Bach as an example of music the interpretation of which depends on the performer's

---

[137] Wilhelm Furtwängler, *Notebooks* 1924-1954, trans. Shaum Whiteside, ed., and with introduction by Michael Tanner (London: Quartet Books, 1989), 9, quoted in Alcantara, 173. (Emphasis added)

[138] Schuller, 14.

[139] *Three Essays by Felix Weingartner*, 3.

[140] Galamian, Ivan (Alexander) (1903-1981), eminent Armenian-born American violinist and pedagogue. *Baker's Biographical Dictionary of 20th Century Classical Musicians*, by Nicolas Slonimsky, Edited by Laura Kuhn. (New York: Schirmer Books, 1997), 442.

personal conceptions of how a particular piece should sound.

> *If we knew (which we do not) exactly how Bach wanted his music to sound, there still would remain the question of whether it should be played precisely in the historical style of Bach's day, or whether the style should be adapted to fit modern ideas, means, and surroundings. This is a highly controversial question, and no conclusive answer is possible.*[141]

Bruno Walter, in his book *Of Music and Music-Making*, discusses his opinion on the tradition of the "accurate" interpretation of a composer's temporal and dynamical marks:

> *To be sure—'only the spirit can give life'. How little, after all, is said by these indications! No **poco ritenuto** can teach me **how** little should I retard; no **forte** how strongly, no **allegro con brio** how quickly, no **largo** how slowly I should play. These markings have only a vague, quantitative meaning which is just sufficient to point out to the interpreter the direction in which he must move to gain an understanding of the work . . . The composer, to be sure, tries his best to make us find the right tempo by his indications. But not even the apparently incontrovertible tempo indication by means of metronome-numbers can give us a reliable idea of the speed. A marking such as half-note = 92*

---

[141] Ivan Galamian, *Principles of Violin Playing and Teaching* (London: Faber and Faber, 1964), 4.

> *gives us a speed that may be right for the first few bars, but must needs lose its validity as soon as a change in expression demands a modification of speed.*[142]

The arguments regarding the acceptable balance between the conductor's own interpretation and the composer's conjectural concept are among the most controversial musicological aspects of conducting practice and methodology.[143] An example of this never-ending debate can be found in the conducting practice of Gustav Mahler.

> *Mahler ... recognized that the musicians found him hard to follow because he altered his tempi from performance to performance, a habit that he adopted because he would have been 'bored to death if [he] constantly had to take a work down the same monotonous beaten track.*'[144]

It would be appropriate to mention Wagner's remarks on this subject from one of his letters: ". . . only the performer is a real artist. All our poetic creations, all compositional works – this is only a certain 'I want,' and not an 'I can': only performance of

---

[142] Walter, 43.

[143] Schuller, 12-30.

[144] H.-J. Schaefer, *Gustav Mahlers Wirken in Kassel* [Gustav Mahler's Work at Kassel], Musica 14: 6 (1960), 355, quoted in Holden, *The Virtuoso Conductors*, 68.

this 'I can' creates art."[145] "I am convinced," said composer Roger Sessions, "that the performer is an essential element in the whole musical picture. ... There is no such thing as a 'definitive performance' of any work whatsoever. This is true even of performances by the composer himself."[146]

> *The concept obtained by the recipient from the work of art is always the recipient's own concept, conditioned by the content of his own life and personality rather than the concept 'put in' by the composer in the texture of the piece; at the same time, the texture of the piece is developed by the composer – consciousness and unconsciousness – thus, for transferring or, more precisely, suggesting to others utterly certain meanings. The presence of common, for most humans, conditions of vital activity and, therefore, mutual tasks upon concept ... conditioned the possibility of a comparable adequate transfer of concept. The thesis of intercommunication of personal concepts may be recognized as rightful with the reckoning of such reservations.*[147]

---

[145] Richard Wagner, *Pis'ma. Dnevniki. Obrashchenie k Druz'yam* [Letters. Diaries. Appeals to the Friends] (Moscow: Jurgensson, 1911), 22, quoted in Erzhemsky, 181.

[146] Roger Sessions, *Questions about Music* (New York: W. W. Norton & Company, 1971), 86, quoted in Frederik Prausnitz, *Score and Podium* (New York, London: W. W. Norton & Company, 1983), 2.

[147] D. A. Leontiev, *Vvedenie v Psihologiyu Iskusstva* [Introduction of the Psychology of Art], 15-16.

Henrich Neuhaus[148] in his book quoted a remark of Nietzsche's about writers:

> *'To perfect a style is to perfect ideas. Anyone who does not at once agree with this is past salvation.' 'This', commented Neuhaus, 'is the true meaning of technique (style). I often tell my pupils that the word "technique" comes from the Greek word "techne" and that it means art. The objective [the "what"] is already an inclination of the means of attaining it [the "how"].*'[149]

The transmission of the conductor's own concept of music requires a specifically 'tuned' psycho-physical technique (or conducting apparatus) for the realization of the conductor's creative intentions. The common assumption of the word *technique* "is the physical means by which one actualizes one's musical conception."[150]

The conductor's technical abilities (mental and physical apparatus) serve as a link between the conductor's own conception of the piece and the musicians' perceptions. Such a

---

[148] Neigauz, Genrich Gustavovich (also Neuhaus), 1888-1964. Soviet pianist, teacher and author of work on music. *Great Soviet Encyclopedia* [Bol'shaya Sovetskaya Entsiklopediia] A Translation of the Third Edition (New York: Macmillan, Inc., London: Collier Macmillan Publishers, 1978), vol. 17, 416.

[149] Heinrich Neuhaus, *The Art of Piano Playing*, trans. K. A, Leibovitch (London: Barrie and Jenkins, 1973), 82, quoted in Alcantara, 174.

[150] Alcantara, 171.

virtual instrument should include the capacity for psychological anticipation, the use of the technique of "divided attention" (such practice is similar to the conductor's "third ear"- a definition proposed by Gunther Schuller in his book *The Complete Conductor*), an ability to form the model inner sound ("imaginary orchestra"), and the imagination to visualize a non-forcible quasi-linguistic action.[151]

> *Busoni ... writes that a great pianist must first and foremost be a great technician. But, he says, **technique does not depend solely on fingers and wrists, strength and persistence. It is seated in the brain**.*[152]

Modern orchestral practice has proven that conducting based on the principles of mental and, consequently, visualized anticipation are of great assistance in realizing artistic tasks.[153] This is especially true given the common practice of limited or even absentee rehearsals (typical for conductors' auditions or competitions), which are out of reach for the "beat-striking method."[154] But such sophisticated practices require a specially

---

[151] The methodology of artistic purpose and practice of division of psychological attention can be found in these resources: 1. Konstantin S. Stanislavsky, *Polnoe Sobranie Sochinenii*, [Complete Edition of Works] (Moscow: GosIzdat, 1954), vol. 1: 54-61; 2. Schuller, 17; 3. Scherchen, 15.

[152] Stuckenschmidt, *Ferruccio Busoni*, 79, quoted in Alcantara, 172. (Emphasis added)

[153] Erzhemsky, 216.

[154] There are quotation marks because such a description is very conditional; later the definition of the beat-striking method will be used instead of the "psychological expectation of occurrence of sound at the breaking point of a physically enforced downward-upward motion."

tuned mental *internal* instrument, an external technical elasticity, a high level of individual professionalism from the orchestral musicians, and a high degree of collective self-organization from a group (orchestra) with a large core of full-time professional players.

In the modern age, the high collective performing standard is common even for non-major orchestras. For conducting a semi-professional or student orchestra with a substandard level of self-organization, a simplified manner of conducting "on the beat" (or physical reinforcements) may still have a reasonable degree of practical implication, but only in the early stages of rehearsals.[155]

The practice of providing musical concepts through mental and visualized anticipation can make a performance very expressive, but requires a particular psychological and physical modification of the conductor's action.

---

[155] The conductor's apparatus should include various sets of techniques (depending on the orchestra's professional and self-organizational level) from the simple alphabetical manifestation of striking strokes and metrical clichés to complex conceptual techniques.

ACTION AND CONCEPT

A comprehension and practical realization of various concepts and developments in the sciences of behavioral psychology, psycholinguistics, and the psychology of communication may assist in the practical realization of the conductor's artistic intentions. The nature of the musician's psychological responses to audible and visual stimuli must be taken into account due to the special and complex feature of the conducting practice as internal and external communication: "For gestured depiction of power and energy, the presentation of muscular tension is not as important as the motion which **forms the conception** about power and energy."[156]

The style of conducting that features visual and mental anticipation was first introduced by Arthur Nikisch and later adopted by Wilhelm Furtwängler, Nikolai Malko, and Herbert von Karajan.[157] The practical differences between the forcible

---

[156] Musin, 62. (Emphasis added)

[157] Two of Malko's most prominent pupils, Evgeny Mravinsky (1906-1987) and Ilia Musin (1903-1999), should be mentioned as well. Evgeny Mravinsky was the music director of the Leningrad Philharmonic Symphony Orchestra from 1936 to 1987, and Ilia Musin was one of the most distinguished conducting teachers and scholars of the twentieth century – the

and non-forcible traditions are rather specific, as the gained practical reflex of expectation at the occurrence of orchestral sound requires a different psycho-physical mechanism. Modern conducting practice has revealed that the tradition of conducting "on the beat" is subject to a variety of shortcomings, mostly because being *on-the-beat* in actuality means **always being behind** the reality of sound.

The expectation of sound at the lower point of the stressed-ahead (clicked) downward-upward motion is a recurrence of psycho-physical actions that belong to the instrumental environment (where the use of muscular tension instantly binds with the occurrence of the sound) and has a correlation with conditioned responses gained by conductors through their primary instrumental practice, or as *dynamic*[158] stereotypes characteristic of instrumental performance. The influence of

---

'father' of the Leningrad/St. Petersburg conducting school. Among his pupils are many prominent modern conductors, including Yury Temirkanov, music director of the St. Petersburg Philharmonic Symphony Orchestra (Russian Federation) and former music director of the Baltimore Symphony Orchestra (United States of America); Mariss Jansons, former music director of the Pittsburgh Symphony Orchestra (USA); Valerie Gergiev, music director of the Mariinsky (Kirov) State Opera House (RF) and principal guest conductor of the New York Metropolitan Opera (USA); and Semeon Bichkov, music director of the Orchestre de Paris (France). Some of Karajan's pupils adopted this manner of sound anticipation as well; Christoph Eschenbach, former music director of the Houston and Philadelphia Symphony Orchestras and at the present time music director of the National Symphony Orchestra, is a notable example.

[158] *Dynamics* [Greek, *dynamis*, force]: 1. The science of motion in response to forces. 2. In psychiatry, used as a contraction of psychodynamics. 3. In the behavioral sciences, any of the numerous intrapersonal and interpersonal influences phenomena associated with personality development and interpersonal processes. *Stedman's Medical Dictionary*, 28th Edition, 594.

that phenomenon on the conducting practice was realized by the prominent German conductor and scholar Heinrich Scherchen; he noticed: "It is an established law that **increased psychical energy tends to show itself in the form of increased physical energy**," but to be able to express inner musical intentions the conductor has to realize that: **"Physical energy is anti-musical:** music, the art of the spirit and spiritual tensions, cannot endure physical energy as an end in itself."[159] For the conducting practice, any physical tension creates an obstacle in the transformation of the conductor's inner artistic impulses.

The forceful physical action (in the form of a strike or click) typical of the generally accepted conducting method is non-informative and non-communicative (at least in the musical context) in itself, and consequently the perception of such an action will be anti-musical as well. In contrast with instrumental practice, where the pattern of physical (muscular) effort always coincides instantaneously with the sound, orchestral leading incorporates an additional psycho-physical pattern of intercommunication, as described by the following: The visual[160] stimulus generated by the conductor's inner creative intentions and designed as a part of the conceptual (non-dynamic) 'informational' action evokes a musician's response which potentially results in the occurrence of sound of a certain character and quality conditioned by the musician's comparable

---

[159] This statement, made by Hermann Scherchen almost a century ago, best expresses the need for the existence of a non-physical (non-dynamic) method of conducting. Scherchen, 24. (Emphasis added)

[160] The phenomenon of inner (intangible) impulse will be discussed in Chapter 5, *Inner Mechanisms. Inner Will.*

reaction onto an appropriately designed action.[161]

> *Herr Mahler holds the reins in his hand with an energy which binds the individual firmly to him [and] draws him ... with magical force into his own world of thoughts.*[162]

At first glance, the complexity of the physical (muscular) interaction during conducting seems to be similar for instrumental playing. Both the instrumentalist and conductor, for the realization of their artistic duty, have to incorporate a complex flow of physical interactions of muscular contractions and relaxations as a necessary part of their techniques. One important divergence should be examined and taken into account by a conductor: "The following factors must include the internal modeling, that is, the anticipation of the desired result

---

[161] In reference to Lev Vygotsky's work on psycho-linguistic development, it would be appropriate to count a gesture-stimulus (motion-impulse) only as a fraction of the complex meaning-formative "lingual" unit. The traditional utilitarian description of the upbeat (as a distinct segment of the conducting activity) does not adequately explain or disclose the innate meaning of the phenomenon and the inner complexity of conducting (as a part of the non-verbal communicative process). In analogy to Vygotsky's claim that only a complex of symbols functioning as a "lingual" unit (with reference to the conducting process - a pattern of 'informative' motions organized by the creative conceptual [goal-oriented] task of the disclosure of inner content of music) forms the necessary internal meaning of the communicative process. Lev S. Vygotsky, *Psihologiya i Uchenie o Lokalizazii Psihicheskih Funkzii* [Psychology and Studies on Localization of Psychological Functions] (Moscow: Znanie, 1980), 168-174, quoted in Erzhemsky, 246.

[162] Josef Sittard's review in the *Hamburgischer Correspondent* on April 1st, 1891 as found in K. and H. Blaufopf, *Mahler: His Life, Work and World* (London: Thames & Hudson, 2000), 93, quoted in Holdend, 82.

as an ideally formulated goal of the conductor's forthcoming activity and the **constant psychological anticipation**[163] [forethought] as a condition for the realization of leadership."[164]

The essence of the forceful motions evoked by a conductor's conditioned stereotypes as an inseparable subconscious component of the primary instrumental experience (the continuous and immediate physical application) have little value from practical and artistic standpoints. The conductor's suitable mental setting for non-forcible physical action will broaden his/her creative abilities; hence the development of specific ingenuous psychological contact (realized as a specific proprioceptive sensation – the conductor's "touché") with the sound, which is one of the most challenging tasks of modern conducting: "By his fingers, a conductor receives a **specific perception of cohesiveness with the sound.** Partly, one of the important technical methods that cause the occurrence of a shade-tone [touché] depends on it."[165]

The lack of a need for direct forcible (muscular) action against

---

[163] It is important to mention the thesis, which is based on research of psychological reactions on signals and temporal connections, that the anticipated reflection of reality is a distinctive characteristic of the unconditioned response. This characteristic is generally recognized as a basic form of the development of living matter. Piotr K Anokhin, *Metodologichaskii Analiz Uzlovich Problem Uslovnogo Refleksa* [Methodological Analysis of Main Problems of Conditioned Response] (Moscow: Institut Filosofii Akademii Nauk SSSR, [Institute of Philosophy Under Supervision of Academy of Science of USSR] 1962), 28-9.

[164] Erzhemsky, 16-17. (Emphasis added)

[165] Musin, 17. (Emphasis added)

any materialized subject is the main psycho-physical dissimilarity between instrumental and conducting practices. In comparison with instrumental performance, the question of the level of muscular contraction or relaxation elaborated by the conductor is not as important as the psychological effect of a suitably designed pattern of actions [tangible or intangible] on the orchestra's musicians. This will form a **comparable conception** of the appropriate tempo, dynamics, and character of the sound.[166] It establishes the different psychological intentions for the use of physical (muscular) tension despite the fact that physical involvement is utilized for both instrumental playing and conducting.

The instrumentalist's mental and physical expectation of sound occurrence is a result of the direct application of stressed muscular tension and is not similar to the conductor's psychological expectations obtained through the process of conducting. Despite this methodological assertion, the simple active elaboration of a certain and standardized combination of gestures designed as a schematic (within the frame and pattern of conventional schemes) depiction of varied levels of muscular exchange (either with very relaxed or extremely intense muscular tone) **will not evoke the musicians' necessary psycho-physical reaction that is required for a vital and expressive performance**:

---

[166] Here I would like to emphasize the principal difference between analyses of the conductor's physical motion (gesture) and his/her complex action in general as indivisible phenomena. In modern conducting methodology, the gesture cannot be taken separately as an isolated motion but rather as a segment of a complex cluster of mental and physical actions (conceptual stimuli).

> *But the decisive and final turn towards the new system occurred only after the general ensemble culture of musical collectives had matured along with their self-consciousness and ability for self-regulation, that is, [the turn occurred] when orchestras **actively** began to "think", having been transformed from objects of a conductor's influence into the subjects of communication and creation, into [an] independent artistic organism.*[167]

For expressive and successful conducting, the amount of physical energy applied toward beat-marking is not so important (though the instrumental conditioned responses provoke responses to this end). What is most important is the musicians' clear impression of the motion (or motion-impulse) as a **conceptual (informational) construct**.[168] The conductor must provide a continuous cycle of such conceptual motions-units as a segment of the communicational tool (in accordance with the dialectic principle of the unity of the part and the whole). It is vitally essential to manifest this cycle of gestures with a communicative anticipatory technique,[169] or else those

---

[167] Erzhemsky, 214.

[168] Or *units of conducting* and *units of communication*, as suggested by Erzhemsky, 246.

[169] It is important to mention the thesis, which is based on research of psychological reaction on signal and temporal connection, that the anticipated reflection of reality is a distinctive characteristic of the unconditioned response. Such a characteristic is generally recognized as a basic form of the development of living matter. Piotr K Anochin, *Metodologichaskii Analiz Uzlovich Problem Uslovnogo Refleksa* [Methodological Analysis of Main Problems of Conditioned Response] (Moscow: Institut Filosofii Akademii Nauk SSSR, [Institute of Philosophy Under Supervision of Academy of Science of USSR] 1962), 28-9.

gestures will not be informational. Though formally such a gesture may resemble the performance of the traditional upbeat, it is important to indicate the inner conflict between the meaning of the traditional terminology (description of the upbeat) and a multifunctional complexity of the anticipatory conceptual motion.[170]

---

[170] For example, Ilia Musin, in an extensive depiction of the multifunctional communicative role of the upbeat, had to describe (with the implementation of specific terminology) over thirty various types of motion-upbeats (i.e., complete and incomplete preparatory, double-meter and triple-meter upbeats, various upbeats for an incomplete measure, upbeats of various modes, [e.g., converted, suspended, converted-suspended, etc.]). Musin, *Technique of Conducting*, 55-129.

PART II

DIMENSIONS OF CONDUCTING

4

THE SYNTAX AND SEMANTICS OF CONDUCTING

During the first half of the nineteenth century, certain traditions of the orchestral arrangements on stage and the conductor's physical presence were eventually reached as mutually accepted principles which were carried into modern times. The paradoxical dilemma, though, persisted through the history of conducting technique into modern times: should the conductor 'operate' (play) the orchestra or lead the orchestra through the landscape of music?[171] Whether the answer is one,

---

[171] As George Erzhemsky suggested, there were three periods in the history of conducting: "The first is the 'strike-bandmaster' period, characterized by the prevalence of mechanistic principles of conducting, which were based on 'battuta-stick techniques.' In this period the orchestra was not yet the

the other, or a combination of both, the clarification of this dilemma is essential.

Presuming that the activity of conducting is a specific (quasi-linguistic) form of communication, it will be appropriate (with some reservations, however) for a description of its fundamental phenomenon to use linguistic terms such as *syntax*[172] and *semantics*.[173] The use of such terms will reveal their meaning

---

conductor's partner in the creative act. For the most part, it was defined as, so to say, a 'living instrument' on which ... the conductor 'played,' beating time. ... The second, 'illustrative-depicting,' stage represents a well-known analogy of the 'art of representation' characteristic for that time – a trend well-known to us from the history of the theater. Here it was already possible to observe attempts at the overcoming of mechanistic techniques and the striving to reveal the informative aspects of music. However, for the most part it did not go further than illustration of the external form and details of the musical fabric by movements specially thought up before a mirror." And finally the modern: "The informational-psychological approach to conducting, in tune with modern scientific notions, was first formulated by Franz Liszt in his famous 'Letter on Conducting.' ... *We are helmsmen, but not oarsmen,* that is, the leader must *manage* the musicians' activities but not attempt somehow, in analogy with actions of the instrumentalists, to directly 'extract' sounds from the orchestra by means of power methods." Erzhemsky, 160-1.

[172] In linguistics, *Syntax* (from Ancient Greek συν- syn-, "together", and τάξις táxis, "arrangement"): 1. The order of words in which they convey meaning collectively by their connection and relation. Also, the established rules and usages of grammatical construction; the branch of grammar that deals with these. ... The order and arrangement of words or symbols forming a logical sentence; the rules by which elements in a formal system, programming language, etc., are combined. *Shorter Oxford English Dictionary. On Historical Principles.* 6th Edition, vol. 2 (New York: Oxford University Press, 2007), 3152.

[173] *Semantic* (Greek sēmantikos, giving signs, significant, symptomatic, from sēma [σῆμα], sign): 2. Relating to meaning in language: relating to connotations of words. *Semantics* 1. The branch of linguistics that deals with meaning; (the study or analysis of) the relationships between linguistic

through discussion of the external and internal intercommunicative sides of conducting (though this division is superficial).

The external aspect of the conductor's complex action can be conditionally described as a phenomenon similar to the linguistic term *syntax*, and the inner (mental) part as *semantic*. The existence of conventional metrical schemes (1/4, 2/4, 3/4, 4/4 and their variations) is an example of the conditional syntax of conducting. This metrical patterns function as a customary tool for a basic vocabulary of gestural communication. After centuries of evolution, orchestral performance has developed this vocabulary as a practical and mutually accepted (conventional) tool of communication. This tool has been refined by the need to perform the complex rhythmic patterns and harmonic innovations that characterized the following:

1. The orchestral compositions of the Viennese Classical School.

2. The music of the early Romantic period.

3. Increasing diversity of the instruments of the orchestra.

---

symbols and their meanings. 2. The interpretation of signs in general. *Shorter Oxford English Dictionary. On Historical Principles*, 6th Edition, vol. 2, 2746.

4. From the middle of the nineteenth century forward, this vocabulary (conventional metrical schemes) has been further developed to include the complicated metrical patterns of meters, abrupt tempo changes, and highly expressive content of works of the late Romantic period, and, finally, innovations in orchestration and instrumentation introduced on by Gustav Mahler and other composers of the late nineteenth and early twentieth centuries.

The current practical styles and methods of conducting could be summarized as follows:

I. A generally accepted tradition of practical (conventional) tools of signs/clichés, which was formed in the first half of the nineteenth century.[174]

II. Communication between conductor and orchestra through the manifestation of *conventional metrical schemes*:[175]

---

[174] The most complete graphical descriptions of existing variations on practical metrical schemes (with extensive references to numerous methodological resources) can be found in: Eliot Galkin, *A History of Orchestral Conducting*, 305-423. The most complete description of the technical application of the metrical schemes can be found in: Musin, *Technique of Conducting*, 32-210.

[175] I prefer the term "conventional metrical schemes," which was used by a

There are several schools of thought regarding the time-beating patterns and several ways of diagramming the beats. One school emphasizes that every beat should touch a given horizontal base line. Another school maintains that every beat-point should land in an identical spot in space.[176]

    A. Striking the provisional horizontal line

    B. Point-centered indication of beats

III.   Modern conducting commonly consists of two practical and methodological approaches: [177]

    A. Dynamically (physically) accentuated manifestations of metrical points (beats)

Professor at the St. Petersburg Conservatory (Russian Federation) and a prominent contemporary scholar, George Erzhemsky, in his books: *Psychological Paradoxes of Conducting*, 88; *Psychologicheskie Mechanizmy Ispolnitel'skikh Deistvii Dirizhyora* [Psychological Mechanisms of Conductor's Performing Activities], Psihologicheskii Jurnal [Journal of Psychology], 2nd ed. (Moscow: APN, 1983), 5; *Dirijirovanie Kak Obschenie I Tvorchestvo* [Conducting as Communication and Creativity] (St. Petersburg: Unpublished Manuscript, 2003), 7; *Psikhologiya Dirijirovaniya* [Psychology of Conducting] (Moscow: Smisl, 1983), 12.

[176] Elizabeth A. H. Green, *The Modern Conductor* (New Jersey: Prentice-Hall, Inc., 1987), 17.

[177] It is important to emphasize that such descriptions illustrate those methods developed through protracted performance. During rehearsal such methods could be applied in a fragmentary fashion, with certain reservations.

       within a conventional pattern of schemes

    B. A tool of intercommunication for the realization of creative (musical) intentions with prevalence of *non-verbal quasi-linguistic intercommunicative principles*[178] through the *non-forcible utilization of conventional metrical schemes*[179]

Thus, modern conducting has two contrasting practical methods. Approach A demonstrates a preservation of a meaningless and forceful usage of conventional schemes without substantial reference to the semantics of conducting; while Approach B, on the contrary, reveals a non-forceful manner which is based on rules of human intercommunication. It is likely that this dilemma has existed since conducting was established as an independent artistic activity. However, the inner conflict between these two approaches remained unsolved throughout the twentieth century, mainly due to the absence of a unified methodological approach.

In the last century, economic and social changes affected the orchestra business in general, and consequently called for significant changes in conducting methods. This contrasts with

---

[178] Lev S. Vygotsky, *Thought and Language* (Cambridge: MIT Press, 1965), 12-21.

[179] Erzhemsky, *Dirijirovanie kak Obschenie I Tvorchestvo* [Conducting as Communication and Creative Process], 19-24.

the nineteenth century, wherein there was tremendous growth in the number of orchestras as well as the number of music education institutions and programs established for instrumental training. Also, socio-political demands were brought on by the musicians' union demanding higher standard service pay, recording regulations, etc., and, consequently increased costs, which (among other issues) reduced the number of rehearsals available to the orchestra and conductor. The limited number (or even absence) of rehearsals in modern times is typical for conductors' auditions and competitions, or for emergency substitution calls.

The forceful (striking) manner is an silent vestige of the "battuta" style with a relocation of the application of the inaudible strike being higher (on the level of the conductor's stand rather than the floor). The word "beat" (with its semantic meaning of beating [striking] against something) is a preserved remnant of the original forceful conducting manner as an etymological trace of its origin to the "battuta" approach. Ironically, this lexical fragment was carried over two centuries into the modern age as part of the forceful tradition even though this characterization of metrical units is dubious for the modern conducting practice.

THE POWER OF SOUND GOVERNANCE

CONTOUR OF SOUND

For centuries, the fundamental issue in conducting practice has revolved around one principal issue: is there a universal technique which gives a possibility of establishing productive communication with the orchestra and taking control over the complexity of the orchestra's sound? At present time, the answer is yes, there is, and has always been; such a practical tool is the phenomenon known as the *contour of sound* and, for modern conducting, it is essential to acquire the specific mental and physical sensations it produces.

The contour (or line) of sound is a vital segment of modern expressive conducting syntax.[180] The practical development of profound comprehension and sensation of the phenomenon of

---

[180] However, the contour of sound includes the innate (semantic) features of conducting as well.

the *vicinity* (contour) of sound is essential for a successful and expressive conducting practice. This phenomenon should develop into an exclusive part of the modern conducting methodology. Its apprehension (and, eventually, sensation) should become a cornerstone of the conductor's inner technique. The presence of the contour of sound emerges in the form of a line of sound within the vicinity of conducting (or in the surrounding area of the manifestation of motions). This contour is a specific provisional zone where the orchestra's sound repeatedly appears in response to the conductor's action: "When the conductor's gesture 'meets' the extracted sound, that is, at the end of the gesture, the hand has a feeling of touching an elastic object. This feeling of touching results in a shock and the hand is thrown a little backwards, or rebounds a little."[181] The sensation of the vicinity (contour) of sound (and consequent connection to it) is an effectual experience which is crucially valuable for successful conducting practice.

The generally-accepted conducting method suggests that this spot (or point) of communication should be located at the "tip of the baton," as if this method assumes that the orchestra's musicians are trained to constantly follow its movements.[182] However, the comprehension of intercommunicative principles of the conductor-orchestra action suggests that this method is causative and artificial. The occurrence of a definite temporal

---

[181] Malko, *The Conductor and His Baton*, 49.

[182] For example, in books of: H. Farberman, *The Art of Conducting Technique: A New Perspective*, 28; E. Green, *The Modern Conductor*, 7; B. Grosbayne, *Techniques of Modern Orchestral Conducting* (Cambridge, Massachusetts: Harvard University Press, 1956), 21; M. Rudolf, *The Grammar of Conducting*, 10.

interval between the action of the conductor and the sound is a manifestation of the phase in natural human reaction to a visual stimulus required for the assessment of the motion originated by the conductor and the execution of the ensemble's combined response.

The observation of the practical occurrence of sound after the lowest point of the conductor's motion (as a consequence of the existence of a time-gap) provides the prospect of tracing a certain location (or line) within the environ of the manifestation of motions (or metrical schemes) when recognized by the orchestra as a identified momentum of the continuous appearance of sound. The examination of this phenomenon reveals that the appearance of this momentum occurs within a similar contour, and that: "Our concept of relations in space comes not only from our binocular vision but above all **from our experience of a fixed eye-level above a fixed ground.**"[183]

However, the level for the occurrence of the sound after the lowest point of the motion is conditioned and may vary depending on the tempo or character of the music. It is likely that many conductors of the past (especially in the nineteenth century) intuitively sensed that there would be a principal technique of connecting the action and the sound. After all, the concept of the presence of the contour of sound materialized (after hundreds of years of trial and error) for the conductor's

---

[183] *The Body and Social Metaphor* by Donald G. MacRae, in *The Body as a Medium of Expression. Essays Based on a Course of Lectures Given at the Institute of Contemporary Arts, London*, Edited by Jonathan Benthall and Ted Polhemus (New York: E. P. Dutton & Co., Inc., 1975), 63-4.

intention **to control the appearance of sound at the lowest end of the beat!**

A factor of the appearance of the contour of sound above the flatness of conducting, which is typical for the application of the striking motion, other than the delay of human reaction on visual stimuli, is the acknowledgement of natural tendencies and practical differences in the performance of orchestral instruments.

> *In a large majority of cases the regular preliminary beat will secure a unified attack. However, certain instrumental combinations present difficulties that require special consideration. The inexperienced conductor may find it difficult, especially in soft entrances, to bring in wind instruments simultaneously, or winds combined with harp, or high strings.* ***The problem is caused by the purely physical difference in the way each instrument "speaks."*** *For instance, the oboe player reacts differently at the attack than the trumpet player, and various other instruments respond differently in very high or very low registers. Despite these differences, a good ensemble must be achieved, or the entrance will be "arpeggiated." This difficulty occurs not only at the beginning but also in the course of a piece, especially after rests.*[184]

---

[184] Rudolf, 246. (Emphasis added)

As was discussed earlier, it is recognizable that stringed instruments are played with different physical and practical approaches than wind instruments and percussion. However, this is not just for the reason that stringed instruments are played by the bow grabbing the strings, wind instruments by the blowing of air, and percussion by striking with mallets. To understand why such differences are essential for the conception of the vicinity of sound we have to recognize that there is an individual temporal delay which is specific for each group: e.g., strings and brass; or within the group: violins and double basses, etc. Such specifics should be taken into account when those instruments are performing together. If we make a simple test for the ability of players of different orchestral instruments to respond to the single downward-upward motion (distinct beat strike), the result will most likely be that different instruments respond with a different time-lag to the same beat.

By putting the results of this test in order, we find that the responses of some instruments are somewhat quicker than others. Timpani and percussion instruments in general, along with piano and harp, respond the fastest of all and it is justifiable to put them at the bottom layer of the conditional contour of the vicinity of sound. This is followed by the thin layer of strings (with the violin at the bottom and the double-bass on the top). Next comes the layer of woodwinds, then brass (in this sequence: trumpets, horns, trombones, and tuba). Finally, the upper 'edge' of the contour of sound culminates (coincides) with the organ (with its natural temporal lag) and the choir[185] (as indicated in the following diagram).

---

[185] The moderation of temporal factors is one of the most challenging techniques of conducting. However, certain technical methods which will be

Conditional Table of Instrumental Temporal Delays[186]

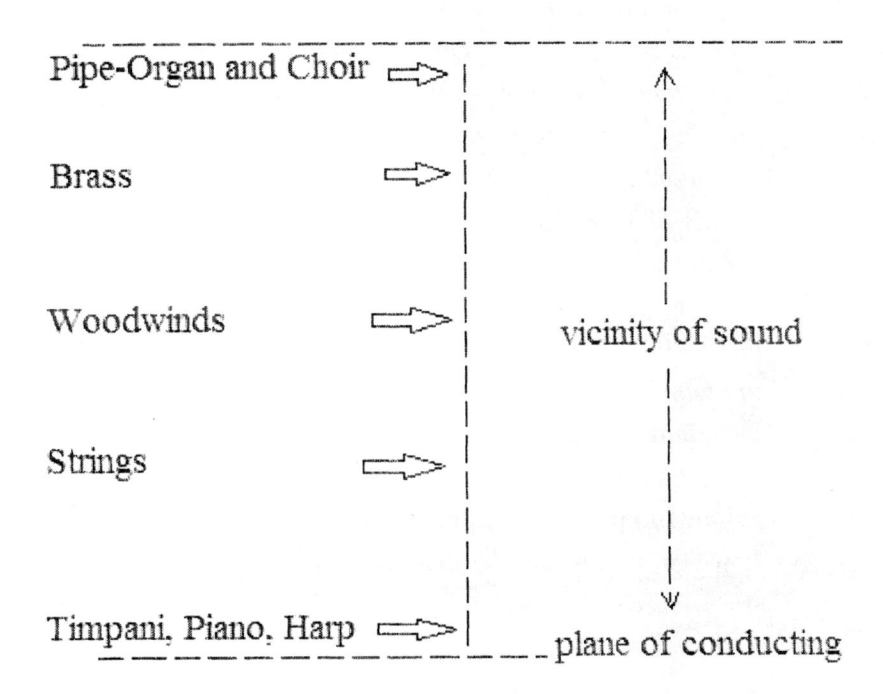

```
- - - - - - - - - - - - - - - - - - - - - - - - -
Pipe-Organ and Choir  ⇒ |            ↑
                        |            |
Brass                 ⇒ |            |
                        |            |
Woodwinds             ⇒ |     vicinity of sound
                        |            |
Strings               ⇒ |            |
                        |            |
                        |            ↓
Timpani, Piano, Harp  ⇒ |_ _ _ plane of conducting
- - - - - - - - - - - - -
```

discussed later (e.g., suspended upbeat, converted upbeat, rhythmically-contingent rebound, etc.) could help to modify or eliminate this negative aspect. The factor of distance also makes its contribution to temporal lag during an orchestra's performance. However, experienced professional orchestral musicians will adjust to it in a simple manner of anticipation, which is sometimes necessary but has a negative effect on the performance if implemented constantly (simply in a manner of anticipation of the conductor's motion).

[186] One may posit that such a table is justifiable under the condition that musicians (especially in the brass section) do not anticipate the conductor's action.

> *The solution of the problem depends to a certain extent upon the understanding between the conductor and his players. ... Some German conductors use an anticipatory beat. The played attack does not coincide with the baton movement but follows it by as much as half a second longer. The conductor uses a rather dry beat (tenuto, or for f attacks, marcato), stops on the opening count and **waits** for the orchestra, then proceeds as usual. ... Some orchestras are accustomed to the use of this technique, either for the entire group or only for certain soft entrances in the winds; the conductor visiting these orchestras will do well to adapt his beat to this well-established habit, for it would take a great deal of training to replace it. **The reason that such an anticipatory beat works is that the players are accustomed to adjusting their attacks so that they follow immediately after the beat.** Many conductors, however, adhere to the principle of always beating with the orchestra.*[187]

The stiff and conditioned stigmata of the forceful technique make it difficult to adjust the conductor's apparatus, which is especially necessary to orchestras with the practical 'habit' of a delayed (time-lagged) occurrence of sound and in some examples it may be treacherous. In general, the practical implementation of the contour of sound is not only beneficial for the conductor's own physical sense of the orchestral sound (the conductor's contact with the sound) but also for specifically establishing the zone of the **synchronized** sound appearance for

---

[187] Rudolf, 247. (Emphasis added)

various orchestral instruments and **the comprehensive continuous maintenance of the concept of this zone**.

On numerous occasions I have witnessed practical situations when conductors (even with names and reputations) were having evident psychological difficulties adjusting themselves to an orchestra's manner (mainly because of the presence of a time-lag), even after their rigorous and unsuccessful appeals to the orchestra to adjust the appearance of sound to the lowest point of the beat. Sometimes such demands could be as humorous as: "Do not play by what you hear, but by what you see!" In reality, such an emotional appeal discloses no more and no less than the conductor's inability to unify the variety of the sound's appearances with appropriate motion-impulse (or an upbeat of suitable *innate* [informative] quintessence). In general, it indicates the lack of his/her concept of the *contour of sound* and consequently the absence of the technique of the unified conceptual upbeat[188] needed due to differences among instruments and/or players' individual perceptions.

Nevertheless, after several measures of music of "correct" playing, the musicians resumed their ordinary manner (with the presence of a time-lag after the conductor's beat), and in the end it continued with a syncopated application of beats by the conductor and the consequent appearance of orchestral sound on the upper edge of the rebound.[189] Sometimes such

---

[188] Again, the presence of a practical time-lag is usual for any large ensemble and not just for orchestras which have this habit as their historical tradition.

[189] Here again, we encounter the deficiency in the terminological narrative of the specific action (i.e., conceptual upbeat or motion-impulse, gesture-unit,

disagreements ended disastrously – with the orchestra stopping during the rehearsal (or even during the performance), or with conductors throwing batons against the conductor's stand in anger, assuming that the musicians were misbehaving or disrupting the rehearsal. In reality the true reason for the predicament was the inability of the conductor to adjust his/her action in accordance with the nature of human perception.[190]

---

etc.) and, consequently, the need for a mutually accepted updated vocabulary for the description of the conducting techniques in accordance with the conditionally new methodological paradigms such as: a time-lag, the constant mental anticipation of the action, and other advanced techniques.

[190] Obviously, those incidents are rare. The conductor's ability to adjust his/her technique also depends on one's personality and the specifics of the interpersonal (conductor-orchestra) psychological 'atmosphere' during rehearsals and performances.

Schematic display of the presence of the contour of sound in a single striking beat:

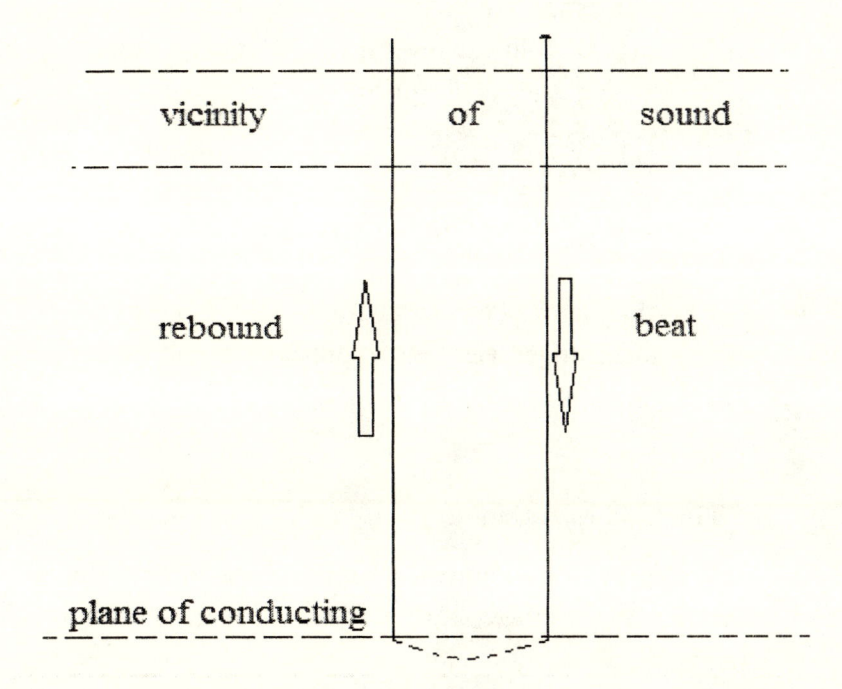

vicinity	of	sound
rebound	⇧ ⇩	beat

plane of conducting

The environs of the contour of sound are approximate and its location is conditioned by:[191]

A. Tempo

For **slower** tempi, the vicinity of sound has a propensity to be located at a **lower** level next to the plane (flatness) of conducting and, consequently, at an **upper** edge for **faster** tempos.

B. Dynamics

For **loud** dynamics, the vertical length of the contour of sound tends to **extend** and, consequently, it becomes **narrower** for **soft** dynamic levels.

C. The Orchestration

For **strings,** the vicinity of sound tends to move to a **lower** plane, and to a **higher** plane for **woodwinds and brass.**

D. The Instrumentation

A greater number of instruments is apt to **expand** the vertical extent of the vicinity of sound (especially for slower tempos).

---

[191] The following outcomes are conditioned by the performance of a simple unmodified striking stroke.

E. The Artistic Traditions of the Orchestra

Some orchestras have a long tradition of a significant (deliberate and excessive) time-lag before the appearance of the sound (e.g., Berlin Philharmonic and St. Petersburg Philharmonic).

The comprehension of this phenomenon (the presence of the contour of sound) is very valuable for various practical purposes, especially in movements with slow tempi and continuous stretched melodies (especially if the melody is presented by a number [or layers] of instruments), for indications of gradual dynamic changes, for non-striking (non-forcible) indications of changing notes, or entrances of instruments (especially if they are enter on weak beats).

For example:

1. Second and fourth beats in a slow 4/4 meter. Tchaikovsky P., "Romeo and Juliet", beginning.

2. A bond between beats and fulfillment of the beat with fast notes (small metrical values such as 16^{ths} or 32^{nds}) – Brahms J., Symphony # 1, Finale.

It is expected that the hidden existence of the contour of sound is evident in forceful (overcoming) conducting styles as well, though more likely without the conductor's awareness (especially if the orchestra is trained to play on-the-beat or in conjunction with an anticipation of the conductor's action). In that instance, the contour of sound is pushed toward the upper edge of the rebound and emerges as an innate and rather unpleasant result of such a forceful (striking) mannerism.

The internal conflict within forcibly performed downward-upward motions (as well as an unmodified performance of the click) is situated in its own principle – it is the expectation of sound at the lower breaking point and its actual likely appearance at the upper edge of the rebound. The application of stronger, harder, 'clearer' beats or the application of any overcoming types of the beat will more likely than not push the location of the vicinity of sound higher. In reality, such actions always put the conductor's motions away (or up higher) from the sound and situate his/her actions behind the orchestra's responses. This contradiction develops a mental fuse and creates a significant obstacle to the progress of the conductor's professional improvement.

Overall, the existence of the contour of sound as a communicative phenomenon is evident for any group of players (bands or orchestras), whether they are composed of amateurs, students, professionals, or combinations of each. This fact justifies the necessity for the development of the sense of the contour of sound, and makes it an important part of a technique which will make the conducting apparatus flexible and instantly adjustable. On the other hand, ignorance of the contour of sound and the conditioned installation of a chart of techniques or clichés will, once and for all, serve a conductor's own reality rather than the reality of sound.

But, how do we find the appropriate method to effectively synchronize the manifestation of the conductor's apparatus in reference to the phenomenon of the contour of sound? How do we locate that line (or provisional zone) within the vicinity of conducting where the orchestra will perform with its best sound? Here one must appeal to the rules of human intercommunication in order to find the location where the communication between the conductor and the orchestra's musicians will be the most satisfied and productive.[192] Orchestral seating was eventually designed in such a way that all musicians could perceive the conductor clearly on a similar and convenient visual line. This visual line can also be described as the *natural* plane within the milieu of communication.

In linguistic terms, the phenomenon of the contour of sound may be conditionally described as a part of the conductor's syntax (along with a set of conventional schemes), but with a semantic (conceptual) connotation. Essentially, **the contour of sound serves as a specific outer sensorial screen** for the reflection of a musician's reaction to the conductor's action. The practical implementation of the contour of sound **is an intangible bond** between the innate constituencies (*semantics*) and practical tools (*syntaxes*) of conducting.

A well-established sense of the contour of sound acts as a dictum of a tight connection to reach the orchestral sound at its best. Also, the contour of sound serves as a melting pot for the application of the conductor's artistic intentions and as a milieu of direct communication with the orchestra. For modern

---

[192] It is important to mention that a similar search is characteristic of instrumental performance, too. A minimal adjustment for the location of the bow, a change of the fingers' pressure on the strings or keys, a slight adjustment in embouchure, etc., may significantly change the 'color' of the sound.

conducting, the technique of a practical sensation of the contour of sound is a cornerstone in the effective communicational cycle between a conductor's actions and an orchestra's responses which they evoke.[193]

It is necessary to mention that the contour of sound is not a fake or artificially imposed line within the utilization of metrical schemes. When the sensation of the contour of sound is established properly, it is as though a confident and firm psycho-physical reaction has been established, and its practical application can be extraordinarily beneficial.[194] It is likely that an intuitive sense of the existence of the contour of sound was evident for many conductors of the past (Arturo Toscanini, Wilhelm Furtwängler, Herbert Karajan, Leonard Bernstein, and others). However, there is vague (if any) evidence that such phenomena have an appropriate conscious tutorial result, or that they are even recognized by the generally accepted conducting methodologies.

The practical utilization of the vicinity of sound itself in general optimizes the conductor's apparatus. The relatively new

---

[193] A technical description of the contour of sound can also be found in: Musin, *Technique of Conducting*, 17, 68-70, 80.

[194] The intercommunicative functions of the vicinity of sound are extremely practical. The conductor not only senses the vicinity of sound as a factual reality but is also actively involved in its future setting. Thus, both the orchestra and conductor actively establish the most productive zone of communication. The layer of the contour of sound can vary (sometimes almost imperceptibly) depending on the practical situation: the acoustics of the new hall, the characteristics of the piece being performed, and the practical relations between the orchestra and conductor.

paradigms, such as the vicinity of sound and advanced mental techniques (which are not particularly new but, rather, recent appropriate methodological descriptions[195]), make the conductor's apparatus flexible, thriving, and aesthetically attractive. With appropriate methodological guidance, those techniques are not arduous to obtain and, with a certain amount of practice, could be available to all conductors for leading a band, choir, and/or orchestra.

The realities and demands of our post-industrial informational time constantly come to mind and require a change from dynamic and forceful to **informational** mannerism. Interestingly enough, in modern times the practical orchestral (instrumental) performing techniques are far more advanced than orchestral conducting, and the demand for successful professional conductors is greater than ever.

Practical approaches and exercises for developing a sense of the contour of sound can be found in the methodological part of this book (see Chapter 10, *The Upbeat as a Conceptual Action. Establishing the Sense of the Contour of Sound*).

---

[195] The prominent Russian psychologist Petr Anokhin developed the theoretical description of functional systems which linked the conductor's practical psychological functions (conductor-orchestra) to a given functional system. Anokhin's concept allowed "the appellant 'system' to be applied to any such complex of selectively involved components in which interaction and mutual relations acquire the character of ***mutual assistance*** towards the achievement of focused useful results." Petr K. Anokhin, *Ocherki po Fisiologii Funktsionalnykh Sistem* [The Essays On Physiology of Functional System] (Mioscow: Akademia Nauk, [Academy of Science] 1975), 35. (Emphasis added)

SEMANTICS OF GESTURE

Any examination of human inter-communication in context must take into account the role of the gesture in the exchange of information. Gesture is perhaps the most obvious means by which communication can take place apart from language.[196] According to Lev Vygotsky:[197] "Concept formation is a creative, not a mechanically passive, process . . . and that the mere presence of external conditions favoring a mechanical linking of word and object does not suffice to produce a concept."[198]

---

[196] *Language Functions and Brain Organization*. Edited by Sidney J. Segalowitz (New York, London: Academic Press, 1983), 55.

[197] Vygotsky, Lev Semenovich (1896-1934). Russian psychologist. ... The range of his activities included research on the history of psychology, experimental study of child language and concept formation, and research and development projects in the area of special education and psychopathology. ... Although Vygotsky's ideas reached the West with much delay, they have informed a wide range of educational (Moll, 1990), cross-cultural (Cole, 1996), and assessment (Lidz, 1987) studies. *Encyclopedia of Psychology*. Alan E Kazdin, Editor in Chief (Oxford: Oxford University Press, 2000), vol. 8, 218-9.

[198] Vygotsky, *Thought and Language*, 99.

> *Human beings could not grow and learn, or even survive, if they did not possess powers of association (imitation). Associated thinking is present in every sphere of human activity, including all aspects of music-making.*[199]

To make conducting an artistically rich and musically expressive experience, the conductor has to apply actions that serve as visual mimics and will evoke comparable conceptual or emotional reactions from the orchestral musicians. The gestures substitute the conductor's verbal communication; it becomes a specific "language", which enhances "the conductor's *talk* with the orchestra and the audience about the content of music."[200]

Some motions applied as decoded external transmitters of inner impulse may resemble the motions derived from common human social practices such as hitting, striking, chopping, tossing, lifting, pulling, rubbing, stretching, scooping, etc. Also, gestures may imitate different actions such as struggling, as in an arm sticking in mud or dough, or an arm struggling to move through free-flowing soil or a jelly-like substance. Or, they may form a concept about "weight" and "space."[201]

The concept-formative effect of such motions may be conditioned by the indirect, subconscious impact of their

---

[199] Alcantara, 249.

[200] Musin, 290.

[201] Ibid, 248-9.

semantic and/or symbolic meanings (as a customarily-emerged, generally comprehensible association): "The artist refers to emotional-acoustical and emotional-visual units as a distinctive code, or language, which attaches to certain meanings and concepts. Thus, high tones, perceived with certain mono-semantic meaning as bright, pointed or thin, and low as dark, massive and thick ...; symmetry is associated with calmness, asymmetry – with anxiety; straight vertical–striving for upwards; horizontal line–passive, diagonal–active."[202]

The human body is basically bilaterally

---

[202] G. Prazdnikov, *Napravlennost' Hudojectvennoi Formi//Hudojnik i Publika* [The Purposefulness of the Artistic Form//The Artist and Audience] (Leningrad: LGITMiK, 1981), 51, quoted in D. A. Leontiev, *Vvedenie v Psihologiyu Iskusstva* [Introduction of the Psychology of Art], 17. It is also appropriate to make a reference to the article of Semen M. Morozov, *Smisloobrazuyushchaya Funkziya Psihologicheskogo Konteksta* [The Concept-formative Function of Psychological Contest]. Morozov revealed the formation of sense for the perceived word, which is characteristic of verbal communication; a similar principle of the formation of meaning is distinctive for non-verbal communication as well, when we get involved in the communicative process, i.e., we presuppose, that words pronounced or described by us fully reflect all "active designs" of the present subjective concept. However, factually the image is awakened by the conductor's own, "individual conceptual design," the part which is mutual to our own conceptual "design" and is the part that we name as "meaningful." So all communicating individuals express through a word and enclose into a perceived word their concept. But those two differential concepts of communicating persons have "one mutual part – the meaning of that word," and only due to this mutual part can we understand each other. Semen Morozov, *Smisloobrazuyushchaya Funkziya Psihologicheskogo Konteksta* [The Concept Formative Function of Psychological Contest] (Moscow: *Poznanie I Lichnost'* [Cognition and Personality], 1984), 56-64, quoted in Dmitri A. Leontiev, *Znachenie I Lichnostnii Smisl: Dve Storoni Odnoi Medali* [The Meaning and Personal Concept: Two Sides of the Same Medal] (Moscow: Rossiiskii Gumanitarnii Fond, [Russian Humanitarian Fund] Smisl, 1995), 8-9.

symmetrical. This external symmetry is imperfect but dominant. ... Both our categories for classifying and dealing with space manipulatively and organizationally, and our emotions about space and the values we attach to direction in space, derive directly from our body form. ... For example, what is superior is up or high and what is inferior is down or low. (Low is often dirty, but high is not necessarily clean.) Right is law, morals, the holy and the strong; left is sinister, profane, weak and (often) feminine. Backward and behind are slow, hence stupid. Forward and in front are active, oriented and intelligent. Besides is confederate or paranoid: it is an ambiguous category of place.[203]

The placement of the arm in a low position (under the waistline) would be associated with dark, somber images and a higher hand position with light and bright images.[204]

These motions are perceived as recognizable visual images and generate certain and, more importantly, comparable and predictable psychological associations. In reality, the appearance of such associations is taken with the realization that "the conductor's action is comprehended by musicians in connection with a certain situation, created through the process of performance. However, it should be taken into account by the

---

[203] *The Body and Social Metaphor* by Donald G. MacRae, in *The Body as a Medium of Expression. Essays Based on a Course of Lectures Given at the Institute of Contemporary Arts*, London, 63-4.

[204] Erzhemsky, *Psychological Paradoxes of Conducting*, 116; Erzhemsky, *Psikhologiya Dirijirovaniya* [Psychology of Conducting], 81.

conductor that the arising of such needed conceptions will not happen if the conductor's motions do not have an association with gestures from the common social practice."[205]

The more profound the psychological impact of the external transformation of the conductor's inner creative intentions, the more colorful and expressive sound the conductor can expect from the orchestra in response. It is important to mention, however, that such visual informative gestures can be effective only if provided with anticipatory modes, especially for the performance of an upbeat of a certain character at the beginning of the movement or phrase, and also if performed with reference to the contour of the sound.[206] This approach to conducting is opposite to the tradition of mechanistic (or surmountable) 'conventional' conducting, which is doomed to be preoccupied with illustrative manifestations and constant post factum mental registrations of pitch, dynamics and tempos: "With its comprehension, and from this, with the recognition of the actual nature of the conductor's performance . . . the conductor can avoid the sad fate of a *living metronome* (Alexander Serov[207]) or, according to the ironic definition of Yury Temirkanov,[208] *a*

---

[205] Musin, 210.

[206] The sophisticated technique of the "converted" mode of the upbeat may be taken as an example of such a practice (directions for performance can be found in Musin, *Technique of Conducting*, 67, 69, and in Chapter 11 of this book).

[207] Serov, Aleksander Nikolaievich, important Russian music critic and composer, 1820-1871. *Baker's Biographical Dictionary of Musicians*, 1687.

[208] At the present time Yury Temirkanov (born 1938) is the music director of the St. Petersburg Philharmonic Symphony Orchestra (Russian Federation) and was formerly the music director of the Baltimore Symphony Orchestra

traffic-controller, and become a musician and creator with a complete foundation."[209]

The prominent German conductor, and Arthur Nikisch's devotee, Wilhelm Furtwängler mocked this type of "traffic-controller" technique as an end unto itself:

> *All of his writing stresses the fact that anybody can develop a clear, 'traditional' up-and-down baton technique. Once, he stopped an orchestra during rehearsal and said, "You think I can't give you an orthodox beat?" He did so, and took the orchestra along for a few measures. Then he stopped. "But it has no quality." As he put it in 1937: Anybody who thinks today that it is possible to impart and develop the 'technique' of a singer, instrumental player or conductor in the absence of close and constant association with the art itself, in the face of which technique can only be a means, is very much mistaken. Problems of 'technique' are exerting a hypnotic influence on us nowadays, and considerable progress has been made in the examination of its foundations - especially by means of the modern biological approach.*[210]

The effective transmission of the conductor's inner creative

(United States of America).

[209] Erzhemsky, 62.

[210] Schonberg, 275.

intentions, which may evoke a certain adequate psychological reaction from the orchestral musicians, is one of the most problematic, and, at the same time, one of the most challenging and inspired parts of the conductor's technique. The arm motions appear as apparently similar gestures but eventually carry diverse conceptual tasks which could generate various reactions. For example: "Compare the motion of an arm executing a strike on any object with the motion of an arm intended to catch a falling object. In the first instance the muscular involvement of the arm is conditioned by the downward motion; in the second, since the arm was not intended to hit, the stopping occurs not as a cause of the arm's contact with the aiming object, but because of its sudden inhibition."[211]

The dissimilar reactions from gestures that depict straight or curved lines may be taken as an example of different psychological interpretations of the hand motion. Because of their redundancy, repeated patterns of straight-line motions (typical for a beat-striking manner) will not generate an enthusiastic response from the orchestra (according to the principal of a "fading" psychological reaction[212] ["principle of

---

[211] Musin, 67.

[212] The function of reticular formation is one example. In the conducting process its mechanism reveals a "fading" subconscious reaction to the pattern of the forcible "dynamic" strike-motion: "Reticular activating system: The alerting system of the brain consisting of the reticular formation, subthalamus, hypothalamus, and medial thalamus. ... This system is essential in initiating and maintaining wakefulness and introspection and in directing attention." *Taber's Medical Dictionary*, 1669.

dominant"[213]] to a forceful but similar type of stimulus), although curved or rounded lines with a range of amplitudes will evoke a variety of musically productive reactions. The practical shortcomings and visual non-expressiveness of the straight line especially reveal themselves in movements (sections) with moderate or slow tempi (*andante, adagio, largo, grave,* etc.); i.e., the straight lined motion has a practical inability to control the substance of a slow beat:

1. In depiction of fulfillment of faster notes (e.g., 16th or 32^{nds}) within the beat

2. For an appropriate depiction of *crescendo*

3. For the indication of *ritenuto* or *rallentando*

Often this inability manifests itself in an unnecessarily practical subdivision of the beats, although such a formal subdivision is perceived as only an artificial smudge on the texture of the musical line.

Gestures derived from common social practices and their subsequent psychological impacts can be commonly understood

---
[213] Erzhemsky, 212.

and interpreted. The motion of "rejection" is one example of such a gesture. This gesture may be used as a visual stimulus in the situation where one person would like to abruptly break a conversation with another person or a group of people. Manually, it is performed with the open palm starting from the upper level of the chest and quickly moving forward. This visual stimulus has a specific psychological reaction and has obvious interpretations - "Stop! Do not move!" - or, in the denotation of the orchestral conducting practice, "Do not play!" or, "Play with an abruptly softer dynamic." Another example of a motion derived from the human social practice is the gesture of "striking,"[214] which is an impression of the action used for a specific labor practice. The motion designed as a "begging" gesture may be useful for modeling an appropriate reaction needed for an instant increase in the loudness of sound or to play with higher emotional involvement. This gesture is performed with the arm straightened completely in the direction of the entire orchestra, a certain section, or an individual player. The "inviting" gesture may serve as a powerful visual depiction in phrasing melodic lines in order to show their attractive points or harmonic resolutions.[215]

It would be appropriate to depict the manifestations of the conductor's creative impulses as a fusion of two operative tools:

---

[214] However, the striking motions will have a productive communicative impact if performed in one of its informative modes (i.e., suspended upbeat, converted suspended upbeat or along with implementation of rounded motion).

[215] An inclusive description of various gestures, which reflects certain commonly comprehensible socio-cultural associations (e.g., "offering," "calling off," "directing," "rejecting," "dismissing," "begging," "tossing," etc.) can be found in: Musin, *Technique of Conducting*, 241-51.

semantically expressive motions and their *conventional* performance (in accordance with traditional schematic framing). Within this tool, the conceptual gesture serves as a unit of a given, as an indivisible combination of the conductor's techniques which blends both internal and outer features and is an inseparable part of the conglomerate of conventional (schematic) and "concept-formative" (expressive) motions. Furthermore this technical tool functions only as a part of the more complex united communicative organism: the conductor-orchestra. At the foundation of the conductor-orchestra intercommunicative nexus lays a situational meaning that requires recognition of the conceptual uniqueness of each performing situation, and consequently, a unique inimitability for each element of the expressive part of the given operative apparatus.

5

INNER MECHANISMS

It is irrefutable that the role of gestures (and therefore the features of techniques of the external apparatus) in conducting was, is and will be essential as long as conductors use them as devices of communication with orchestras. Nevertheless, in the modern conducting methodology there should be a principal recognition of a distinctive separation between a gesture as a formal decorous physical motion and a gesture as a **segment** of a complex concept-formative[216] action. Paradoxically enough, however, the traditional methodology

---

[216] I use the terms "concept-formative" and "conceptual" to differ conditionally the motions typical for a force-coming mode (strike, stroke, click, "flick," ictus, etc.) from motions which reflect the innate (intercommunicative) nature of conducting.

mostly concentrates on the external (illustrative) segments of conducting such as: premeditated fixed metrical schemes, various outlines of schematic gestures, graphics, etc.[217]

> *There is a need **to distinguish motion from action**. The action is a motion which is applied to achieve a certain task. **There is a limited number of arm motions**: up – down, left – right, through the circle. ... **The number of actions performed by the motions is unlimited**.*[218]

In accordance with the principles of human intercommunication, the external (visual) act is a projection and extension of the intangible (inner) activity of a conductor's mental apparatus. The conductor's motions never lie. Rather,

---

[217] Numerous methodological books on conducting have been published since it became an independent profession; some of those publications could include up to 100 diagrams (with descriptions of the external, or decorative, aspect of the conducting practice) and even more graphics of various metrical schemes and glossaries of symbols, which, according to their authors, could serve as a model for any 'inner' content of music. The following is one of Arturo Toscanini's appropriate comments which may serve as an example of his emotional reflection on such traditional illustrative methodological approaches. As Giuseppe Valdengo (1914-2007), Italian baritone, remembered: "Just think, today I received a book sent to me by one conductor from the Metropolitan in which he teaches conducting... You should see what kind of book it is. The devil knows what is it! Some kind of little circles, small lines, graphics and drawings for baton movements... An extremely ridiculous thing. And that is recommended as a guidance for young conductors? And there are even people who take it seriously. Such an absurdity and illiteracy!" Valdengo, Giuseppe, *Ya Pel s Toskanini* [I Was Singing for Toscanini], (Leningrad: MuzGiz, 1989), 86, quoted in Erzhemsky, *Psychological Paradoxes of Conducting*, 219.

[218] Musin, *Vado Mecum*, 16. (Emphasis added)

they initially reveal the significance of the conductor's inner (mental) techniques and, in many instances, an outer manifestation of the absence of effective artistic intentions. Despite the evident importance of the external (visual) technique, it is still a secondary (subordinate) part of a conductor's actions - in much the same way that the vocal cords, tongue, and lips serve as physical "materialization of thoughts (inner speech)."[219]

Thus, the assertion that the conductor *conducts with the hands* incompletely defines the complexity of his/her action (despite the visually indisputable reality of this fact): "The rules of speech functioning, which are developed on the foundation of psycho-motor skills, absolutely common for all types of interpersonal communication, including communication of conductor and orchestra."[220] Functioning similarly to linguistic principles, the primary mission of a conductor's hands is to materialize and transmit the conductor's inner thoughts and his/her creative intentions.[221] This chapter analyzes the inner, hidden engine of conducting and its essential role in the management of a successful performance.

---

[219] Vygotsky, 217-226.

[220] Erzhemsky. *Dirijeru 21 Veka. Psiholingvistika Professii.* [To the Conductor of the 21st Century. The Psycholinguistic of the Profession], 67.

[221] Ibid, 90.

INNER AND OUTER: FUNDAMENTAL METHODOLOGICAL PREDICAMENTS

Recognition of the complexity of the inner (mental) practical skills (the inseparable blend of physical and mental proactive techniques which are supposed to govern the performance) leads into the basic methodological disagreements between schools of conducting. The fundamental method of predominantly forceful and illustrative manners includes the traditional way, which uses as its goal: "The specially formulated collection of dynamic 'cliché-symbols' called out with the help of home schematic preparation to illustrate one characteristic or another of the music being performed, or …" in contrast with the dynamic method, the non-forceful approach should be founded on: "… the principle of the natural transmission of the creative impulses, which establishes objective conditions for the **involuntary, and, therefore, the most adequate** external codification of the conductor's artistic ideas."[222] Such methodological contradictions still generate controversies among scholars and acting conductors, mainly because the greatest part of conducting techniques lies beyond

---

[222] Erzhemsky, 74. (Emphasis added)

empiricism since the evident (external) characteristics are not the equivalents of the innate (intangible) features of the phenomenon.

As profound and meaningful as are the musical ideas generated by a conductor, so sophisticated and complex should be the palette of his/her techniques for the realization of individual artistic phenomena. During the execution of the performance, one of the artistic leader's main duties is to lead the orchestral musicians through the expressive points of the essence of musical texture. Although this concept seems obvious, the present orchestral practice reveals that satisfactory performance of the main artistic task is problematic for many professional conductors due to the absence of specific psychological training. These methodological predicaments exist mainly because of the absence of the cardinal restructuring of the conductor's primary psycho-physical reflexes. It is necessary to accept that in the process of orchestral leading there is never to be any physical action against any subject, since the conductor has no physical contact with either the musicians or their instruments.

Conducting is based predominantly on the conductor's mental abilities and their visual expression through characteristic movements. This approach assumes that the art of gestural supervision is not a fixed (standardized) self-dependent pattern of graphical (conventional) clichés/schemes or a certain independently active physical object, but an organic system of psycho-physical functions designed for an intercommunicative realization of the conductor's artistic intentions:

> *All of human linguistic experience convincingly showed the fallacy of the striving to create non-verbal codes, dictionaries or some kind of "alphabets" . . . consisting of separate formalized pseudo-linguistic elements, in so far as they unavoidably – whether we want or not – will close their body to the reality they describe.*[223]

It would be appropriate to affirm that there is a need for a revised methodology for the external features of the conducting apparatus, and that these re-designed characteristics would eliminate non-communicative dynamic approaches once and for all: "The link between different sciences and musical practice has been up to now insufficiently established and developed," Herbert Karajan states, "It is necessary, therefore, to stimulate creation of works in the fields of physiology, psychology, and other disciplines, connected with musical themes."[224]

Comprehension of the superiority of inner creative impulses and amplified practical utilization of a conductor's mental potency forces the modern conducting methodology to re-design the outer (physical) apparatus (and consequently its methods). At its best, modern conducting **requires advanced mental techniques** for instant assessment and adjustment of the conductor's action. The practical development of an inner

---

[223] Vygotsky, *Psihologiya Iskusstva*, [Psychology of the Art] (Mioscow: Iskusstvo, 1968), quoted in Erzhemsky, *Psychological Paradoxes of Conducting*, 81.

[224] Erzhemsky, 14.

apparatus of high velocity is the most challenging part of the current conducting practice. Modern conducting needs an interdisciplinary development in its methodology that will lead to the perception of conducting and its techniques mainly as an **informative action** (though a specifically musical one). This method helps to incorporate external techniques which justify the informative (conceptual) intent of the innate creative impulse. And, it also builds the apparatus of complex non-forceful techniques which fundamentally anticipate the occurrence of orchestral sound as a pre-assumed (pre-modeled) result of the musician's comparable reaction to the action.

A lack of mental comprehension or an attempt to forcibly fuse the moment of the occurrence of sound and the marking point of the motion will generate the effect of constant psychological lateness, especially if the conductor coordinates his/her actions with his/her stiff and inflexible technical tool, which is established irrevocably once and for all. In the absence of an appropriate intercommunicative dialogue between conductor and orchestra, the experienced collective of musicians may ignore (partially or fully) the conductor's actions and redirect their attention to the backup linear connections of orchestral collective self-organization:

If Koussevitzky's[225] *cues were inadequate or incorrect,* ***they learned to understand his wishes in***

---

[225] Koussevitzky [Kusevitsky], Sergey (Aleksandrovich) (1874-1951). American conductor and double bass player of Russian birth. ... He took over the Boston SO from Monteux in 1924 and remained there for a quarter of a century, rivaling Stokowski and Toscanini in his influence on American concert life. *New Grove Dictionary*, 2nd ed. (2001), vol. 13, 844-5.

*spite of his mistakes. If his upbeat was uncertain, they learned to watch one another. They worked out a set of signals to insure their playing together. The orchestra, which followed its leader when **he knew how to express his intentions**, played like a superb conductor - less ensemble when he didn't.*[226]

"All of us do our best just to make you look good!" was a retort by an angry player at a very uncomfortable rehearsal under one of the author's more aggressive students. The remark, though rarely quite true, should be engraved on every conducting stand - perhaps together with another by the concertmaster of a great orchestra: "We'll play well for any one, better than he deserves, as long as he doesn't come on strong."[227]

If any of the elements are not included in the stroke, the fabric of the first sound will suffer, and the players will compensate by adding the missing part or parts. The result will be **an unregulated sound created by committee** rather than a unified one guided by the conductor's intent.[228]

There is a scale of practical communicative methods, ranging

---

[226] Schonberg, *The Great Conductors*, 306. (Emphasis added)

[227] Prausnitz, *Score and Podium*, 467.

[228] Farberman, 61. (Emphasis added)

from following the signals of different section leaders and the concertmaster (collective internal leaders and "underground conductors")[229] to factorial anticipation of the conductor's marking chops (particularly if the performance of beats and metrical schemes is relatively predictable and there is a sufficient number of rehearsals for adaptation to the conductor's manner). Gunther Schuller supports this statement as follows: "Musicians also know that, even with very famous and popular conductors, many times **they save the conductor from serious embarrassment by not playing what the maestro conducts**."[230]

Paradoxically, a lack of comprehension of such collective self-organizational mechanisms creates the illusion of artistic monitoring of the orchestra's sound, as: "There is among the conductors' views of themselves a sizable gap between perception and reality, that is, between their perception of themselves and the reality as seen by others ..."[231]

Though a satisfactory performance may still result (especially with an orchestra that has a high level of self-organization and a conductor of certain talent), it will not achieve the suitable artistic level. Factually, to act (or to be) at the same time with the orchestra (in modern time, this style is still the prevailing mechanistic methodological approach) in actuality means to be

---

[229] Erzhemsky, 282.

[230] Schuller, 19. (Emphasis added)

[231] Erzhemsky, 282.

behind and mainly just register the reality of sound (instead of creating it). This constant lateness (or absence of the technique of constant active mental anticipation) is one of the key practical contradictions. The practical demand for the conductor's technique of the active (constant) mental anticipation is revealing the communicative (quasi-linguistic) and non-verbal nature of the conducting as a creative intercommunicative process.

In contrast with the practice of audible time beating that prevailed during the seventeenth, and part of the eighteenth, century and its 'silent' preservation through the nineteenth and twentieth centuries, successful modern orchestral leading requires an intercommunicative realization of inner creative intentions. The conductor's external setting (manifestation of conventional metrical schemes) is a subordinate segment of the indivisible conglomerate of inner and external techniques.[232] In addition to the quasi-linguistic development in modern methods the emergence of a "para-linguistic"[233] phenomenon and its analyses was suggested by Professor George Erzhemsky as

---

[232] The non-verbal 'linguistic' features of conducting mainly include a small amount of "external symbolic *supervisory* actions," which bear nominative and designative functions, i.e., certain mono-semantic tasks may be translated as: play louder, softer, faster, slower, stop the sound, play a *fermata*, concentrate your attention on such and such momentum, etc., and more complex "concept formative bonds" may also be found within a given pattern of gestures. Erzhemsky, *Dirijirovanie kak Obschenie* [Conducting As A Communication], 22; Musin, *Technique of Conducting*, 190.

[233] *Para-*, in English, is an affix of [Origin Greek *para, par* - beside, beyond, past, (in comb. also) to one side, amiss, irregular, and expr. subsidiary relation, alteration, etc.] *Shorter Oxford English Dictionary. On Historical Principles*, 2092.

another important feature of a conductor's technique.[234] It is valuable to mention again as an example of such para-communicative conducting the quote of Romain Rolland's[235] on the conducting manner of Richard Strauss whose visual manifestation of technique was very minimal, yet his ability to transmit an inner thrill of his musical intentions was enormous.

Some conductors with whom particular orchestral musicians have never before performed are amazingly able to establish a positive communicational bridge with the musicians from their first step up to the podium. A similar phenomenon occurs when an orchestra performs the same piece with a remarkably different quality of sound and overall performance for two conductors who both demonstrate a relatively comparable level of technical skills. I have a personal recollection of one of my respected colleagues, an experienced orchestral musician, who expressed his wonder at how "magically" the sound of his orchestra was "amplified" under the direction of one well-known conductor: "It felt as though the orchestra somehow was hooked up into a high voltage circuit," he recalled with amazement.

The answer to such surprising phenomena is simple - the conductor's external emergence reflects the validity of his/her inner psychological and emotional state. This is an example of the manifestation of an artistic will with an elevated preeminent

---

[234] Erzhemsky, *Dirijeru 21 veka* [To the Conductor of the 21st Century], 99.

[235] Rolland, Romain. Famous French author and musicologist, 1866-1944. *Baker's Biographical Dictionary of Musicians*, 1530.

inner intensity and, most importantly, the conductor's external techniques did not block the projection of such intensity. On the contrary, even if the conductor is capable of generating a valuable inner impulse, his/her continuous forced actions (i.e., a redundant hammering of the strikes throughout metrical schemes) simply chop and suppress the inner impulse, or at least greatly diminish its strength.

Practically speaking, the strain-free apparatus which is cleared from bad dynamic reflexes allows the maintainability of the mental abilities of the conductor at their highest degree with their continuous uninterrupted utilization. Again, during the process of conducting, the presence of unmodified physical tension should be minimized as much as possible. Instead, the application of techniques of external (biomechanical) natural strengths (e.g., centrifugal, centripetal motions or the principle of a pendulum, etc.) could be a vital and productive practical resource for non-forceful conducting.[236]

During the execution of the performance, the conductor may count on the quality, precision, and expressive fulfillment of **conceptual actions** that will be similarly interpreted and accepted by all of the orchestral musicians (an appropriate [without exaggeration] facial expression may support the conductor's approach to leading, though it usually just reflects the conductor's own experience of the performance). For example, for the depiction of power or force by the use of a

---

[236] Such a methodology is discussed in Erzhemsky's manuscript: *Dirijirovanie kak Obschenie* [Conducting as Communication], 46-54, 62.

gesture, the presence of muscular tension in the conductor's gesture is not as important as the recipient's (musician's) psychological impact on the performance of such action, which may (or may not, if it is performed inappropriately) evoke a psychological conception (or an appropriate image) of the intensity.[237]

The conceptual motion[238] designed to evoke a predestined emotional reaction serves as a pledge for the creation of an artistically productive intercommunicative bridge between conductor and orchestra. The search for the action that would carry a predetermined psychological impact is a major quest for the modern conductor and, after centuries of conducting practice, this goal remains the most challenging task of conducting methods.

---

[237] Musin, 242.

[238] Again, the term "conceptual" is used to contrast a formal operational gesture from the gesture which reflects the inner strength of the informational action. I prefer to use this term even though it may not be methodologically accurate.

CONCEPTUAL MOTIONS

The relationship between the motion of the conductor, the precision of an ensemble, and the character of the orchestral sound (as a result of the conductor's action) has to be viewed as a transmission of the conductor's inner creative impulses which are broadcast as an advanced **informational inner impulse**. This transmitted motion-impulse evokes a reaction conditioned mainly upon the conductor's **mental performance**. Yet, essentially **only the innate strength and determined confidence of such specific mental actions**[239] (which portend the actual gesture) affect the precision of the ensemble and **the quality and character of sound generated by the orchestra** as a reaction in turn (and **never** the decorous formal performance of the motion). This is followed by the conductor's rapid assumption and analysis of the orchestra's response and subsequent further manifestation of appropriately adjusted clusters (mental and physical) of actions.

The predetermination of the outcome of the orchestral

---

[239] Such inner (mental) action also may be described as a manifestation (projection) of a creative will.

musicians' reactions is one of the greatest challenges in conducting (the technique of mental anticipation of desired orchestral sound [as a part of the preliminary "inner modeling of ideal sound"[240]]).

> *I was on stage when Maestro George Szell, a master conductor, tried, but could not begin, Beethoven's Fifth Symphony with the New York Philharmonic. His upbeat veiled his intent and the opening kept coming out solsol; solsol; solsol; mimi; instead of sol, sol, sol, mi. His wonderful orchestra in Cleveland had no trouble deciphering his upbeat;* **he had trained them to respond to his movements over a period of twenty-plus years.** *But in New York he was a one-week guest.* [241]

---

[240] Erzhemsky. *Psychological Paradoxes of Conducting*, 28-9.

[241] Farberman. *The Art of Conducting Technique: A New Perspective*, 59. (Emphasis added) This example with George Szell is very significant; even famous conductors can fail to establish **instant** (or at least prompt) **productive** communication with orchestras they are guest conducting. Despite Szell's fame and reputation, he was likely not able to adjust his manner in an appropriate way to the sound (and more importantly to the responses) of the host group but rather expected the orchestra to adjust to him. Evgeny Mravinsky was another example of a 'one orchestra' conductor: he was extremely successful with and authoritatively ruled the St. Petersburg Philharmonic for almost 50 years, but he did very little guest conducting, mainly at the beginning of his career. The ability to establish instant productive communication with an orchestra has become crucial in our time. This is despite the talent and respect some conductors of the recent past have achieved by demonstrating their abilities, mainly under the condition of a large number of rehearsals. To be fair, it should be said that adjustments should be made by both the orchestra and the conductor. Sometimes, though, an expected incoming adjustment from the orchestra may take a while, especially if musicians have been trained by an authoritative music director to play what they 'see' rather than what they 'hear.'

Similar to Pandora's Box, there is no predictable outcome of such predetermination within the intercommunicative cycle (conductor-via-orchestra). It is known that the motions of each instrumentalist have precise and specific audible results, which sub-organize the specifics and techniques in achievement of such results. Thus, audible results are achieved strictly in accordance with the technique of performance of such actions: "For a conductor, such accordance, between a technique (performance of gesture) and its audible result (for exclusion of the indication of tempo), practically cannot exist. Similar motions can cause different results and vise-versa, similar results can be achieved by different [technical] approaches."[242]

In some instances a conductor considers the collection of specific technical clichés as a certain complex of pre-arranged special techniques, which will guarantee certain reaction of the performers (orchestral musicians) and, consequently, certain audible results. Practical conducting suggests, however, that **no results (if any) can be determined or guaranteed** in general. **The orchestral response (reaction) to one or another particular gesture is indeterminate**. Similar technical approaches "can be perceived differently" and, consequently, "performed differently by different orchestras."[243]

Therefore, the audible result depends on a combination of factors: the precision and **inner strength of the conductor's motion-impulse** by itself and on the musicians' psychological

---

[242] Musin, 290.

[243] Ibid.

reactions based upon qualification and experience, level of collective self-organization and adaptation to the conductor's mannerisms in general.[244] This non-verbal mode of intercommunication needs a distinctive type of **informational advanced inner impulse** in order to evoke a prerequisite set of mental (imagistic) reactions. The perception of the impact of this conceptual motion-impulse[245] gives a powerful emotional design to the conducting technique. Also, this motion-transmitter may be interpreted as a motion-image (conceptual motion) that can evoke a specific psychological reaction.

As was discussed earlier in Chapter 4, subchapter: *Semantics of Gesture*, some of these motion-impulses may have connotations to common human activities (professional, domestic, social, etc.) and their implementation is presumed to imitate or resemble a variety of labor and/or social biomechanics (or kinetics).[246] The recognizable (semantic) meaning of those motions will have a comparable psychological impact on each orchestral musician. The inner strength and meaning of this

---

[244] Nikolai Malko in his *Vospominaniya* [Remembrance] made an interesting comment about the conducting practice of the German conductor Felix Motl: "Those things which now seem to be a conductor's and orchestra's routine at the time of Motl were nothing but courageous experiments and Motl along with Richter, Mahler and Nikish was the conductor who made a big step on the way from doubtful playing, when musicians were afraid to dissolve their ensemble at any moment, to the modern 'organic' artistic orchestral performance." Malko, *Vospominaniya, Stat'i, Pis'ma* [Memoirs, Articles, Letters] (Leningrad, Izdatel'stvo Muzika, 1972), 94.

[245] Also, for the description of such action, I would like to suggest other terms: "concept-formative motion" or "conceptual motion-unit."

[246] Kinetics: The forces acting on the body during movement and the interactions of sequence of motion with respect to time and forces present. *Taber's Medical Dictionary*, 976.

motion, in association with the contents of the music, may evoke an effective reaction from the musicians. By achieving that technique, a conductor would have the ability to reach an immensely high level of collective creativity. And this achievement is one of the greatest challenges of conducting because: "... each orchestra exists as a distinct conglomerate of personalities. For each, the conductor must be able to devise a technique, a **means** of communication that is eloquent and undeniable ... His gestures must be first and always **meaningful** in terms of the music."[247]

However, it is important to emphasize that the innate meaning of the motion evoked by the appropriate inner impulse is entirely different from the illustrious upbeat – the formal downward-upward motion or an operational cliché.[248] Some prominent conductors are of the opinion that the immediate connection between the illustrative manifestation of arm movements and the demonstration of the conductor's expressive inner intentions is rather uncertain, as Karl Ancherl[249] emphasized: "The external features of gestures are not as essential as many suppose,"[250] R. Kahn-Speyer[251] agrees, "What

---

[247] Leonard Bernstein, *The Joy of Music* (New York: Simon and Shuster, 1959), 150, as quoted in Galkin, 768. (Emphases added)

[248] Here it is necessary to emphasize, though, that any conductor's motion, even the most formal one, is still somewhat informational. As operational tools such gestures were in use for over two centuries. However, currently, due to various objective reasons, the innate 'informational' practical insufficiency of these gestures has led to their malfunctioned use.

[249] Ancerl, Karel. 1908-1973, Czech conductor, *Baker's Biographical Dictionary of Musicians*, 36.

[250] *Karel Ancherl's Interview* (Moscow: Sovetskaya Muzika, [Soviet Music],

opens up to the gaze of the audience can in no way be considered a criterion of a conductor's achievements."[252] Finally, Nikolai Malko noted that, "The chief task is to adjust two extremes: **to want** and **to be able to**; the composition and the fulfillment. This means to know how to carry out this plan to action: to be able to brush away all the obstacles along the path from the impulse of the will for the final aim, to the conductorial movement executing this will."[253]

Though professional (as well as semi-professional and even non-professional) orchestras may be conducted with only a pictographic demonstration of the external features of conducting, such formal manifestations will have little (if any) artistic value if they do not serve as transmitters of the intensity of the conductor's inner creativity:

> *The more surely a conductor uses the techniques of his business, the less 'wasteful' are the gestures he uses to achieve the desired results. A shining example of this is the activity of distinguished modern conductors such as Toscanini, Mahler and Richard Strauss.*

6th ed., 1967), 121, quoted in Erzhemsky, *Psychological Paradoxes of Conducting*, 117.

[251] Kahn-Speyer (Cahn-Speyer), Rudolf, 1881-1940, Austrian conductor and musicologist. *Baker's Biographical Dictionary of Musicians*, 6th ed. (1978), 268.

[252] A. M. Pazovsky, *Zapiski Dirijera* [Conductor's Notes], (MuzGiz, Moskow, 1966), 302-3, quoted in Erzhemsky, 117.

[253] Malko, 29.

As is known, all of them, to one degree or another, significantly simplified the external manner of conducting in the process of the perfection of their skills. Thus Toscanini over the years arrived at the simple 'circular movement', which, however, fascinated the audiences and evoked everything he wanted in the orchestra. Mahler ... even more frequently resorted to only one glance, a slight turn of the head, and suggestive gestures. Richard Strauss' manner of conducting underwent an analogous metamorphosis. If Romain Rolland earlier wrote about him as a young conductor who performs a striving dance while conducting the orchestra, then simplicity and stinginess of movement became the distinguishing characteristics of this master in his maturity. His face and figure recalled a sculpture. Only up close were the nervous tremors and the **radiation of powerful force, attractive as a magnet**.[254]

The more informative the conductor's technique, enhanced by a diversity of expressive innate (non-dynamic) preparatory motion-impulses (functioning as a transmitter that evokes prolific reactions), the more likely accurate and precise will be the orchestra's response to the conductor's creative impulses. Wilhelm Furtwängler expressed the thesis that "there can be no movements of the conductor which have an end in themselves; only those which pursue a fully practical goal – a high quality sound in the orchestra – are important. Only from this position,

---

[254] Erzhemsky, 117-118. (Emphasis added) In the context of this quote it would be appropriate to mention Fritz Reiner's approach as well.

from the position of the music ... should one assess a conductor's movements."[255]

The intensity of the psychological fulfillment of the conductor's advanced motion-impulses **improves** the possibility of the consequent orchestral response with good ensemble playing, cohesion, and colorful sound. Evoked by the inner creative impulse, conceptual gestures, despite their likely methodological wrongness and non-conventionality, enrich conducting ability, in that they may express much more about the content of the music than a formally correct and clear conducting style or detailed verbal description. Orchestral musicians mutually comprehend and follow them as soon as they generate corresponding associations:

> *Rehearsal work is generally overestimated in our time, which places everything mechanical excessively high," Furtwängler asserts. "What can be taught to the orchestra in rehearsals, even though they be quite lengthy, quite strenuous, and quite painstaking, is utterly insignificant in comparison with what* ***can be communicated to the orchestra in [the] course of minutes, thanks to the character of the arm wave and the way of direct transmission connected with it.***[256]

---

[255] Wilhelm Furtwängler, *Iz Literaturnogo Naslediya* [The Legacy of Writings], 412, quoted in Erzhemsky, *Psychological Paradoxes of Conducting*, 117.

[256] Wilhelm Furtwängler, *Iz Literaturnogo Naslediya* [The Legacy of Writings], 150, quoted in Erzhemsky, 275. (Emphasis added)

Conducting is a specific creative form of non-verbal intercommunication, and, as with any communicative act, conducting presumes to transmit the conductor's own (innate) creative information. This method of non-forcible communication with the orchestra is opposite to the style that is obtained when the supposed communicative cycle is turned upside-down: the conductor's physical action is followed by his/her post factum mental/physical registration of the resulting sound.[257] And despite the fact that the bodily kinesthetic[258] is associated with the utilization of muscular energy, the development of the conductor's kinetics should be based on **linguistic** and **informational** principles. This information by itself does not consist of any force or tension; it is only the transformation or reception of certain messages: **"INFORMATION IS INFORMATION, NOT MATTER OR ENERGY."**[259] Thus Norbert Wiener's short sentence should become a mantra of the modern orchestral conducting methodological paradigm!

---

[257] Though the meanings of pitch registration techniques are different, the mental/physical precept of such an approach may be somewhat similar. Farberman, 75.

[258] *Kinesthesia.* The sense perception of movement; the muscular sense. *Kinesthetic.* Relating to Kinesthesia. *Stedman's Medical Dictionary*, 1031.

[259] Norbert Wiener, *Cybernetic. Or Control and Communication in the Animal and the Machine* (New York: The Technology Press, John Wiley & Sons, Inc., Paris: Herman et Cie, 1949), 155.

Exercises that result in a practical transformation of the formal operational upbeat into the conceptual motion can be found in Part III, *Methodology*.

INNER WILL

As was discussed earlier, it is often said that with one conductor an orchestra plays with a great reach and a vibrant sound, and oddly enough the same group of musicians does not sound the same under the direction of other conductors. To be a conductor, one should be able to project a potent creative will (or inner creative impulse).

> *The will of the conductor,* **with the knowledge of how to use it** *towards himself and towards the performing instrument, - the orchestra or chorus, - is one of the most essential factors of conducting.*[260]

A correct but formal or outwardly illustrious performance of a motion results in an unsatisfactory practical and artistic outcome.

> *The preliminary process of the movement of an arm, i.e., the course of the impulse of will originating in*

---

[260] Malko, 24. (Emphasis added)

the cerebral center to the actual movement itself, is rather complicated and is often accompanied by handicaps of a psychical or a physical nature or both.[261]

The recognition of the concept of creative will, as a vital part of a conductor's inner apparatus, reshapes the whole methodological concept of modern conducting. This concept leads to a recognition that the impediments lie not only in the physical misuse of conducting techniques (the visual manifestation of schemes, various preparatory upbeats, intermediate [within the scheme] upbeats, etc.) but, more importantly, **in the misuse of psychological motivations.**

The principles of group leadership (either social or musical) suggest that an 'inner' action always precedes its visual (outer) manifestation. **Every conductor's gesture should be ignited and motivated by an uncompromised strength of the inner creative impulse.** This impulse prompts the actions, once the conductor has formed an appropriate model of how a work should both sound and proceed through this concept in an actual performance.

Prominent Austrian conductor Felix Weingartner, in his book *About Conducting*, recalled the memory of one old respectable musician - Dresdner's flutist Fürstenau: "... when Wagner conducted, orchestral musicians surely did not have a feeling that someone was directing them. Every one of them had the

---

[261] Malko, 35.

impression that he was being led only by his own musical intuition and, indeed, it was a magnificent ensemble. So was the mighty Wagner's willpower, which subconsciously but persistently seized the will of each musician and each performer with their own sense of freedom, while in reality they just followed directions of the leader."[262]

An example of how a formal gesture which is not supported by an innate creative impulse can disorient musicians even from the highest level of professional ensembles can be found in Kirill Kondrashin's (one of the prominent soviet conductors of the twentieth century[263]) book *Mir Dirijera* [The Conductor's World]. Kondrashin remembered one stunning episode from the early stages of his career during a performance of Puccini's "Madame Butterfly." While Kondrashin was conducting from memory, at the end of one scene he realized that he had suddenly forgotten the opening of the next one and he decided to give a mechanistic but "strong" upbeat suggesting that with the very first note he "will instantly recognize the rest of the music."[264] To Kondrashin's amazement, this mechanistic

---

[262] Felix Weingartner, *About Conducting*, 15, quoted in Musin, *Technique of Conducting*, 152.

[263] Kondraschin, Kirill (Petrovich), 1914-1981. Russian conductor. ... Kondrashin saw himself in the same tradition as the great conductors of the past, who strove to produce their own unique sound and style with their orchestras. He was a brilliant interpreter of Russian music, always showing an immense panache and commitment to the music. He was equally at home in the music of Mahler, Beethoven, Brahms and Hindemith. His interpretations showed an extraordinary balance of texture of the orchestral sound, an acute dynamic control, and a warmth and kinship with the music not often found in interpretations of Western music by Russian conductors. *New Grove Dictionary of Music and Musicians*, vol. 13, 773-4.

[264] Kondraschin, Kirill. *Mir Dirijera* [The Conductor's World] (Moscow:

gesture elicited a devastating result – some of the musicians were confused by such an unexpected formality of action and simply couldn't begin, despite the fact that the orchestra had performed that opera numerous times previously.

One of the cornerstones of a conductor's mental techniques is a **continuous advanced projection of firm potent leadership**.[265] The principal features of such leadership are inner confidence and a proper manifestation of a robust creative will for the accomplishment of all musical goals dictated by the composer's score.

> *The inner (mental) preparation is a **psychophysical exercise in imagination, visualization, and overall the modeling of all actions** that will allow a conductor "to conceive" of* [himself/herself] *as an accomplished performer before* [he/she] *becomes one.*[266]

As one of the methods of the practical enhancement of the inner impulse, and to achieve and preserve an adequate leader's type of psychological and emotional state, one should deeply analyze and comprehend the style and character of the piece — "to

---

Muzika, 1976), p. 89.

[265] The conductor's inner (mental) techniques were profoundly analyzed (with the inclusion of suggested practical methods) by prominent conductor and scholar George Erzhemsky in his books: *Psychological Paradoxes of Conducting, Theory and Practice of the Profession*, and *Dirijeru 21 Veka* [To the Conductor of the 21st Century].

[266] Alcantara, 263. (Emphasis added)

compose the piece again as yours," as George Erzhemsky suggested.[267] The prevalence of a superimposed musical conception (and the technique of its proper advanced exhibition), which affects overall the manifestation of both the creative inner impulse/stimulus and the mental nourishment of such a creative impulse, gives a conductor and, consequently, the orchestra musicians, an **essential confidence** in all of their collective performances.[268] These goals include the important **social** and **cultural** components of the orchestral business in general: the conductor and the orchestra perform not for their own enjoyment but rather for an audience of music lovers. Overall, artistically productive and vibrant performances positively affect the life of the local community. Their influence on the cultural, social and educational aspects of the community's life is hard to overestimate.

However, we often hear of instances in which a conductor, after a successful first appearance with the orchestra, later has certain difficulties maintaining a similar level of interest for the orchestral musicians; in a few years he/she cannot offer any fresh ideas to the orchestra.[269] The conductor's manner, which

---

[267] Erzhemsky, *Dirijeru 21 Veka* [To the Conductor of the 21st Century], 216-220.

[268] It is an interesting fact that after an artistically successful performance orchestral musicians experience the specific 'job-well-done' satisfaction of the individual as a part of the collective performance, and, on the contrary, after an unsatisfactory performance (even for high level orchestral musicians), they are left with a discomfited feeling of unacceptable personal and collective performance.

[269] This could be another reason for the revision of the current conducting methodology. The lack of potential professional growth is one of the hidden pitfalls of the traditional training. Rather than focusing on the further

seems attractive at first, becomes predictable and boring. Even if musicians cannot distinguish the intangible significance of a conductor's inner intentions beyond the screen of his/her manner at the beginning, later, this significance (or rather its absence) becomes obvious.

Ultimately, the concept of the hidden prevalence of inner impulses over gestures suggests that patterns of motions, even the most correct ones, which are not ignited by the appropriate inner impulses, **are just collections of formal clichés**.

The practical nourishment of the inner impulse should be implemented from the very beginning of conducting study. In general, along with other interactive techniques (i.e., utilization of the sense of the contour of sound, mental anticipation, proper management of the physical apparatus, etc.), the proper realization of the technique of the inner impulse positively optimizes the conductor's performance at all stages of his/her career.

---

development of innate techniques, conductors instead continue to search for 'attractive' illustrious gestures. Thus incorrect methodological maxims may crush an otherwise successfully begun career. I personally remember one colleague of mine who, at the beginning of his career, won several prestigious conducting competitions (including a competition to be the music director in one of the regional orchestras). At that time his main concerns were: "I have to find new attractive gestures that will keep an orchestra interested in me," and, "I have to go to this conductor's performance to see if I can pick up some expressive gestures." When I pointed out to him the danger of such a principle and suggested rather that he consider his inner 'attractive' pathways, his answer was always: "I have to proceed in such a way because it is the way I was trained and it was good." However, pursuing this pathway ultimately 'fed up' the orchestra and audience and eventually damaged his position as a music director.

Exercises for the practical development of the Inner Will/Stimulus can be found in Part III, *Methodology*.

6

INTERACTIVE TECHNIQUES

In the previous chapters, an effort was made to analyze the historical and practical roots of the traditional conducting methods and styles. It is appropriate now to discuss principles which would suggest a method for developing an updated methodological and practical paradigm. These advanced conducting techniques should not be seen as **causative, speculative or hypothetical principles**, but rather as based strictly on the scientific discoveries of human nature, and following the rules of human communication.

Put simply, the development of an updated conducting methodological paradigm should be founded on one principle:

none of the techniques of the complex conducting apparatus refer to **opinion** or **tradition** but rather correspond with the **rules of psychology, physiology and communication**. When we are equipped with the appropriate methodological tools, only then will it be possible to unify and eventually justify all the features of modern conducting methods.

The next two chapters will summarize the previously discussed material as a provisionally applicable methodological pattern.

RELAXATION

For the purpose of our routine day-by-day social needs, or for any special occasions (formal and informal), we manage to express our thoughts mainly with our focus on the contents of speech rather than with a concentration on the verbal apparatus which translates our thoughts into words (the muscular function of the mouth, lips, tongue, vocal cords, etc.). We use a necessary or normal functional minimum of muscular tension to accomplish the means of thought and without paying much attention (if any) to how we actually physically manage this complex process. Our verbal apparatus serves as a physical decoder of our inner thoughts, and as soon as this apparatus provides an appropriate tone and articulation, our acknowledgement of the apparatus's functions is submerged by the necessities of thought. Similarly to the function of the verbal apparatus, to be able to manage a productive action of both the inner and outer segments of conducting, an appropriate organization of their functions in accordance with the basics of communication is vital.

As mentioned in previous chapters, there should be a distinction made between a gesture as a formal *operational* physical motion and a meaningful gesture (conceptual action).

> As a conductor's gestures would be able to actively manage the performance, the conductor has to **sense the 'texture' of sound** and musical content as directly as an instrumentalist. ... The strong-willed character of the gesture **is not tied to any physical tension, big amplitude, harshness or other traces of volitional exertions.**[270]

In conducting, the performance of meaningful action (evoking an image or a concept) suggests the dominance (prevalence) of inner intentions over their outer manifestations. However, none of the most creative inner intentions will be expressed if their outer manifestations are not organized properly. The achievement of a flexible, agile, and organic physical apparatus is challenging. However, the natural physiological design of the human arm demonstrates extreme degrees of freedom: "... **the main task of the motion coordination [is] to overcome the excessive number of extensions of freedom** that is reduction of the variable quantities managing the motion."[271] However, the benefits of such natural freedom will not be available to the conductor if he/she does not possess the technique of muscular relaxation.

---

[270] Musin, *Vado Mecum*, 16. (Emphasis added)

[271] Alexei Alexeevich Leontiev, *Deyatel'nii Um. Deyatel'nost'. Znak. Lichnost'* [The Active Mind. Activity. Sign. Personality] (Moscow, Smisl, 2001), 123. (Emphasis added)

The psychological response to the technical and musical challenges of orchestral conducting (as a specific form of creative performing activity) **provokes** an unnecessary physical strain. The presence of unmanaged excessive muscular tension **sufficiently suppresses and diminishes a conductor's mental abilities**.

For the successful manifestation of the inner intention (or even to amplify its meaning), the outer feature of the conducting apparatus should include the technique of active muscular relaxation. The management of instant inclusive or partial muscular relaxation is a vitally important part of the conductor's apparatus (a complex blend of mental and physical features).

As was mentioned in Chapter 2, the science of physiology suggests that there are two types of responses (reflexes): unconditioned, which are inherent to the human body, and conditioned, which develop throughout life. The way we are able to function physiologically throughout the day is, for the most part, unconsciously and, consequently, subconsciously determined. In general, our body's reflexive responses are carried out with minimal or no thought.

If each time we made such a movement we had to consciously work out the countless neuromuscular responses involved, there wouldn't be enough hours in the day to get us through breakfast. ***But these same habitual and reflex behaviors which simplify life can also cause many difficulties. Among them are undue tension, excessive fatigue, inefficient muscular*** *coordination, poor posture, and backache.*[272]

It is noted that intensive physical activity affects mental performance. K. Stanislavsky,[273] in his book *An Actor Prepares (The Self Preparation in Creative Means of Agitation)* described how the actor's studio mentor, Arkady Torzov, demonstrated to his pupils how extensive physical tension affects the actor's performance. Torzov asked one student to lift and hold one side of the piano and then to perform a simple mental task: multiply double digit and single digit numbers, recollect the names of all the stores on a nearby street (starting from a nearby corner), sing the tune of a popular song, remember the taste of common cuisine, recollect the sense of the texture of silk or the smell of ashes. The student was able to answer these questions only after he lowered the piano and took a moment to relax his muscles.[274]

> *Pupils sometimes mistake the concept of "favourable position," "convenience," for the concept of "inertia" [i. e. relaxation], wrote Neuhaus. 'These are not only two entirely different things, they are also*

---

[272] Leibowitz and Connington, 36. (Emphasis added)

[273] Konstantin Sergeyevich Stanislavsky (Константин Сергеевич Станиславский) (1863 – 1938). Was a director and acting innovator, responsible for a great deal of the acting technique used during the 20th century, all over the world. Pickering, David, ed. *International Dictionary of Theatre - 3. Actors. Directors and Designers* (New York, London: St. James Press, 1996), 716.

[274] Konstantin S. Stanislavsky, *Polnoe Sobranie Sochnenii* [Complete Edition of Works], vol. 2, *An Actor Prepares*. Part 1, *The Self Preparation in Creative Means of Agitation* (Moscow: Iskusstvo, 1989), 185-6.

contradictory. The attention required for ensuring well-ordered, organized playing ... excludes both physical and spiritual inertia.' The word 'tension' has acquired an unwarranted negative connotation. When somebody complains of tension, he really means too much tension or, more precisely, **the wrong kind and amount of tension**, *in the wrong places, for the wrong length of time.* **In itself tension is not negative.** *Tension is a proper adjunct of human behavior – one cannot live without it ... Tension creates and sustains life, and carries it forward. Tension – of the right kind – is a prerequisite of dynamic, energetic, vital human endeavor. The cause of wrong tension is most often the lack of right tension. In such case it is fruitless to try to relax these wrong tensions directly; the solution lies in creating the right tensions, and letting relaxation come about on its own ...* **right tension – right in type, amount, placing and timing** *... If a human being is truly one and whole, then surely there is no distinction between 'the thing controlled and the control itself.*[275]

From the standpoint of conducting methodology, it is especially important to manage and to sort out bad reflexes from useful ones at the beginning of acquaintance with practical approaches. Proper tutorial guidance is particularly important for novice or inexperienced conductors if their 'bad' reflexes subconsciously provoke paroxysmal, seizure-like gestures.

---

[275] Alcantara, 15-16. (Emphasis added)

> *The condition only becomes a problem as soon as it is **automatic, harmful, and beyond the control of the conscious will.***[276]

As part of the conducting technique, it is especially important to achieve and master the technique of the management of different levels of muscular relaxation, from large muscular systems (arms, shoulders, back, abdomen/diaphragm, etc.) down to relaxation of the smaller muscles of the different parts of the arm (fingers, wrists, forearms and shoulders).

> *There is a constant connection between brain and muscle—between what I think and what I do. It is impossible to say of an act that it is purely 'mental' or purely 'physical.'*[277]

The efficient utilization of a body's appropriately relaxed muscular background (though with active external manifestations of posture) is an assurance of having achieved a **specific mental and physical sensation of *connection* to the sound**. Such an interactive combination of mental and physical techniques is crucial for a productive conductor-via-orchestra communicational cycle.

> *The freer a body part is, the better able it is to*

---

[276] Alcantara, 21. (Emphasis added)

[277] Ibid, 55.

sense accurately what it is doing.[278]

In some instances, conductors with the strength of well-developed musculature (naturally inherited or developed through certain physical exercises) may struggle with making a certain progress with techniques of active muscular relaxation. The constant presence of augmented muscular *tonus*[279] may be an obstacle on the path to complete muscular relaxation. However, to a certain extent, the presence of a developed musculature could be very beneficial to conducting in general (i.e., it may have a good natural 'impact' on orchestral sound).

Once, I personally made a remarkable observation while watching a conversation between deaf-mute individuals. For the outside observer, it was easy to discern that the emotional heat over the subject of their conversation was very intense. As the conversation continued to heat up, their hands, fingers, and lips moved with increased speed and excitement. However, what amazed me was that despite the recognizable manifestation of an elevated degree of emotions, the overall muscular tone of their body parts which conducted the conversation (fingers, hands, and facial muscles) was relatively minimal; that is, **it was just enough to articulate the subject**. A comparable

---

[278] Alcantara, 42. (Emphasis added)

[279] *Tonicity. Tonus* [Greek *tonos*]. A state of normal tension of the tissues by virtue of which the parts are kept in shape, alert, and ready to function in response to a suitable stimulus. In the case of muscle, it refers to a state of continuous activity or tension beyond that related to the physical properties; i.e., it is active resistance to stretch; in skeletal muscle it is dependent upon the efferent innervation. *Stedman's Medical Dictionary*, 28th ed., 1998-9.

approach can be applied in conducting, as well.

The management of the instant exchanges of inclusive or partial muscular relaxation in combination with advanced mental techniques (perpetual mental anticipation) is a necessary basis for productive conducting. When motions are directly connected (without fusing with excessive muscular tension) to the conductor's intentions, the spontaneous variety of conceptual motions is limitless and the value of the pre-requisite (prepared throughout study of the score) construction of schemes is minimal.

INCORPORATING RELAXATION

During the performance of a strike at the lowest (breaking) point of the motion, the primary instrumental response – the sound coupled with the applied physical effort – provides expectations of the occurrence of the sound on the edge of the exchange of the arm's muscular contraction and relaxation, or at the point of the instant change in direction at the lower breaking point of the "strike" as suggested by the generally accepted methodology. This stereotype sharply contrasts with the validity of the mental and physical aspects of conducting as a communicational act. To be able to eliminate or diminish the negative influence of such a primary instrumental response, the conductor has to implement the technique of dynamic muscular relaxation.

In contrast with instrumental practice, conductors do not have a practical opportunity to affect sound with direct physical action (at least not in ways similar to instrumentalists on their instruments). Although visual and emotional contact with musicians is an essential component of their professional tasks, conductors have to move their hands (with or without the baton) in space without the possibility of tactile (physical) contact with their virtual instrument – the orchestra (though the physical sensation of connection to the orchestral sound is practical and valuable [phenomenon of contour of sound]). This activity is founded exclusively on psychological (communicative) principles.

Recognition of the fundamental differences between the forceful (overcoming) and communicative conducting performances will lead to the acceptance of an adjusted mode of the practical implementation of a specific type of supervision.

> *The body functions with maximum efficiency when all parts are in dynamic balance with one another. When excess tension is released, it is as if a heavy weight is lifted off the body; there is often a sense of relief and of wonder at how much easier movement can be.*[280]

As was mentioned in the previous chapter, the technique of instant muscular relaxation of the various parts of the body (arms and their parts, shoulders, back, legs, abdomen [diaphragm], etc.), as well as the body as a whole (which, however, should be outwardly manifested in an active and dynamic mode) is an inseparable part of the conductor's psycho-physical action. Every external feature of a conductor's actions (arm motions, gestures, and overall body movements) should be carried out and then should return to the appropriately **relaxed primary physical mode**.

---

[280] Leibowitz and Connington, xvii.

The mastered management of instant muscular relaxation immediately after an action (e.g., cues to different instruments [or sections], the manifestation of abrupt tempo or dynamic changes, phrasing [especially with reference to the contour of sound], performance of various conceptual upbeats [converted, suspended and converted-suspended, etc.]) is one of the most vital psycho-physical conducting techniques. Also, the technique of instant muscular relaxation is a necessary part in getting a sense of connection to the sound and, consequently, a **sense of the practical management of the contour of sound**.

In principle, every advanced conductor's psycho-physical action should be **carried out with an appropriate level of muscular relaxation** (that is, they should return to a primary relaxed physique [though, again, manifested in a visually expressive mode!]). The duration of this relaxed mode could vary from a fraction of a second to a longer interval - its duration is determined by the specifics of the piece being performed: its character, dynamics, tempi, orchestration, etc.

The non-tactile manipulation of sound is a particularly delicate psycho-physical process, which requires **the utilization of unobstructed physical channels for the sensation of orchestral sound and its mental apprehension**. The control of an actively relaxed physical stature of a conductor's body provides a sufficient and instantaneous analysis of this accomplishment and, consequently, a proper foresight to an upcoming action.

During a performance, the physical apparatus, which is

uninterruptedly coordinated with the conductor's mind, will amplify the spontaneous liberalization of the inner intentions. Due to the specific emotional drive of a public performance, such a release can make the performance especially vibrant and add a specific zest which is not present during rehearsals.[281] These inversions in direct spontaneous (unprepared) manifestation of the motions/impulses are what make the conducting profession so creative and musically charming.

Suggested exercises for the appropriate development and management of the physical apparatus (techniques of *Dynamic Muscular Relaxation*) can be found in Part III of this book, in Chapter 12: *Active Muscular Relaxation*.

---

[281] Even the most successful rehearsal will not guarantee a successful performance (e.g., some of Arturo Toscanini's contemporaries recalled that many of the musical achievements he made during rehearsals were "missed during a performance"). Erzhemsky, *Psychological Paradoxes of Conducting*, 158.

7

MILIEU OF COMMUNICATION

MODIFICATION OF THE BEAT

As was discussed in previous chapters, the practical method of mental anticipation of the occurrence of sound at the lowest point of the stressed forward-downward-upward motion (or on the beat-strike) serves as an outdated vestige of audible time beating. The distinctive features of this traditional method are: the stressed physical act as an element of time-beating, and the manifestation of the visual strike, which is also described as the *ictus* (though again, as mentioned earlier, among scholars there is no unified methodological description of it). This mode was initially intended for establishing proper tempo, meter and dynamics, as well as for the transmission of the emotional content of music; all of those elements are supposed to coincide in time. The last two centuries of silent orchestral leading have revealed that the tradition of conducting "on the beat" is subject to a variety of severe practical and artistic shortcomings.

The whole concept of an upward-downward, reinforced application of impulses should be reconsidered. In general, the intercommunicative execution of the downbeat (or any beat of a metrical scheme) as a rule should not be continuously applied downward. For example: there is a multiplicity of instances when it should be reversed from downward to upward, to the spot where the actual line of sound is found.

It is important to mention, however, that even with this upward conversion, the formal (visual) contour of the gesture is preserved and is similar to the typical forced one (directed downward), though with absolute modification of the conductor's inner intent of the expectation of sound on the way to the upper point of motion instead of at the lowest breaking point; this consequently demands a practical (physical) re-setting of its application.

Historical evidence suggests that the practical approach of conducting which features psychological and, consequently, visual anticipation was first introduced by Arthur Nikisch and was later adopted by other conductors (among them were Wilhelm Furtwängler, Nikolai Malko, Ilia Musin, Herbert von Karajan and others).

> *Nikish was a great virtuoso of the orchestra. He was profoundly a musician. ... But he had a manner of conducting which is not ours today. He was conducting always before the time. That is the first example of what happened later with Furtwängler, who gave the beat and the moment after came the playing. It was very difficult for a conductor like myself to conduct the Philharmonic in Berlin because they had this habit.[282]*

The practical dissimilarities between the two traditions diverge particularly on one fundamental principle: the acquired practical reflex of expectation of the occurrence of the orchestral sound requires a different mental and physiological precept. Modern conducting practice has revealed that the tradition of conducting on the beat is subject to a variety of limitations. The expectation of sound at the breaking point of the stressed downward-upward motion (strike) is a psycho-physical reoccurrence of actions that belong to instrumental reflexology (where the use of muscular tension instantly binds with the appearance of sound) and that has a correlation with conditioned responses gained by conductors through their primary instrumental practice, or as dynamic stereotypes characteristic of instrumental performance.

From a practical standpoint, the creation of the still generally accepted forced manner of conducting - the old battuta style – in its time was nothing but an additional (artificial and non-scored!) drumming instrument of the orchestra (though with a specific 'operational' implement).

---

[282] *Conversations with Conductors*, Ernest Ansermet, 78.

Again, it is necessary to emphasize that the external appearance of conductor's gestures **is only a reflection of the fusion of his/her mental and physical activity**. Visual (tangible) momentum is an important element of conducting, but it is still only a **subordinate segment** of complex psycho-physical actions (the conversion of formal gestures into 'conceptual' motions) and should be organized consequently in reference to the rules of interactive communication.

The inner initiation of valid creative impulses should always precede the manifestation of the external (visual) operational tool, the execution of which is consequently supposed to precede the orchestra's response to the sound. An important part of this inner technique is that the *time-lag* between actions, or the amount of succession or anticipation, should be constantly monitored. From a methodological view (as suggested by George Erzhemsky in accordance with the research of known psycho-physiologist Nikolai Bernstein[283]), such a complex pattern of mental and physical actions can be most adequately depicted (or visualized) as a **rounded pattern** of actions.[284] The description of this hidden technique is a relatively new approach in conducting methodology, and it is meant to emancipate conductor's innate creative impulse.

The forceful approach of conducting (manifested in the

---

[283] Bernstein, Nikolai Aleksandrovich (1896-1966). Soviet psychophysiologist and physiologist, creator of a new research specialization – the physiology of activity. *Great Soviet Encyclopedia*, vol. 3, 214.

[284] Erzhemsky, 84-5.

application of a physically repressed downward-upward pattern of gestures) contains the unsolved inner conflict within itself. The mental expectation of the audible response at the bottom (or breaking point) of the motion and its actual appearance at the upper part of the motion (or at the top of the rebound) **creates the effect of syncopated conducting**. The reflex effort to correct or adjust the line of sound (that is, to lower it) with additional downward re-enforcement will exacerbate the situation and will actually push the line of sound even higher. In reality, such an effort will situate the conductor's actions perpetually **beyond the control** of the orchestral sound.

Here, I have to mention again the most important problem in observing the obstructive power of instrumental reflexes: why is such a useful tool as a technique of constant psychological and visual anticipation still not mutually accepted by conducting tutors as a practical method? The answer may depend on the specifics of human psychology rather than on methodological clichés. Without a proper tutorial to guide one through the modification of primary (instrumental) reflexes, a certain conscious (and subconscious) discomfort and confusion will not be overcome (though the formal application of mental and visual anticipation will not be useful but, rather, confusing).

At practically every moment of anticipation, a conductor psychologically acts in front of the "vacant" space.[285] For example, imagine a pianist who 'plays' the piano 10 feet away from the instrument's keyboard and with absolute sincerity! Apparently, the number of conductors who consciously (and

---
[285] This terminology was suggested by G. Erzhemsky.

subconsciously) managed to overcome such discomfort was (and still is!) much smaller than that of those who could not subdue it, and instead preferred to correct the human nature and create their own proper on-the-beat or, rather, a "how-I-believe-it-should-be-done" reality (the phenomenon of an assumed correctness of an incorrect nature in conducting).

EMANCIPATION OF METRICAL SCHEMES

The manifestation of the conductor's intentions (in the form of the quasi-vertical application of visual strikes) as a predominant (or merely) practical skill not only affects the performance of the beat itself but also shatters the flow of the musical line. Presumably, in such an approach, the vertical depiction of the stressed (lowest) point of the downward-upward motion throughout the metrical schemes is supposed to serve as a transmitter of the conductor's inner impulses to the orchestra. A technique such as this traces its nature to the instrumental type of conducting (audible beating). A common example of this approach is the motion of conductors who stick to the beat-emphasis (striking) manner of leading the orchestra:

> *In their actions they proceed from the precept that music exists and is developed only in time, and not*

> ***both in time and space***, *as the latter would seem to contradict the notions of 'common sense.' From this, the basis of management for them is the constant accentuated emphasis of metric points, which almost fully excludes the possibility of transmitting information about the subtlest artistic aspects of the work being performed.*[286]

Another important reason for modifying the forced strike motion is to overcome the primary (traditional) stiffness of the metrical schemes and to create a meaningful connection between metrical points (beats) in accordance with the flow of music (instead of the manifestation of logically connected structures, the conductor's mechanical measuring breaks down the musical flow).

The emphasized marking of every beat, which is underlined by the upbeat strike, isolates the beat, so as the indication of each beat in different sides of the metrical schemes.

"Metrical schemes by themselves accept that a metrical measure acquires the structure of a fixed constancy of strong and weak beats. Thus, a gestural depiction of such measurement consists of the pattern of repeated cycles of motion which separate one beat from another. As such, a conductor repeats the same gesture over and over, though with different directions, to unconnected points. In music, though, sounds [notes] are

---

[286] Erzhemsky, 109. (Emphasis added)

connected and form the unbroken musical complex."[287]

Besides the quasi-vertical application (predominantly directed from above down to the floor - next to the conductor's feet) of an impulse (strike or click) throughout the metrical schemes[288] there are varieties of other (non-vertical) visualized planes (or dimensions) where impulses may be applied (even though Harold Farberman's "flick," is performed sideways, the principle of the motion's performance is similar to the click).[289]

Leading a large ensemble has always required a complex combination of physical and mental (though specifically musical) actions. Modern conducting as a communicative (quasi-lingual) performance has to contain a multi-dimensional practical tool which aids **in connecting metrical points in accordance with the needs of the musical texture** and in overcoming the stiffness of the conventional metrical schemes. Utilization of the contour of sound as a part of the practical tool exclusively revises the design of a conductor's external manifestation of technique. For practical modern conducting

---

[287] Musin, 189.

[288] In modern methodology, the vertical principle of an enforced beat application is predominant for emphasized (dynamic) indication of the beats on various sides of the conducting schemes (e.g., for 3/4, 4/4 metrical patterns). Allan A. Ross, *Technique for Beginning Conductors* (Belmont, California: Wadsworth Publishing Company, 1976), 3-4; Rudolf, *The Grammar of Conducting*, 9; Prausnitz, *Score and Podium*, 51-2; Emil Kahn, *Elements of Conducting*, Second Edition (New York: Schirmer Books, A Division of Macmillan Publishing Co., Inc., London: Macmillan Publishing Co., 1965), 10-12; Lumley and Springthorpe, *The Art of Conducting*, 24-5.

[289] Farberman, 24-6.

methods, the implementation of horizontal (not just from one side to another [left-to-right] but also in an inward-outward direction) or diagonal dimension throughout a performance of metrical schemes has more practical significance than a reliance on quasi-vertically applied beats.

Most features of the prevailing conducting methodology could be useful if **modified in accordance with communicative principles**. However, any technical elements of the conducting methodology should not serve themselves but should be applied as a part of the productive communicational tool.[290] For an appropriate non forced modification of the beat, which consequently affects the performance of the metrical schemes (among other features), the principle of sound appearance for various orchestral instruments should be taken into consideration.

The multi-dimensional modification of all visual technical features allows for certain amalgamating divergences in orchestral instruments' attacks. All orchestral instruments (with certain conditions based on their performing techniques) can be divided in three categories:

1. **Linear** or **'Horizontal'** – strings' predominantly technical approach

---

[290] For example, the striking elements of the widespread tradition of conducting "on the beat" may become a part of the advanced techniques if modified in correspondence with communicative principles (e.g., the technique of the suspended mode of upbeats).

> The tone color of the string group is fairly homogeneous from top to bottom, variations in the different registers being much more subtle than in the winds. At the same time, stringed instruments are the most versatile in producing different kinds of sound. As string tone is rich in overtones all manner of close and open spacing is practical.[291]

2. **Striking or 'Vertical'** - all percussion and some keyboard instruments (e.g., celesta)

> Instruments of percussion may be simply defined as those instruments in which sound is produced by striking one object with another. ... A more scientific classification distinguishes those with a vibrating membrane (membranophones), such as the various drums, and those of metal, wood or other substances capable of sounding when struck (idiophones), such as cymbals and triangle.[292]

3. **Diverse** – includes the combination of **Linear** and **quasi-Vertical** elements - all winds (breathing), piano, harp, guitar and organ

> The vibration of air enclosed in a pipe may be

---

[291] Piston, *Orchestration*, 3.

[292] Ibid, 296.

compared to the vibration of a string stretched between two points. One important difference is that whereas the pitch of a string is affected by length, density of materials, and amount of tension, the pitch of vibrating air column depends upon its length alone. This rule is not perfectly accurate in a scientific sense, but it is the basis for the custom of speaking of pitches in terms of length. ... The function of sound generator ... is fulfilled in a brass instrument by the player's lips, held against a more or less cup-shaped metal mouthpiece fitted to the small end of the main tube of the instrument. As the air stream is forced through the lips, they are set in vibration, and these vibrations are communicated to the column of air enclosed in the brass tube. [293]

Plucking (harp, guitar, or pizzicato in string sections) is closer to Striking or Vertical: "... first the stringed instruments (harp and piano, together with the guitar, mandolin, etc.) mentioned ... as contrasting with the 'stroked' instruments of the true string orchestral group; and then the keyboard instruments (piano again, of course, but thence celesta, organ, etc.)." [294] The pipe-organ is close to winds (Diverse) with certain reservations due to the stable temporal delay (time-lag). The occurrence of sound during singing (vocal soloists or choir) is close to winds (Diverse), also with certain reservations.

To unify the divergence of instruments' attacks, the

---

[293] Piston, 115, 208.

[294] Del Mar, *Anatomy of the Orchestra*, 431.

performance of the striking stroke must be modified. A flexible and more communicative approach is needed to secure a good ensemble at those various attacks which, in reality, means that musicians need a certain amount of time to respond mutually to a conductor's action. With a flexible and elastic motion-impulse, the conductor "breathe[s]" with the players and almost "put[s] the notes in their mouth[s]."[295] Communicative modification of the gesture should be made in the form of rounded motion. This mode (rounded motion) as a primary element in the organization of the conductor's gestures, (external apparatus) and proves to be an essential principal for the development of the conductor's communicative apparatus.

ROUNDED MOTION

To coordinate the various entrances of sound (or various orchestral time-lags) and interactive conjunction of the metrical points, the proper utilization of **rounded motion** is vital confluence of the vertical and horizontal dimensions. The

---

[295] Rudolf, 247. The technique of *Breath Control* is one of the most important segments of a conductor's apparatus. A combination of breath control and active relaxation produces a specific psycho-physical sensation. Such techniques are essential for the development of communicative modes of motions (Chapter 12, *Active Muscular Relaxation. Breath Control, Active Muscular Relaxation and the Contour of Sound*).

appropriate implementation of rounded motion (especially with reference to the contour of sound and, consequently, its effect on the musician's perception) will unify all fragmentation of instrumental attacks, and this technique could serve as a coordinating device for connecting the horizontal and vertical dimensions.[296]

The implementation of rounded motion with reference to the contour of sound is an interactive practical substitution of the archaic and artificial striking stroke, click, or traditional *ictus*.

Rather than a monotonous hammering of the ictus throughout the metrical schemes, with the manifestation of the gesture applied towards the floor, the visual impulse could be productively redirected and applied upward with the performance of a rounded motion from right to left (see Diagram A).

---

[296] It is necessary to emphasize that some conductors who are vaguely familiar with the practical methods of Ilia Musin often mistakenly substitute the concept of rounded motion with the simple "Musin's circles." Apparently the term 'rounded' expresses the concept of curved motion (and its endless variations) more appropriately.

A.*

left side   right side

Contour of sound

← Time-lag momentum

beginning of sound

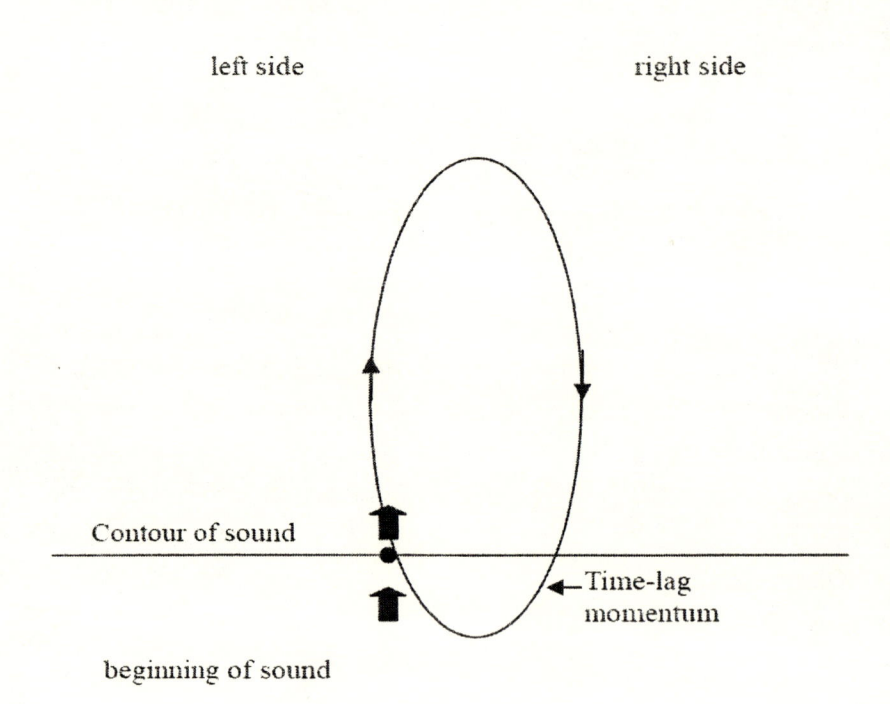

A more complex modification of the rounded motion when impulse could be applied outward towards the orchestra as in diagram B below.

B.*

outward   inward

Contour of sound

Time-lag momentum

The beginning of sound

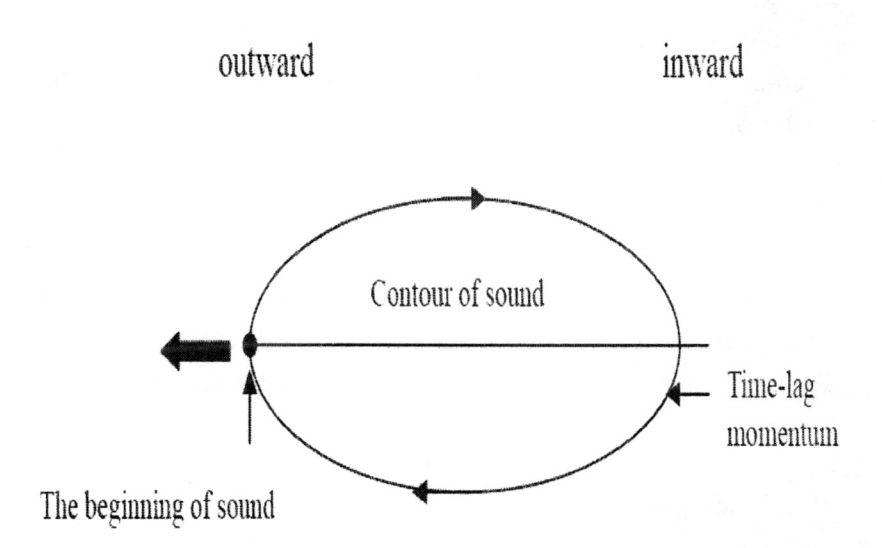

* For practical reasons, both diagrams demonstrate the single metrical unit in one (e.g., quarter note in 1/4 meter). Notice that in both instances (upward and forward motions, diagrams A and B) the beginning of sound coincides with the beginning of the beat, in such way that **the hand always arrives next to the point of the beginning of the sound** – on the contrast, with the forceful style the arm is bounced away from the sound after the strike. Also, it is necessary to mention that modification of the strike has to be considered in its complexity in regards to tempi, dynamics, and textural thicknesses of the musical material.

Despite the apparent (evident) simplicity of rounded motion, it makes available the wide spectrum of sophisticated intercommunicative techniques. The development of complex advanced techniques within the rounded motion could dramatically expand the technical tools of the conductor. For example, during the performance, the rounded motion can function as an interactive complex with a multifunctional utilization of various segments of the arm:

1. The application of various accents by the wrist or wrist and forearm. This technique is especially practical because the performance of accents does not disconnect the meaningful (rhythmical and linear) ties between metrical points (beats) of the scheme as soon as they are applied within the performance of the rounded motion.

2. The interactive modification of the upbeats within the mode of rounded motion: e.g., converted, suspended (delayed) upbeats, etc.

3. The interactive modification of rounded motion for the utilization of various types of rhythmically-contingent rebounds. This technique allows managing the rhythm and the dynamic of the upcoming beat during the performance (without a negative disturbance) of the current.

4. The interactive utilization of the various parts of the arm within the rounded motion: e.g., wrist, fore-arm, and shoulder are in parallel control of the melodic lines and rhythmic patterns of the orchestral sections.*

*For example: Brahms Symphony # 3, I movement, measures 3-14.

The most practical benefit of the utilization of rounded motion is that it naturally manifests continuity (that is, it prevents fractures) and facilitates the interactive connection of the beats (metrical points) throughout metrical schemes. The technique of rounded motion (and its modifications: elliptical, circled, varied eights, etc.) is especially practical if it stays in an interactive connection with the contour of sound. This connection brings a sense of firm control of the orchestra's sound (instead of bouncing off the sound each time after the strike), allowing a conductor to control the intermediate beat within the metrical pattern and sense the fulfillment of the metrical unit (beat or measure), especially in scores with thick orchestration (e.g., Gustav Mahler's Symphonies, Richard Strauss's "Tone Poems").

The mode of the rounded motion-impulse is a primary communicative feature for the organization of the conductor's gestures and it demonstrates an essential element for the development of the agile physical apparatus. In general, performances of beats (motion-impulses) and metrical schemes exhibit the inner essentials of the conductor's apparatus. An informative conducting manner instantly creates a productive atmosphere into conductor-orchestra collaboration. The methodological utilization of such communicative principles allows one to organically unify such interactive dialogue at its best for the service of the musical piece.

THE ZONE OF COMMUNICATION

THE TECHNIQUE OF ATTENTION GATHERING

For tutorial purposes, the conductor's complex techniques can be divided into two conditionally independent segments: inner (psychological) and outer (visual.) The conductor's inner creative impulses are manifested through the external (physical) features of the conducting apparatus. Despite the apparatus's visual complexity, there is a certain narrow communicative zone which is responsible for the suitable 'broadcast' of musical images. This place would be recognized by the orchestra's musicians (consciously or subconsciously) as a zone of communication. Due to the characteristics of human perception, and the specifics of orchestral linear communication,[297] the proper placement of a communicational

---

[297] The phenomenon of fixed eye-level linear perception was discussed earlier in the subchapter: *Contour of Sound*. Also, related aspects of the human communication will be touched later in subchapter: *Dimensions of Perception*.

transmitter within the conductor's apparatus is a necessity of successful interaction. Consequently, the conductor's external (physical) apparatus has to be organized in reference to this place of intercommunicative connection between him/her and the orchestra's musicians: "The physical placement of the beat - the spot where information is passed on to the orchestra - is very important for effective communication."[298]

This communicational spot is not the same as the constant "focus-on-the-tip-of-the-baton" (though the various parts of the baton can function with reference to the communicational spot) type of technique suggested by the generally accepted conducting methodology, without the analysis of the arm's functions and, most importantly, its perception by musicians.[299] The delineation of an attention gathering zone[300] requires the specific adjustment of the external part of a conductor's apparatus with proper communicational positions of the arms, which would unify the performance of beats within the pattern of metrical schemes.

---

[298] Meier, 6.

[299] Another common shortcoming **(especially typical for novice conductors)** is an impulsive forehead nod along with the manifestation of the upbeat/motion-impulse **(particularly along with the preparatory)**. Such a forehead nod serves as a supplementary upbeat and, consequently, an additional point of communication.

[300] The practical role of such a zone (or place) to a certain extent, could be perceived in the same order as other methodological approaches such as "conductor's space" as suggested by Harold Farberman in his book *The Art of Conducting Technique: A New Perspective*, 1-2.

Along with other communicative phenomena (e.g., contour of sound, time-lag, various communicative modes of motions, etc.), the technical implementation of the zone of attention gathering resets the whole concept of the performance of conducting metrical schemes, as is suggested by the force-overcoming method. For example (as suggested by forceful methods), in a 3/4 metrical pattern, after the performance of a downbeat, the arm bounces up to the left 'corner' (next to the left shoulder) to prepare a reinforced tangent 'slam' (by fisted fingers with or without the baton or by the open palm) to the right side against the second beat, and then with a similar 'slam' to the left side and up for the third, etc.

The performance of 4/4 is analogous in the performance of such a 'slammed' manner, but with a redirection of sides of the beats – first going to the right instead of the left, and so on.[301] The intercommunicative shortcomings of such a performance are evident: striking with a slam (forcible or reinforced motion) provokes a fracture of the **linear** manifestation of the arm and, consequently, instantly represents several contradicting, rapidly changing and fluctuating spots of communication – i.e., from wrist to elbow or from wrist through elbow to forearm or shoulder and then back to the wrist, or the parallel presence of two, three or even four points of communication (wrists and elbows of both arms in mirrored motions, etc.).

Another important addition to the proper delineation of the zone

---

[301] For example: Allan A. Ross, *Technique for Beginning Conductors*, 3-4; Rudolf (Third Edition), 9; Prausnitz, *Score and Podium*, 51-2; Kahn, *Elements of Conducting*, 10-12; Lumley and Springthorpe, *The Art of Conducting*, 24-5.

of attention gathering is to manifest it with reference to (and more importantly with a sense of) the contour (vicinity) of sound. **Ultimately the development of a firm sense of the contour of sound itself will lead the arm to the right spot of communication.**

The spot of attention gathering could be located either:

A. At the outer edge of the fingers. The thumb is slightly clasped along the palm. The index, middle, ring and pinkie fingers are straight and form a unit, but without the presence of excessive tension (not squeezed) and with the palm slightly angled downward and to the left side. This position is suggested (especially at the beginning of practice) for conducting without a baton.

B. At the point of connection of the tip of the thumb and index finger (next to the index finger's first joint), which is joined with the other fingers, all slightly bent towards the palm. This position is suggested for conducting with or without a baton. The use of the baton, however, expands (widens) the presence of the zone of attention gathering, which is conditioned by the position of the wrist and arm. In general, because the manifestation of the communicative zone remains inseparably connected to the contour of sound, the use of the baton is suggested once a good sense of the line of sound has been developed.

The active manifestation of the wrist along the unbroken conditional line can be visually drawn from the top of the shoulder, through the elbow, and to the wrist. The preservation of the arm's unbroken line is essential to the proper manifestation of a spot of communication. On the other hand, a non-linear manifestation of the arm (which is typical for the performance of schemes with the striking manner) results in the abrupt exchange of different parts of the arm (i.e., a common shortcoming is a sudden exposition of the elbow during the performance of the first and third beats within 3/4, and the second and fourth beats within 4/4 conducting schemes).

THE COMMUNICATIVE POSITIONING OF THE ARM

The generally accepted conducting methodology suggests that a primary down beat position should be located somewhat in front of the abdomen. Such a subjective and artificial methodological principle is not effective if conducting is considered as an intercommunicative process. A downbeat position "in front of the body"[302] (or near the center) with the elbow "jutting to the right"[303] is one of the methodological cornerstones of the generally accepted conducting practice. Because of its primary artificial setting, it negatively affects the whole appearance of the external apparatus - the right arm's manifestation is sustained in a weak position (with the presence of excessive muscular tension due to the arm's position itself).

Among its many shortcomings, there is the constant presence of

---

[302] Paul Van Bodegraven and Harry Robert Wilson, *The School Music Conductor* (Chicago: Hall and McCreary Company, 1942), 5.

[303] Grosbayne, *Techniques of Modern Orchestral Conducting*, 20; Albert Stoessel, *The Technic of the Baton* (New York: Carl Fisher, Inc., 1928), 24.

a breaking visual line of the arm from the top of the shoulder through the elbow to the wrist, constantly and unnecessarily crossing the front of the chest during the execution of schemes (especially on the way from the downbeat to the second beat and from the second beat to the third beat in 4/4 meter) and during the manifestation of a hammer-like strike in front of the chest (especially for the down beat or second beat in 4/4 meter).

Another major shortcoming of the center position is the constant suppression of sound with the elbow (when the arm has a broken linear position, the elbow operates individually, upward-downward on the side). It is especially unproductive for beats which move to the side of the metrical schemes (for example, in a 3/4 pattern for the second beat and in 4/4 patterns for the second and third beats). This mainly occurs because the visual 'unbroken' line of the arm is not preserved throughout the metrical scheme, and consequently each point within the scheme is manifested in a separate manner.

The deliberate likeness (or unification) of the manner in performance of each metrical point within a pattern (especially for 3/4 and 4/4) is critically important for the maintenance of productive communication with the orchestra.

In general, the methodical unification of all features of the conducting apparatus (and beats in particular) is a tool of constructive communication with the orchestra. This is in contrast with the predominant methodological approach, in which each beat of a pattern is performed dissimilarly (e.g., in a

4/4 pattern: 1st beat – arm is lined up perpendicular to the body and the beat impulse is directed by the wrist down towards the conductors feet (in the mode of a strike); 2nd beat – the forearm and arm form a broken line [letter L shape] and the beat impulse is directed to the left corner (in the mode of a slam); 3rd beat – arm shape is similar to the previous beat [L shape], directed to the right corner (another slam), and the 4th beat is a tangent motion from up above, downward, to the left side (strike), and then back to the 1st beat, etc.). Along with performance of the strike, a non-linear manifestation of the arm is especially confusing for a comparable orchestral texture or articulation, and it is just another example of inadequate traditional practical intention conflicting with the rules of human perception.

Another deficiency for the arm at a non-linear (centered) position is a constant covering of the chest during conducting of metrical schemes (especially for 4/4 meter). It is important to acknowledge that the continuous manifestation of an open chest has an enormous intercommunicative value. This visual presentation has a positive subconscious psychological impact on musicians and literally means that the conductor is **sincere** and **honest** in all his/her intentions. The manifestation of the conductor's apparatus should not be hindered by constant chest crossing, which is typical for the enforced methodology (the downbeat is set somewhat at the center or in front of the abdomen). To avoid the presence of such a constant communicative obstacle, the intercommunicative center of the conductor's external apparatus should be place according to this intercommunicative phenomenon.

The arm's linear manifestation allows all members of the orchestra to perceive it more or less comparably and all motions within the metrical scheme should be unified by the concept of the arm's linear preservation. Appropriate linear management of the arm is an important segment of the productive tool of communication.

Suggested exercises for an appropriate linear arm position can be found in the following Part III, Chapter 8, and subchapter *Primary Arm Position*.

THE CYCLE OF INTERACTION

The conductor-via-orchestra continuous interaction is a constant interactive collaboration and, if illustrated schematically, this interaction could resemble the pattern of discrete circled sequences, which include not only musical elements but social aspects as well. Thus, on one side we have a collective or group of musicians – an orchestra and section leaders – and the conductor on the other. The actions of both sides (mental and physical), with the support of their talents and professional skills, are **unified by a mutual goal, the performance of the musical piece.**[304] However, for a successful achievement of the task, this specific social organism can function productively only under one condition: if both sides (the orchestra and the conductor) are able to communicate through a comprehensive and productive communicational tool.

To succeed in establishing a productive communicational bridge

---

[304] Despite the obviousness of this statement, the specific social aspects of large ensemble performance are often ignored. A musical piece itself suggests the grounds for communication through the specific musical language. The motivation, the emotional and psychological state of the individuals, which are gathered for performance of a musical piece, is distinct from a social or formal gathering for other occasions at various work places (e.g., office, factory, public services, churches, political events, etc.).

on the conductor's side, an inner, firm, potent creative impulse is required, which will ignite an inspirational musical concept. The projection of creative will in an anticipated and continuous mode is vital for communication with an orchestra because only then will the musicians have a chance to uncompromisingly comprehend, accept, and mutually (appropriately) respond to the conductor's artistic conceptual actions. Another fundamental part of a conductor's inner (mental) *apparatus* is the ability to instantly comprehend and evaluate the orchestra's response to the previous round of actions, and then to appropriately modify (if necessary) the upcoming action. This intercommunicative cycle of actions can be conditionally depicted through the following scheme.

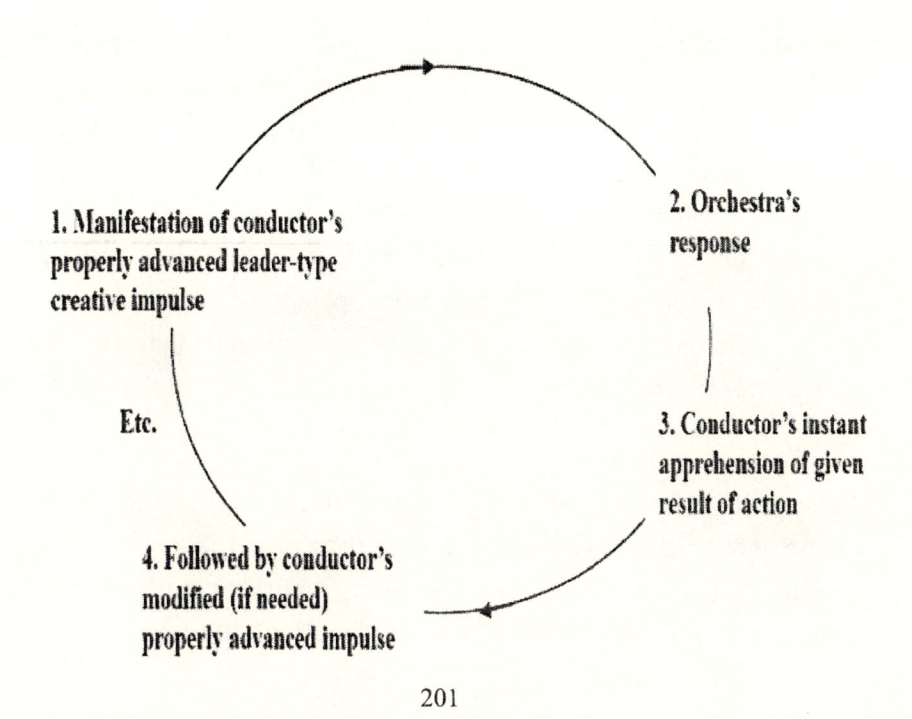

1. Manifestation of conductor's properly advanced leader-type creative impulse

2. Orchestra's response

3. Conductor's instant apprehension of given result of action

4. Followed by conductor's modified (if needed) properly advanced impulse

Etc.

It is necessary, though, to emphasize that the conductor's position immediately in front of the orchestra is not ideal for reliable acoustical perception. The acoustical focus of the orchestral sound in standard concert hall settings (stage in front of the audience hall) is located between 30-40 feet away from the edge of the stage. The conductor's acoustically inferior location in itself determines the specific ear training and adjustments to the sound of different groups of instruments. Naturally, this scheme is conditional, and only schematically outlines the complexity of the intercommunicative, conductor-orchestra sequence of interactions. It is important to realize that, psychologically and physically, the process itself is complex, indivisible, and **constant** (continuous from the beginning to the end) on both sides.

If we tried to analyze the inner nature of the conductor-orchestra interaction as a multi-leveled, collective, complex psycho-physical and social process, we would find ourselves using such words as: continuous, incessant, uninterrupted, rounded, curved, etc., terms which are common in the description of any cycled sociological phenomenon. It is hard to imagine that during a performance (especially of large complex scores) there is any place where orchestral musicians or the conductor can take even a short (seconds-long) mental vacation.

The performance of a work requires an enormous amount of **continuous** and **unbroken** mental intensity - for both the orchestra and conductor. There is simply no practical possibility for a **mental break** (or stop-start) **throughout the piece** (even in between movements the orchestra and conductor tune their minds for the character [images] and the technical challenges of the upcoming music).

Thus, it is appropriate to describe the sociological, and, consequently, the psychological aspects of conducting in such terms as: continuous, unbreakable, uninterrupted, rounded, spiral, etc., due to the dialectic rules of the unity of "the part and the whole." It is also logical to assume that the manifestation of the external (visual) features of conducting techniques should match their internal phenomena as well. This contrasts with the prevailing pedagogical formula, which conversely suggests a continuity of the force-overcoming mode, as well as a monotonous, endless, and shattered perpetual sequence of anti-musical hammering (breaking) moments typical of the striking modes of conducting. In reality, the practical admiration of this style creates no less and no more than a stable conceptual (cognitive) dissonance for musicians' perceptions.

The act of collective orchestral performance not only consists of a specific musical and creative phenomenon but it also includes a definite social component when different personalities are united by a mutual goal - the performance of a musical piece. Comprehension of the sociological aspects of conducting gives us an important acknowledgement of the inner (innate) intangible forces which reveal hidden mechanisms (the inner springs) of collective orchestral performance. Even when some orchestra musicians or groups of players (orchestral sections) are not engaged in actual playing, during a performance they are still **continuously mentally (and consequently physically)**

actively involved in the performance. Again, for musicians as well as for the conductor, there is no moment of psychological absence during the performance once their physical presence is required on stage.

DIMENSIONS OF PERCEPTION

It is important to emphasize the social aspect of the conductor's duty. The setting of a fertile creative psychological atmosphere is a pledge of successful conductor-orchestra interaction. Productive communication between a conductor and the orchestra is primarily a psychological interaction - the musician's perception and responses occur via the conductor's mental forethought and analysis. To be a successful conductor, one should realize and acknowledge the main principles of human communication and perception which will allow him/her to maintain a productive, practical relationship with the orchestra from the first moment of the conductor's appearance. This is especially important for auditions or guest conducting.

The technique of establishing productive psychological communication with an orchestra is important as a visual manifestation of the conducting apparatus itself. For successful conducting, an acknowledgement of human perception and its specifics is important and should be seriously learned. Such knowledge is important for establishing productive linear, horizontal, and psychological dimensions based on the recognition of the inner mental connection with the musicians.

This connection is rooted to a conductor constant monitoring by a musicians' emotional and psychological state.

Research in human communication suggests that 65% of a normal two-person conversation consists of nonverbal communicational channels (i.e., gestures, body language, facial expressions, etc.), while less than 35% of the information is communicated verbally. By analyzing nonverbal cues, a person can enhance his/her understanding of what is really being said.[305] Outer appearance also conveys information about conductor's personality and attitude. Every detail is important for establishing a first positive impression (the impression made at first glance **is the most stable psychological stereotype of person-to-person communication**): from the way the conductor dresses to his/her tone of voice, actions, and gestures.

According to sociological paradigms analyzed by Freud[306] and Jung,[307] "instinctive and, emotional tendencies prevail within a group."[308] Orchestral musicians consciously and (more importantly) subconsciously perceive negative or positive

---

[305] Teri Kwal Gamble and Michael Gamble, *Communication Works,* 3rd ed. (NY: McGraw-Hill Inc., 1990), 103-4.

[306] Freud, Sigmund (1856-1939). Austrian neurologist and psychiatrist, who invented the technique of PSYCHOANALYSIS. *APA Dictionary of Psychology*, Gary R. VandenBos, Editor in Chief. (Washington, DC: American Psychological Association, 2007), 390.

[307] Jung, Carl Gustav (1875-1961). Swiss psychiatrist, founder of "analytic psychology" .... *Dictionary of Behavioral Science*, 2nd ed. Benjamin B. Wolman, ed. (New York, New York: Academic Press, Inc., 1989), 190.

[308] V. Yu. Bolshakov, *Evolutionary Theory of Behavior*, 53.

connotations from a conductor. Such details include bright (louder) spots in the conductor's dress, dominant vivid colors (red, yellow, green) or inappropriate combinations within his/her outfit (e.g., a dark suit and bright sneakers), the position and movement of hands (i.e., if the conductor's palm is positioned upward [this is perceived as friendly], downward [dominating], or sideways [neutral] when greeting the concertmaster) or the position of arms (crossed [defensive], often touching the chin [unconfident] or nose [nervousness, stress]). "Hand movements are not the only physical manifestations of cognitive processing in communication;" the conductor's outer appearance in general is an important part in creating a positive impression: "There are postural shifts, facial display, head nods, or foot movements."[309]

In general, the conductor's elevated position on the podium above the orchestra is perceived as an aggressive and dominant position. It should, therefore, be the conductor's goal to diminish (or at least not to intensify) such a negative perception. The modern conductor does not have the practical reasons to exercise an authoritarian leadership model (due to economical [orchestras' shrinking budgets] and social [musicians' union] issues). This type of conductor succeeded in the past, when authoritative ruling of the orchestra gave many conductors the opportunity to blame the orchestra for their (his/her[310]) own

---

[309] *Hands, Words, and Mind: On the Structuralization of Body Movements During Discourse and the Capacity for Verbal Representation* by Freedman, Norbert in *The Downstate Series of Research in Psychiatry and Psychology*, v. 1, *Communicative Structures and Psychic Structures. A Psychoanalytic Interpretation of Communication,* Edited by Norbert Freedman and Stanley Grand (NY, London: Plenum Press, 1976), 112.

[310] Beginning from the middle of the twentieth century, there are also

shortcomings (that is, "I am conducting correctly but you are playing incorrectly"). This style of conducting also required extended time for rehearsals to reach suitable musical results.

In appearance as a guest conductor, it is especially important to establish a productive algorithm of the rehearsal (e.g., an excessive number of repetitions for a technically difficult spot may not give the desired practical result due to the state of musicians' mental concentration and its natural tendency to fade [especially towards the end of the rehearsal]). The amount of time spent with a particular section may put the rest of the orchestra out of the spotlight and redirect musicians' attention to other objects - they may check their watches (a typical nonverbal sign of lost communicational ties with the conductor) or start informal conversations with their stand partners, etc.

There are also various dimensions belonging to the conductor's inner apparatus. To maintain productive intercommunicative (psychological) bridges with an orchestra's musicians during a performance is an essential inner task of a conductor's role as a leader. It is important to develop the mental technique of the conductor's division of attention[311] for multi-layered and multi-sectional awareness of orchestral performance as an important part of such an internal apparatus. During a performance, the conductor should be able to monitor (along with performance of

---

examples of authoritarian styles of ruling by female conductors - e.g., Soviet/Russian conductor Veronica Dudarova.

[311] Such a technique is similar to Stanislavsky's method of paying attention to "internal" and "external" circles: Stanislavsky, *An Actor Prepares*. And to Erzhemsky's *principle of octopus* type of the attention division. Erzhemsky, *Psychological Paradoxes of Conducting*, 164-5.

anticipated action) the different sections of the orchestra simultaneously (in contrast with the common shortcoming of the perception of an orchestra's sound as a unified whole). Such an inner technique allows the conductor to appropriately supervise the performance.

Other features of this apparatus include: "vertical" harmonic hearing,[312] and simultaneous awareness of the quality of multi-ranged pitches and timbres. The linear dimensions of the mental apparatus include instant analysis of a melodic line and its quality, the maintenance of appropriate tempi (or an applicable combination of tempi), and their relationship and correspondence and, overall, the maintenance of an appropriate character of the performance of a piece from the beginning to the end, and continuous maintenance of the inner creative impulse.

---

[312] Nina Aleksandrovna Berger, *Garmonia Kak Prostranstvennaja Kategorija Muziki* [Harmony as a Dimentional Category of Music] *Dissertazija na soiskanie uchenoi stepeni kandidata iskusstvovedenija* [PhD Dissertation] (Leningrad Conservatory of Music after Nikolai Rimsky-Korsakov, Leningrad, 1979).

PART III

METHODOLOGY

8

DEVELOPMENT OF THE APPARATUS

The following part of this book is meant to assist in obtaining the practical external and mental techniques of anticipation. By acquiring this technique, one will be able to establish an artistically productive conductor/orchestra interaction that is crucial for the conductor's successful career.

Conducting is a complex psycho-physical intercommunicative action. The complexity of a conductor's interactive techniques should include the scale of specific conducting reflexes, an appropriate intercommunicative implementation of the body and its parts (development of meaningful [informative] and elastic mental/physical apparatus), and most importantly, the developed mental techniques, such as anticipation of texture, advanced inner formation of the orchestra's ideal sound, advanced manifestation of the creative inner impulse, and multi-layered hearing of the orchestral score.

For methodological purposes, this section of the book is separated (conditionally) into the external (visible) and internal (intangible) sides of conducting techniques. However, the final practical basis of the suggested material is meant to harmonize the external and inner features of conducting.[313]

---

[313] A well-developed system of modern conducting methodology can also be found in Ilia Musin's book, *The Technique of Conducting*.

EXTERNAL FEATURES OF THE APPARATUS

This chapter emphasizes the importance of suitable posture and the primary position of the arms in the establishment of the external features of a conductor's apparatus. The practical goals of the following exercises are simple: to make the external[314] emergence of a conductor's inner intentions as supple and elastic as possible, and to achieve an uncompromised connection with the conductor's creative impulses. All technical achievements (inner and outer) will transmit and amplify the conductor's thoughts and spontaneous inner creative impulses.

The conductor's apparatus includes: "... typical motions that convey meaning as a basis for all modes of conducting techniques. **The establishment of the apparatus entails the development of such motions, which are the most rational**

---

[314] The term 'external' is conditional and is employed for practical purposes. In actuality, the 'external' and 'internal' environs of a conductor's apparatus are indivisible. Similarly, for convenience, the terms 'visible' and 'invisible' are employed.

and natural, and are based on inner physical (muscular) relaxation. The arms and their diverse movements, systematized in a harmoniously shaped system are the means of the apparatus by which the conductor leads the orchestra. However, the facial expression, body and head posture, and even disposition of the feet, are not insignificant for a conductor."[315]

Conducting is an intercommunicative process, a creative exchange of musical information. The conductor's body in general and his/her external (physical) apparatus in particular should be organized as part of a unified communicative process and in accordance with its rules. The external apparatus and the body (as a part of it) must serve as an external (physical) transmitter of inner creative impulses (in the form of a specific 'decoder' of musical information). The continuous intercommunicative connection between mind and body (arms, feet, and head) should be one that will allow for the efficient execution of conducting. This is necessarily one of the essential criteria for the rightness of any conductor's action and the proper relationship between indivisible inner and external parts of the conductor's apparatus. Overall, as a practical method, achievement of communicative (linguistic) principles of conducting enhances all features of the conductor's toolkit.

In the following chapters, the conductor's apparatus will be revealed as a combination of interactive modes and techniques characteristic of the advanced methodology.

---

[315] Musin, 15.

BODY POSTURE

Body posture is the most important feature of the conductor's apparatus. The proper posture of the body in general and the posture of the torso (trunk) in particular must be controlled: "to provide a foundation from which the limb muscles can act."[316] The following exercises assist in producing a stable vertically aligned position which places the body in an appropriate posture. Practical accomplishment of these exercises aids in finding an expressive body posture and avoiding (eliminating) excessive muscular tension.

Exercise # 1

1. Place feet slightly apart with toes slightly extended. Make sure that the feet are not together or widely spread, but on the same vertical line with your shoulders. Establish a comfortable breathing rhythm.

2. From the centered (vertically aligned) position, slowly tilt the body forward to the point where the angled position cannot be held without moving one of the feet forward - this is a border position (during the exercise make sure that the waist is not bent). Also make sure

---

[316] Rodney A. Rhoades and George A. Tanner, *Medical Physiology*, 2nd ed. (Philadelphia, Lippincott Williams & Wilkins, 2003), 97.

that the soles of the feet still have full connection with the floor (from toes to heels). Hold for a few seconds to notice this point. Note that some parts of the body will develop a certain degree of muscular tension. This is the forward bordered position. Move back to the vertically aligned position.

Repeat 6 times

3. From a centered (vertically aligned) position, slowly tilt the body back nearly to the point where the feet cannot balance the body's angled position. Hold for a few seconds to notice this point. This is the back bordered position. Move back to the vertically aligned position.

Repeat 6 times

Exercise # 2

Repeat Exercise 1 for the left and right sides. Come back to the centered position each time. Note the left and right sides' bordered positions (again making sure that during the exercise the waist is not bent).

Repeat 3 times for each side

Exercise # 3

>Slowly swing the body between all four bordered positions (forward to back and left to right) at a slow pace. Locate and preserve the body's most comfortably situated, physically balanced, and centered position. Reestablish a comfortable rhythm of breathing at the end of each exercise.

Note the development of muscular tension on all four border positions. The motions which are responsible for the development of excessive tension should be avoided during conducting. Also note that, while at a border position, there is a certain discomfort in breathing.

>*Occasionally, during conducting, one of the feet can be moved forward. If, at some stage of the performance, the conductor refers mainly to the left side, the right foot should move forward and the left foot to the opposite side. Exchanging the feet is performed unnoticeably.*[317]

---

[317] Musin, 16.

Exercise # 4

1. From the centered position, slowly turn the torso and head to the left until a border position is reached. Make sure that the feet stay in the same position. After 5 seconds, turn back to the centered position. Reestablish comfortable breathing rhythm.

Repeat 5-6 times

2. From the centered position, slowly turn the torso and head to the right side until a border position is reached. Make sure that the feet stay in the same position. After 5 seconds, turn back to the centered position. Reestablish comfortable breathing rhythm.

Repeat 5-6 times

Exercise # 5

From the centered position, slowly move the shoulders forward, then up, back, and down to the starting point (a full circled motion). Breathe freely at a slow but stable speed. Make sure that the motion of the shoulders does not affect the 'centered' position of the body.

Repeat 5-6 times

During the exercise, note the position that supports the most comfortable breathing.

Do not stoop. From the centered position, move the shoulders a bit up and slightly back - this will naturally move (open) your chest more forward and increase expressive manifestation of body posture.

The head's position is an important part of the body's basic posture. Look straight ahead - the face must be clearly seen by the orchestra's members. **An unbroken (virtual) vertical line should 'connect' the top of your head to the bottom of your soles.**

This is the primary body posture.

Notice that the most comfortable body position (appropriately relaxed, balanced and with comfortable breathing) is usually perceived as the most natural and/or expressive as well.

At the end of each practice session, take a moment to recognize the body's balanced and aligned position. Make sure next time to start the exercise from the balanced primary body posture. At first, repeated reference to the edged (bordered) positions is a good practical tool to check the balance and correctness of the primary body posture.

> *It is commonly known that a person's outward appearance and posture mirrors his/her mental abilities, emotional state and temperament.* **The conductor's outward appearance must represent the possession of will, activity, determination and energy.**[318]

Appropriate facial expressiveness is of the utmost importance during conducting. No expressive motion is complete without the support of appropriate facial expression. While conducting, prevent any facial expressions indicating displeasure, bewilderment, confusion, etc. Usually improper facial expressions, in general, are a visual sign of the innate shortcomings of the conducting apparatus (i.e., the presence of excessive physical tension and/or improperly organized inner [mental] techniques). On the other hand, natural facial expressiveness is the result of a conductor's effective inner inspiration, profound penetration into the context of the music and its concepts, and their appropriate projection.

---

[318] Musin, 15. (Emphasis added)

PRIMARY ARM POSITION

As was mentioned in the introduction of this book, today there are various views on the conducting methodology. Some approaches suggest that, in the beginning, emphasis on conducting techniques is not so important, as development of these techniques will soon be learned through the act of conducting. According to such methodologies, the study must start with immediate performance of symphonic pieces. But this method must be avoided as unfruitful.

> *The arms' primary positions during conducting have the significant importance of the acquisition of the typical conductor's motions. The freedom, naturalness and character of the motions mainly depend on them [primary positions].*[319]

An appropriate concept of the arms' role and their function 'within' a conductor's apparatus is crucially important from the very beginning: "Hand movements have a critical developmental root. ... Wolff (1952) considered the hands the fundamental vehicle for the study of the structure of thought."[320]

---

[319] Musin, 16.

[320] *Hands, Words, and Mind*, 112.

In the beginning an ample amount of learning should be dedicated to the development of technical skills. It has to be taken into account that some beginners may already have a certain acquaintance with conducting, usually in the form of the schematic techniques of elemental measuring; acquired independently, such techniques, as a rule, are imperfect and consequently cannot be a foundation for continuous technical development. Insufficiently mastered motions not only prohibit the improvement of the conducting technique but also limit the possibility of getting rid of the present [technical] shortcomings. More often, such attempts are manifested as a pattern of chaotic and uncoordinated motions in the form of inexpressive, constrained and seizure-like gestures that make conducting graphically unreadable.

But, on the contrary, continuous study without musical excerpts should be avoided too; since the gestures are not conjoined with certain artistic tasks of performance, such movements become senseless and could resemble abstract gymnastics. The first exercises for establishing arm position, body posture and the learning of basic movements and modes of measuring would be better studied through special exercises without musical excerpts.[321]

---

[321] Musin, 14.

DOWNBEAT POSITION

A suitable primary arm position is an impo<u>rt</u>ant part of the conductor's apparatus and an important factor of natural balance, physical freedom, and the customary essence of the gestures.

> *The arms' position must be **intermediate**,*[322] *which will grant an opportunity to perform motions to any side - up, down, toward and outward from the body.*[323]

Exercise # 1

1. Body in the Primary Posture - a relatively relaxed position of the body with an outward active manifestation of the head, shoulders, chest and overall posture. Position both arms along the body without excessive tension. Note the natural space between the body and arm (natural position). Lift the right arm straight forward: keep the arm parallel to the ground. Note the limit of this border position. Then move the

---

[322] Arms should be in a neutral position equidistant from any bordered positions.

[323] Musin, 16.

arm all the way back with a bent elbow (with the palm facing the ground, forearm in a horizontal position). Note the bordered position at this edge. Resume the starting position.

Repeat 5-6 times.

2. Position both arms naturally along the body. Lift the right wrist and forearm up to a horizontal position (the forearm and shoulder should form a 90 degree angle), then move the arm slowly forward. Stop halfway before reaching the border position and align all parts of the arm - the wrist, elbow and shoulder should be on the same line. Note the need for a slight adjustment (twist) of the elbow to the left. The palm should be facing the ground, with the forearm in a horizontally lined position. Slightly bend the fingers and keep the thumb at the meeting of the first and second joints of the index finger (while adjusting the fingers, make sure that the forearm is horizontal).

This is the arm's **Primary Position** (or **Downbeat** position). Depending on the scheme of conducting being used, the downbeat position may be slightly adjusted either to the left for 3/4 or right for 4/4 metrical schemes.

Repeat 8-10 times

Practice this exercise for both arms.

It is important to preserve a linear manifestation of the arm from the wrist to the shoulder, though there is a methodology suggesting a downbeat placed at the provisional "center" of the abdomen. **Avoid** the downbeat position with the arm completely or partially **overlapping the chest or abdomen**. The use of a conductor's arm should not be compromised by the perpetual performance of a sudden shattering of the arm's linear contour. This contour is breaking by the segmented manifestation of the arm - the elbow, wrist and shoulder appear as separate units and consequently provide contradictory or conflicting messages.

Exercise # 2

Test for the downbeat position.

> From the downbeat position, slowly move the arm from right to left: in the process, at a certain point one will feel a natural limit on motion. At this point, move back to the right, to a point about 45 degrees between the arm and body. The arm's motion should be similar to a ∪ line. This motion is natural to the arm's physiological

structure and has an interactive reference with the vicinity (contour) of sound. Find the most comfortable (maximally non-tense) position. The wrist, elbow, and shoulder should be lined up, with the forearm in a horizontal position.

Repeat 8-10 times

At the end of each exercise, test the arm for release of excessive muscular tension. Such an examination is valuable for tension release and a reassessment of active muscular relaxation:

> Lift both arms over the head and inhale deeply at the same time. Shake both wrists for 2-3 seconds, and then drop the arms down with a simultaneous quick exhalation. At the bottom, shake both hands (like throwing water drops).

This and other active relaxation exercises are discussed later in the subchapter: *Active Muscular Relaxation.*

At the end of each practice session, take a moment to recognize the arm's primary position. Make sure each time to start the exercise from the proper (primary) position. At first, the repeated reference to the edged (bordered) position is always a good practical tool with which to check the balance and correctness of the arm's primary downbeat position.

THE PLANE OF CONDUCTING

The virtual plane (or flat surface) of conducting is an imaginary horizontal line to which the beats (impulses)[324] of a conducting scheme are applied. This plane is usually matched with the lowest (bottom) edge of the vicinity and contour of sound. Though the line of flatness of conducting is conditional, it is important in the beginning of training to establish a sense of a linear application of beats (impulses).

Exercise # 1

> Place the right arm in the downbeat position (the forearm is linear and horizontal). Lift the wrist up to the bordered position and then perform a quick spring-like striking

---

[324] As was discussed previously, the term "beat" in our time is a tribute to a traditional terminology, which does not reflect all the features of the intercommunicative aspects of the utilization of conducting metrical schemes. For methodological purposes I will use the term "impulse" as well.

motion. Make sure that the wrist comes back to the upper bordered position as quickly as possible.

Exercise # 2

Similar to Exercise # 1: combine the wrist and forearm motions.

Exercise # 3

Similar to Exercises #s 1 and 2 for the entire arm.

In both exercises # 2 and # 3, the wrist must conclude the downward motion after a slight delay before the strike follows with a quick rebound. At first, for practical purpose, these exercises could be performed on an appropriately adjusted music stand or a table of suitable height.

Exercise # 4

1. Use an arm motion similar to that of exercise # 2 in the

previous chapter - from the downbeat position, slowly move the arm from right to left. In the process, at a certain point you will experience a natural limit of motion. At this point, move back to the right, to a point about 45 degrees between the arm and body. The arm's motion should be similar to a line with ∪ shape.

2. Starting from the left to the right, apply quick and spring-like wrist motions to the imaginary plane. For practical convenience, apply four times on the way to each side (left and then right). Make sure that during practice, spring-like quick applications of the wrist do not interrupt the arm's overall motion.

Exercise # 5

Similar to Exercise # 4: combine the wrist quick spring-like motion and forearm motions.

Exercise # 6

Similar to Exercises #s 4 and 5: at this time practice with the entire arm.

The use of the metronome will help. Start the practice with a slow (50-60 BPM) rhythm. At the end of each exercise, test the arm for release of excessive muscular tension.

MODIFICATION OF THE WRIST STRIKE

These exercises are more advanced. It is suggested that practice of the following exercises begin after the previous exercises have been achieved comfortably.

In the previous exercises, the wrist strike was directed downward. Such an approach is useful to achieve a rudimentary sense of the plane of conducting, but has a limited practical application since the downward spring component has an unproductive sticking due to the breaking (quick stop and re-start) momentum at the bottom. The wrist's spring-like motion itself could be very useful. However, in utilizing this motion in an interactive mode, the wrist's final strike (impulse) **should be converted from a downward direction to an upward one.**

Exercise # 1

The arm should be in the downbeat position, with the wrist slightly turned inward (the outer edge of the palm should be pointed downward: the index finger should be on top and pinkie on the bottom). Start the motion (wrist only) from the plane of conducting to the upward edge (wrist upper physical limit), then down, falling slightly beneath the line of flatness of conducting. Round out the motion at the top and bottom points. Notice that the wrist's muscles may experience a slight uncontrolled tremor (especially on the way down when muscles are expected to relax). After further practice, the aforementioned tremor will lessen in severity and eventually brought under control.

Exercise # 2

This exercise is similar to Exercise # 1. However, on the way down, relax the wrist's muscles and at the lowest (turning) point make a quick scooping type of motion on the way up. During this motion, on the way up, due to the wrist's small twist inward the pinkie and ring fingers will move slightly upward. In early attempts, practice this exercise slowly in order to control the exchange between complete wrist relaxation (in the downward motion) and the quick scooping. To get a sense of scooping, focus on the tips of the three fingers – pinkie, ring and middle.

Exercise # 3

Similar to Exercise # 2: combine the wrist and forearm motions.

Exercise # 4

Similar to Exercises numbers 2 and 3: for the motion with entire arm.

It is important that for exercises numbers 2 and 3 the wrist concludes the upward strike motion after a slight delay before scooping. Make sure that during all exercises a linear manifestation of the arm is preserved. For better results, at the beginning of practice use a metronome at slow tempos. Match the metronome's beat with the moment of scooping. At the end of each exercise, test the arm for release of excessive muscular tension.

9

THE PREPARATORY MOTION-IMPULSE

The unity of an ensemble, and the precision and embodiment of a conductor's artistic intentions depend entirely upon the significance, precision and definition of his/her preparatory motions. The upbeat is a complex movement which prepares and organizes players for an action. It is a specific action which, for a particular moment, precedes the occurrence of sound.

The upbeat is not just a gesture similar to a traffic-controller's signal, but rather it is a complex combination of mental and physical processes which precede the starting moment of the beat at the beginning of the piece and then each beat within the measure (the inner (intermediary) upbeat).

It is commonly known that any action mutually performed by a number of individuals can be started precisely together only by either an audible signal (a word, a knock, singing, etc.) or by the **innate power of a motion** (by the visualized force of the inner impulse). However, no single abrupt isolated sound or motion will serve as a sufficient sign if it is performed inappropriately. Any signal which pretends to be associated with its intention must consciously incorporate all the personalities involved and develop a similar rhythmic action from them (conceptual unity). It is important to mention again that a mechanistic performance of an upbeat without the support of an appropriate inner action has limited practical value.

The following three chapters will discuss the diversity of upbeats and suggest some practical exercises. Due to the specifics of terminology customarily used in conducting methodology and the format of this book, all suggested material is an effort to describe the communicative phenomenon of the upbeat in the traditional language of conducting methodology.

THE PREPARATORY UPBEAT-IMPULSE

The preparatory upbeat is an action which precedes the launch of the very first sound, the temporal performance of which is equal to the upcoming beat value. The suitable performance of the preparatory-impulse is eminently important. The meaningful psychological and emotional fulfillment of the preparatory-impulse not only launches a certain section or movement with proper tempi and character but also justifies the realization of the piece or even the entire performance.

In his book, *Technique of Conducting*, Ilia Musin provides an extensive description of the anticipatory, multifunctional, and interactive nature of the preparatory upbeat:

a) definition of the initial moment of the performance (preparation for mutual activity, breathing) and the beginning of every beat in the measure;

b) definition of tempo;

c) definition of beat's rhythm [metrical value] *as doubled or tripled;**

d) definition of dynamic;

e) *definition of the character of the attack of the sound (the degree of its acuteness and length);*

f) *definition of the imaginary content of the music.*[325]

* Those important differences are often ignored. The principal intercommunicative dissimilarity between the performance of doubled and triplet upbeats will be discussed in the following subchapter.

For the execution of a preparatory upbeat of an incomplete measure, the arm, as a rule, should be in the position of the preceding beat (in accordance with the upcoming metrical scheme). For the execution of the downbeat, the arm should be placed slightly off to the right and a bit higher than the preceding downbeat on the plane of conducting. The degree of such remoteness (from the forthcoming downbeat location) is conditioned by dynamics and tempo.

To meet all of the above characteristics of the preparatory-impulse, the performance of the upbeat-impulse should be supported by the conductor's appropriate psychological condition. It is important to mention that, from a practical point, the **suitable performance of the preparatory upbeat-impulse**

---

[325] Musin, 55. Musin has suggested, though, that these enumerated functions of the upbeat could vary for the performance of the preparatory and intermediary upbeats (see the subchapter: *Beat Connection* [*Intermediary Upbeat*]).

will be justified by the following beat. After the performance of the upbeat, the conductor **should not wait** for the entrance of orchestral sound but rather clasp it on the way to the next metrical point. Among other features, the complexity of informative meanings of the preparatory-impulse reveals the communicative (linguistic) nature of conducting.

DOUBLE- AND TRIPLE-METER PREPARATORY MOTIONS/UPBEATS

The preparatory upbeat is sub-divided into two types - doubled and tripled (or for double and triple meters).

It is important to emphasize the principal intercommunicative dissimilarity between the performance of doubled and tripled upbeats and, consequently, their practical results (due to their dissimilar perception).

A typical shortcoming (not only for the novice but for experienced conductors as well) is that during the alteration from doubled meter to tripled meter and backward, the conductor does not assist performers but rather confuses them instead. To adapt the gesture to a doubled rhythm in the moment of switching to a tripled meter, he/she does not adjust the gesture, and, as a result, disorganizes the performance. The problems increase if changes of rhythm continue one after another and combine with the change of tempo.[326]

It is also necessary to mention that the predominantly dynamic (enforced) practical method mainly ignores this difference, performing both in similar fashion.

DOUBLE-METER MOTION

The preparatory doubled upbeat includes three elements: **lifting** - up, or up and slightly to the right side; **falling** (or gradually enforced descending according to the tempo) - down (or down and then outward), with or without the application of a strike (impulse) at the end; and a monitored **rebound** – to control the arm's natural reflex on the falling motion. The starting point of the preparatory double beat (the moment which precedes lifting) **should be located slightly below and to the right side of the plane of conducting**, next to the downbeat. For the beginning of the beat, the lifting and falling components are connected to each other with an appropriate curvature-

---

[326] Musin, 131.

round-off (which provide the motions' gradual transition into each other at the upper and the lower points). Their proper execution is crucial for the controlled occurrence of sound. The performance of the rebound affects the appearance of sound.[327]

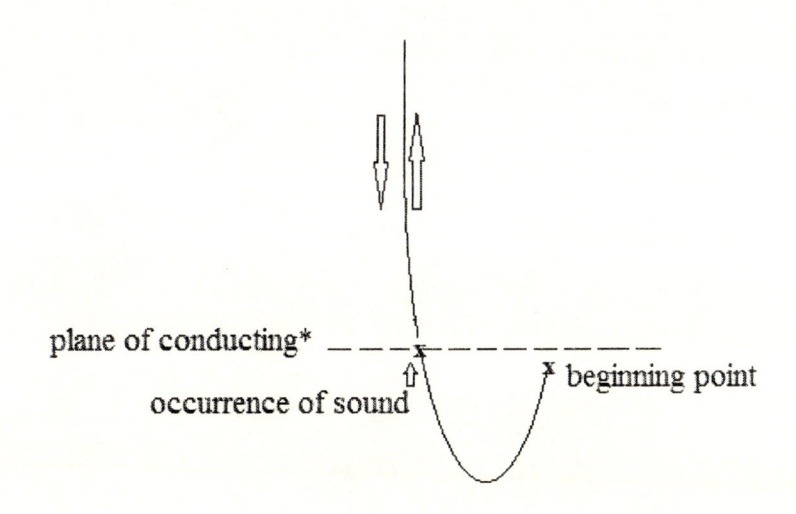

plane of conducting*

occurrence of sound

beginning point

*Here and later this line depicts the provisional plane of conducting.

However, such a depiction of the doubled upbeat is schematic and conditional - increased inner rhythmical diversity (e.g., dotted rhythms) complicates the immediate control of the

---

[327] The important role of the rebound is explained later in the subchapter, *Rebound*.

doubled upbeat. Also, the application of the downbeat within a double beat scheme could vary in dimensions – from the upper left down to the bottom right, from the upper right to the bottom left (graphics A and B), inward from the left side directed outward to the right, or the performance of a doubled upbeat with both hands (a pendulum resembling motion), etc.

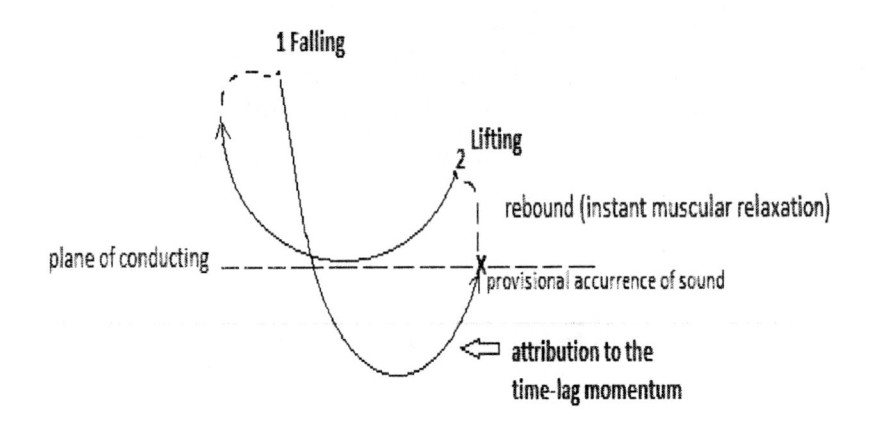

A.

B.

rebound (instant relaxation)
occurrence of sound

⇔time-lag

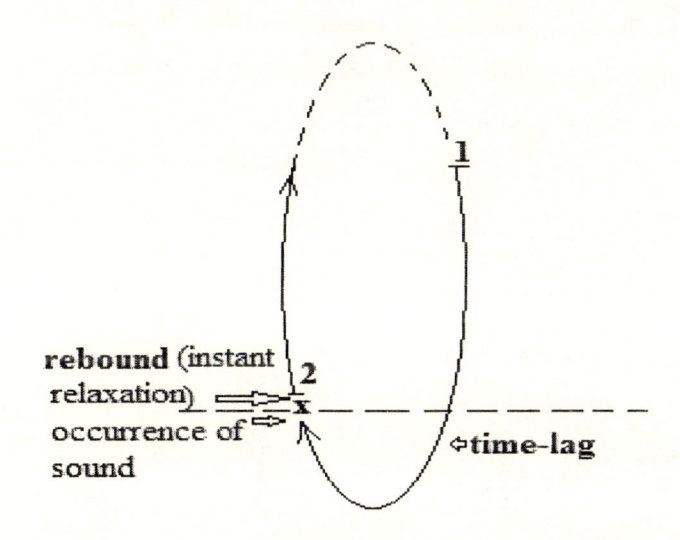

ONE-PATTERN TRIPLE-METER MOTION

    The preparatory upbeat for a single tripled metrical figure "**should be based on the principle of rounded motion**,"[328] since, as the rounded motion (in contrast with the commonly used reinforced vertical down-up gesture), it can be

---

[328] Musin, 58. (Emphasis added)

divided in three parts. Such a simple fact is frequently ignored by the predominant conducting methods.[329] An improperly designed tripled upbeat is among the main causes of professional shortcomings in practical conducting - simply in the manner of the doubled upbeat but with the hold of the 2nd and 3rd beats on the top and repeated reinforced performance of the 1st beat; see graphic A below.[330]

A.

```
          2, 3
           ↑
           |
           |
           |
           ↓
 — — — — — — — — — —
           1
```

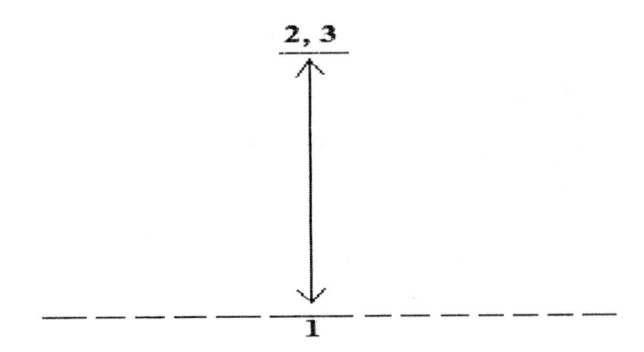

[329] The generally accepted methodological approach does not suggest the difference between the motions applied for duple and triple meters. The rhythmical figure with a triple meter is simply performed in the same manner as duple: a fast reinforced downward-upward motion (or wrist "click") for one, and then a suspension for the second and third beats on the upper edge of the rebound (e.g., Kahn, *Elements of Conducting,* 13; Hunsberger and Ernst, *The Art of Conducting*, 35; Kohut and Grant, *Learning to Conduct and Rehearse*, 26-7).

[330] This common use of doubled motion for the utilization of the one pattern tripled-meter upbeat is another example of the conditional and artificial design of certain motions in generally accepted traditional methods. So far, the best argument I have heard from colleagues who use such a technique has been: "That is the only way it could be done," or "Everyone is doing that." It is especially ironic if it is stated by a group of three, four or more colleagues.

The main characteristic of a tripled upbeat is a curvature (round-off), a smooth and continuous transition of the motion between the *lifting* and *falling* parts of the upbeat and a proper 'distribution' of counts within the motion (graphics B and C). The graphic depicts this singular motion. Depending on musical (textural) content, the motion's direction could vary: from **right to left**, performed **diagonally** with the 1st beat at the left 'corner', directed almost perpendicularly from **inward to outward** and from **outward to inward**. At all instances, the rounded contour of the motion is performed similarly and the first beat is always slightly under the plane of conducting. The common shortcoming in the performance of a single tripled motion from left to right (with the first beat at the right 'corner') is unproductive due to several deficiencies:

1. The manifestation of a 3/4 scheme is converted inside-out

2. Linear preservation of the arm is problematic because the elbow will naturally bend at beat three and that will weaken the manifestation of the arm.

B.

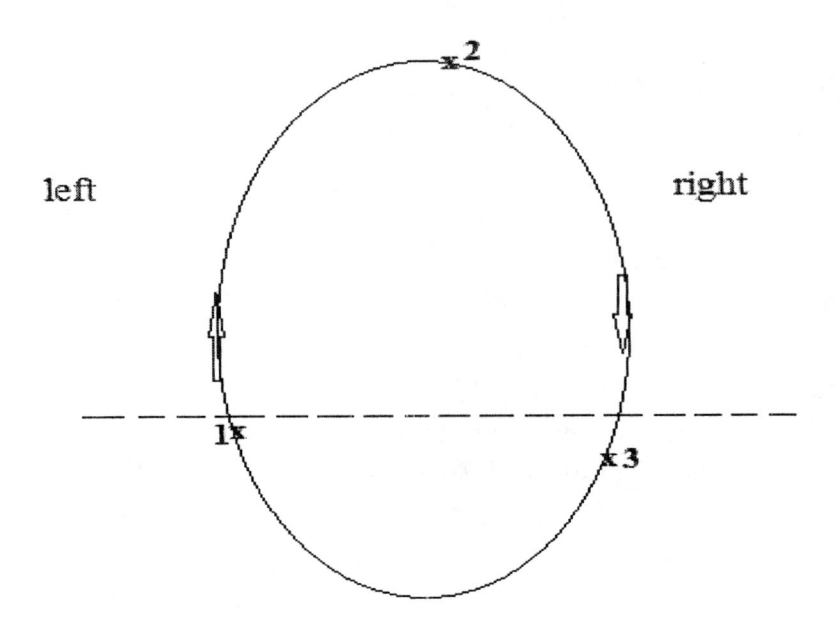

left right

C.

outward inward

246

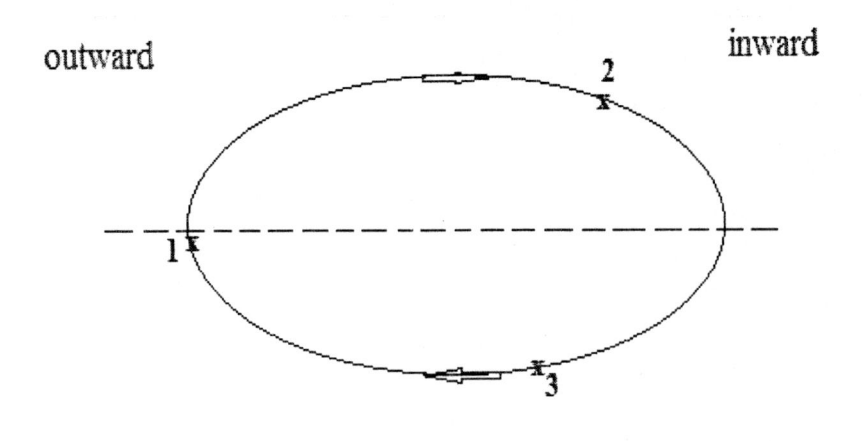

The following exercise assists in obtaining the principle, as well as the sensation (in performance) of the tripled upbeat.

Exercise

> Start the motion from the arm's downbeat position and slightly to the right side - from the traditional place of the third beat. On count three, perform a rounded motion to the left side, up and down. **All three counts have to be equally divided throughout the motion with the location of the first beat slightly above the plane of conducting.** Start each beat (at 1) with a slight 'push' upward (outward or inward) at the bottom - the beginning of the tripled upbeat is a rounded-off motion with the intention of a pick up on the way back to the first beat. Initially, practice at a slow tempo.

Practice until a complete smoothness of the motion is accomplished (without uncontrolled muscular trembling or jerking). Use a metronome at first with one slow beat and then three faster beats per motion.

As with the doubled upbeat, the increased number of sounds (multi-layered musical texture) and inner rhythmical diversity (e.g., dotted and syncopated rhythms) complicate the control of the tripled upbeat.

> *The beat with three sounds is the simplest example of the tripled upbeat - waltzes, scherzos. The beats containing six notes are more complicated for conducting (Schubert: Seventh Symphony, Scherzo). And finally, the triple metrical beat with a syncopated rhythm needs the most attention (Glinka: "Knyaz' Kholmsky", Overture; Brahms: 3rd Symphony, movement I).*[331]

Notice that the performance of the single tripled upbeat is executed only in a mode of rounded motion, as well as that of the doubled upbeat; thus the conceptual 'reason' for roundness in both instances may be diverse. The intercommunicative effect of a rounded motion and its reference to the phenomenon of the vicinity (contour) of sound will be discussed later in the subchapter: *Fusing of the Upbeat and the Contour of Sound*.

Suggested musical material:

1. Tchaikovsky, Serenade for Strings. I movement - from A to H. II movement – beginning

2. Rimsky-Korsakov - Scheherazade, 3rd movement - beginning

---
[331] Musin, 59.

Later, after a certain practical comfort in performance of the tripled motion is achieved, the more complex inner[332] (within the tripled single motion) subdivision may be applied. For example: the application of a rounded motion will facilitate performance of the Allegro section of Ludwig van Beethoven's "Egmont" Overture in one pattern (instead of overelaborated in three), with employment of the wrist' sub-division (within the motion) for accents on the inner beats - **three**-one, one-**two**-three-**one**, etc.

COMBINATION OF DOUBLE- AND TRIPLE-METER MOTIONS

As was mentioned in the previous chapter, conductors often, during the change from doubled meter to tripled meter (and back) with a similar technical approach in performance of upbeats (as a perpetual undifferentiated manifestation of the doubled [with the hold for 2 and 3 on the 'top' of the beat for 3/4]), do not assist the performers but, rather, confuse them. To adapt the gesture to doubled rhythm "in the moment of switching to tripled meter a conductor is not adjusting that

---

[332] Such an inner subdivision, though, will not obliterate the one-pattern triple-meter motion contour.

gesture and therefore disorganizes the performance."[333] The problems are increased if changes of rhythm continue one after another and are combined with a change of tempo.

The perception of the triple-meter is more complex than double-meter and therefore requires the musicians' distinctive mental effort. So often during the transition from the double-meter to the triple-meter due to the improper performance of the tripled motion/upbeat (graphic A in the previous chapter), the rhythmical performance of one-pattern triple-meter motions is incorrect (e.g., first two counts [eighths] are performed faster, almost as sixteenths).

The use of a combination of rapid exchanges from doubled and tripled-meter motions is common in the music of the twentieth century (e.g., in scores of Igor Stravinsky ["Petrushka"] and Aaron Copland ["Appalachian Spring").

---

[333] Musin, 131-2.

Stravinsky: *Petrushka*

Courtesy of Dover Publications

Copland: *Appalachian Spring*

Courtesy of Boosey and Hawks

In these examples, the performance of one pattern doubled and tripled-meter motions must be modified. Principally, the difference between 2/4 and 3/4 (or similar meters) is that during performance of 2/4 (before switching to 3/4) the arm (or wrist) suddenly slows down (inhibits) just above the provisional plane of conducting (instead of the performance of full rebound for 2/4), and a small rebound is used as a short intermediary upbeat before the beginning of 3/4. Another important detail concerns the first beat of 3/4 performed under the plane of conducting as a pick-up or scoop. Before switching to 2/4 the arm considerably inhibits itself at the same point of the second beat for the third beat and then continues downward.

BEAT CONNECTION
(INTERMEDIARY UPBEAT)

The important difference between the preparatory and the inner/intermediary upbeats (upbeats [motion-impulses] between the points of metrical schemes) is that the inner upbeat not only affects the preceding beat (in accordance with the methodological principles of anticipation that all artistic messages in conducting **happen before the beat**) but also influences presently sounding music. As a result, with the effective use of the intermediary upbeat, a conductor could

create a future (upcoming) sound and at the same time continuously manage the present sound as well.

Additionally, as was discussed previously in Chapter 7 (*Modification of the Beat* and *Emancipation of Metrical Scheme*), the interactive modification of the traditional forceful strike assists in overcoming the original stiffness of the metrical schemes and creates a meaningful connection between metrical points. It is important to mention, though, that despite the external (visual) resemblance of the following beat-connecting exercises to the traditional performance of "legato motions," their characteristic differences are principally: as soon as "legato motions" formally contrast the "staccato strikes" with curvatures instead of interrupted points, the further mastering of the beat-connecting motions will not be useful without their reference to the contour of sound (the technique of taking and transferring sound).

Well-developed management of the different parts of the arm and their combinations (wrist, wrist/forearm, and/or whole arm) is paramount to the effective performance of the beats' connection within the metrical scheme.

During conducting, the arm works as a harmonious and well-coordinated apparatus in which all elements interact with one another. Any motion of one or another part of the arm cannot proceed without the participation of the other parts. The most isolated (as it would seem) wrist motion is always supported by the forearm and shoulder. Therefore, seemingly isolated

> *motions of the wrist or forearm are merely dominating throughout the motion. Each part of the arm has its own expressive potentials and specific functions.*[334]

The following suggested exercises assist in establishing control over the wrist, which is the most flexible and agile part of the arm. To establish a well-developed flexibility of the wrist is crucial for the effective performance of the inner upbeat as well as an effective connection of beats.

> *The wrist is a transformer of various impulses, gentle motion senses, which allows the decoding of a conductor's musical intentions into expressive gesture.*[335]

Exercise # 1

> The arm should be in the downbeat position with slightly straightened fingers. Slowly move the wrist with a rounded motion - to the left, up, and then down and then to the right, up, and down. Make sure that the wrist motion does not affect the rest of the arm (the fore-arm and shoulder should not move). The wrist should not cross (go beneath) the provisional plane of conducting (see graphic below).

---

[334] Musin, 17.

[335] Ibid.

left   right

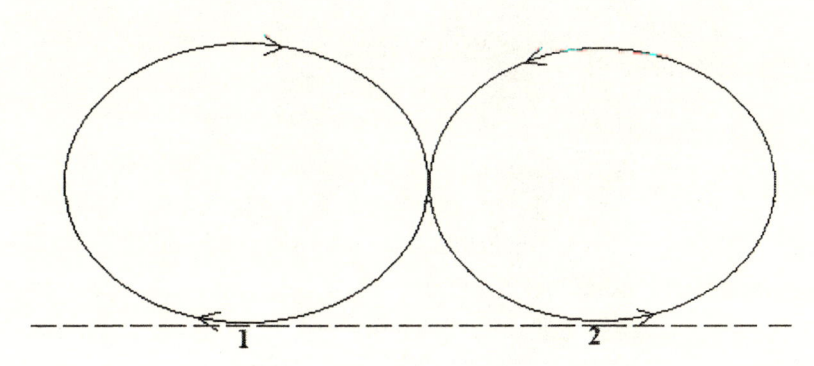

Exercise # 2

Move the forearm and wrist in the combined rounded motion. Make sure that the end the fingers 'lead' the motion.

Repeat 10 times

Exercise # 3

Use the shoulder, forearm, and wrist in the combined rounded motion. Make sure that the ends of the fingers are still leading the motion. During exercise **keep the arm aligned** (make sure that the elbow is not bent excessively and 'sticking out' to the right side).

Repeat 10 times

Initially, all three exercises should be practiced slowly. It is important to achieve appropriate management over uncontrolled muscular tremors for all three types of motions (wrist, wrist/forearm, and arm). A significant amount of practices may be necessary before the wrist's involuntary jerking or the arm's muscular trembling is eliminated.

Exercise # 4

This exercise is similar to Exercise # 1. However, it is a bit more complex. Slowly move the wrist with a rounded motion as in the previous exercise, but with deeper emphasis on the left side - at the place of 1. At this time the wrist should go beneath the provisional line of conducting for beat 1 only - with the wrist's deeper scooping on the way down.

left   right

1

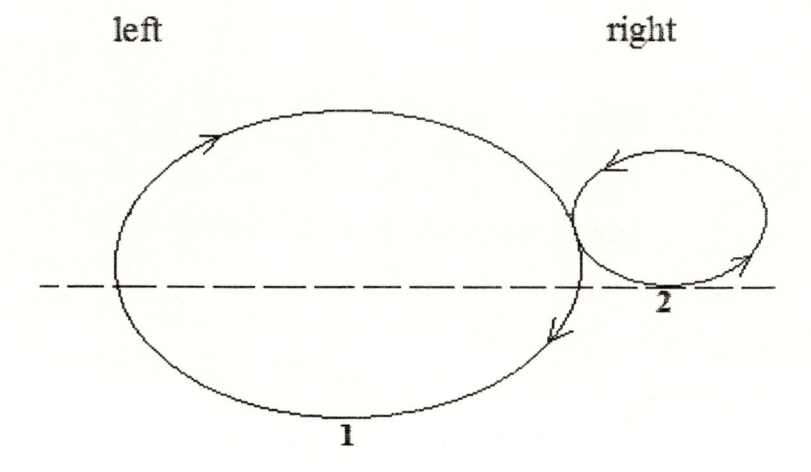

At the beginning of practice, get a sense of the 1st beat's scooping by the tips (distal phalanges) of pinkie, ring and middle fingers (by the *palmar* [inner] side) - similar to Exercise # 2 in *Modification of the Wrist Strike*).

Repeat 10 times

Exercise # 5

Similar to Exercise # 4: combine the wrist and forearm motions.

Repeat 10 times

Exercise # 6

    A. Similar to Exercises #s 4 and 5 for the entire arm. Make sure that the ends of the fingers are still leading the motion. **Keep the arm aligned.**

Repeat 10 times

    B. Similar to Exercises #s 1, 2 and 3. At first, all three of the last exercises should be practiced slowly to achieve appropriate muscular control for all the various types of motions (wrist, wrist/forearm, and arm).

Exercise # 7

    This is similar to all previous exercises. However at this time the wrist's rounded motion will expand to the right side first and then to left - the motion must fill the provisional space between the 2nd and 3rd beats (e.g., within ¾ and 4/4 metrical schemes) with more emphasis (deeper scooping) on the left side (at the place of the 2nd beat). Also, at this time (in contrast with Exercise # 4), scooping is made by the dorsal (outer) side of the pinkie and ring and fingers (by their distal phalanges). Make sure that the ends of the fingers are still leading the motion.

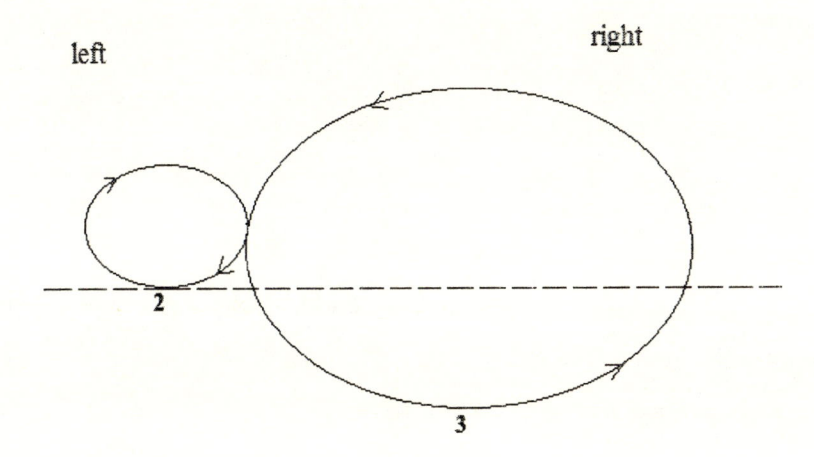

left   right

2

3

Repeat 10 times

Exercise # 8

This is similar to # 1. However, combine the forearm and the wrist in the rounded motion. Move with rounded motion through the plane (flatness) of conducting.

Repeat 10 times

Exercise # 9

Use a similar technique with the entire arm (a similar motion to the previous exercises).

Repeat 10 times

During these exercises, make sure that the ends of the fingers lead the motion, and that the arm is kept aligned throughout the motion.

Later, appropriate practice should convert the formal 'scooping' gesture into an advanced 'conceptual' motion which is combined with the sense of the contour of sound ('taking' motion) - see Chapter: *The Upbeat as a Conceptual Action. Establishing a Sense of the Vicinity (Contour) of Sound.* Also, the rounded motion for the connection of beats (inner upbeat) can diverge from a more elliptic-like motion (for an even [doubled] rhythm) to a motion which is more expansive in width (for an uneven [tripled] rhythm). At the beginning the practical implication of the inner upbeat is more useful for simple meters - 2/4, 3/4 and 4/4 and then later to the more complex meters - 3/2, 6/4, 6/8, 12/8, etc.

The technique of the beats' connection (inner upbeat) is

particularly useful for the indication of the instruments' entrances when the conductor's upbeat breathes along with the musicians. For example: L. Beethoven, "Egmont" Overture, Introduction (3/2 section before Allegro), Brahms, Symphony No 1, movement IV, Introduction (Adagio).

BEATS' CONNECTION THROUGHOUT METRICAL SCHEMES IN VARIOUS DIMENTIONS

The following exercises assist in obtaining multi-dimensional performance of the intermediate upbeats and their intercommunicative convergence from primarily quasi vertical applications. These techniques are useful in creating a meaningful connection between metrical points (beats) in correlation with the structure of musical phrases. The multi-dimensional connection of the beats helps to overcome the original 'stiffness' of the metrical schemes, but without simultaneous disruption of the schemes 'conventional' contour.

Exercise # 1

Start from the primary (downbeat) position with the arm aligned (similar to Exercise # 1 in *Modification of the Wrist Strike*). Slowly move the arm straight forward and then slightly up (similar to the 'push-forward' gesture). Make the contour of the gesture a rounded ellipse. Notice that on the way back to the downbeat position the elbow, while being naturally bent, may extend further to the right side. **Maintain the arm's linearity throughout the motion.** Move the arm horizontally (with slight curvatures at both sides) upon the plane of the provisional flatness of conducting (do not go beneath the conditional line of plane of conducting).

Repeat 10 times

Exercise # 2

This is similar to the previous exercise. However, instead of a 'pushing-forward' gesture, perform it in the opposite direction: from the outward position, slightly up with a curvature at the lower point, and then inward, etc.

Exercise # 3

Slightly push each beat to the left and then right sides with a rounded forwarded motion through the provisional plane (flatness) of conducting. After each round, come back inward to the beginning point of each beat. The motion should fill the space between the first and second beats in a ¾ metrical scheme (or the second and third in 4/4). The contour of the motion should resemble a bent inward figure ∞ (see graphic).

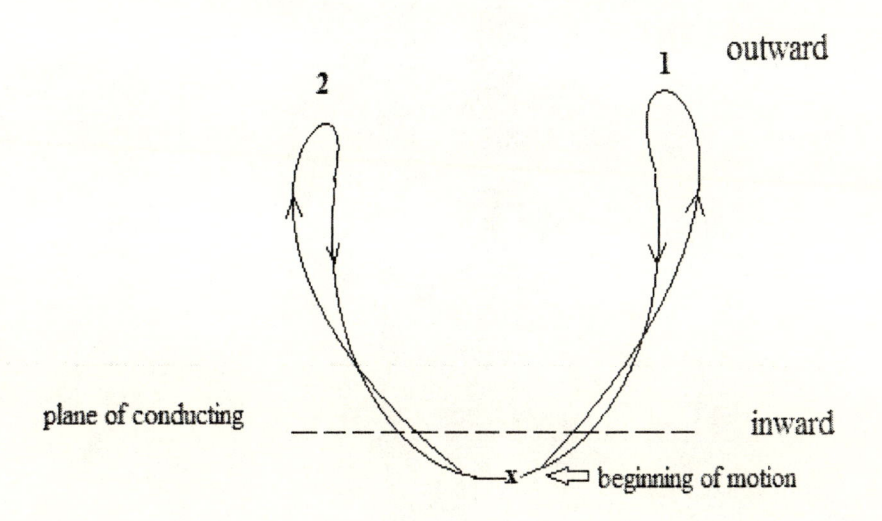

Repeat 10 times

Exercise # 4

This is similar to # 3, but the contour of the motion resembles a bent 'outward' figure ∞. After each round, come back out to the beginning point of each beat (see graphic).

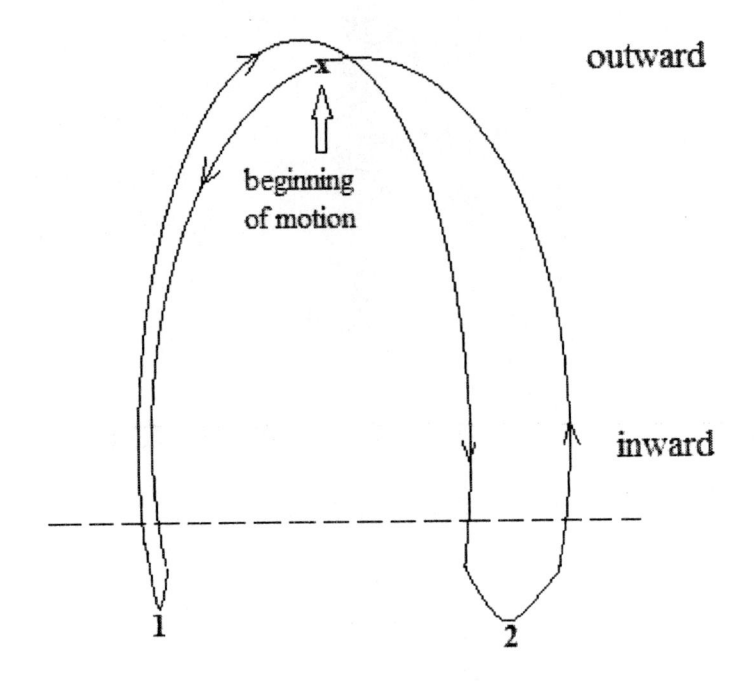

Again, it is important at first to practice all described exercises at a slow speed to gain control over the motions. For better results, use a metronome (one beat for a complete round of motion). At first, use slow tempos between 45 and 60 beats per minute. After an appropriate performance of the exercises of beat-connection is reached the more advanced exercises can be practiced as well: i.e., along with performance of the *beat connecting* motion 'take' ('grab') and transfer the sound from beat to beat by the different parts of the arm: by the fingers (pinkie, ring, and middle), by the upper (outer) part of the wrist (at the connection of the thumb and the index finger), by the outer part of the fore-arm, and eventually the entire arm. The technique of sound 'taking' will be discussed in the following subchapter: *The Upbeat as a Conceptual Action.*

For better results, after every exercise in this subchapter, use the active relaxation exercise from the subchapter: *Active Muscular Relaxation.*

Exercise # 5

>Practice the *beats connecting* motion of all types (the 'plain' figure ∞ (as in the previous chapter) as well as bended inward and outward) throughout the different metrical schemes - 2/4, 3/4 and 4/4. Start with wrist motions only.

Repeat 6-8 times for each scheme

Exercise # 6

A similar exercise for combined fore-arm and wrist motions.

Repeat 6-8 times for each scheme

Exercise # 7

A similar exercise for the entire arm.

Repeat 6-8 times for each scheme

Suggested musical material:

1. Mozart - *Eine Kleine Nacht Musik* (*The Little Night Music*), movement II - first eight measures

2. Beethoven - Symphony # 1, movement II - first seven measures

3. Brahms - Symphony # 1, movement II - first twelve measures

Suggested musical excerpts can be used for each exercise.

Thorough achievement of these suggested exercises will have useful practical implications in encouraging flexibility of the interactive exchange and the combination of intermediate upbeats of various dimensions as soon as the content of the music requires an interactive transformation of conventional metrical schemes.

10

THE UPBEAT AS A CONCEPTUAL ACTION

As mentioned at the beginning of Chapter 9: *The Preparatory Motion-Impulse*, the formal mechanistic (illustrative) performance of the upbeat has a limited practical value. The performance of the upbeat should be implemented as an interactive action with reference to the nature of musicians' (human) perceptions. The innate complexity of an upbeat-impulse as an informative (conceptual) action has, as a rule, revealed both the sense of its connection to the sound and its clear reflection of the strength of conductor's inner impulse.

This chapter suggests some exercises for the development of a sense of the vicinity of sound, and for the collection of upbeats which serve to fulfill the needs of intercommunicative modes. It is important to mention that this technique is challenging, especially for beginners; however, the possession of such an approach may amplify one's professional abilities.

ESTABLISHING A SENSE OF THE VICINITY (CONTOUR) OF SOUND

The phenomenon of the vicinity (contour) of sound and its practical importance were discussed in Chapter 4. Here are some practical suggestions for establishing a sense of the vicinity (contour) of sound. These suggested exercises also assist in conditioning the practical reflex of 'getting' (or 'taking') the sound instead of 'placing' upon, and striking or 'pressing' against the sound (predominant practical manners). Establishing such a sense as a practical reflex (sensation) will be vital for an interactive modification of the upbeat into advanced modes: e.g., suspended upbeat, converted upbeat, etc.

For the following exercises you will need several half-full plastic bottles (16 - 20 oz. or 0.25 liter).

Exercise # 1

Place the bottle on a horizontal surface next to the line of the waist: a table of appropriate height, a music stand, etc. Hold the arm in the primary (downbeat) position next to the bottle. With a small rounded preparatory motion (move the arm left just over the bottle, up and then down), at the bottom turning point of the motion, grab the bottle and drop it half-way up. Stop the arm immediately after dropping. Take a moment to assess the arm's muscular performance and sensation (especially for fingers, wrist and fore-arm).

Repeat 15 times

Relax arm muscles by a gentle arm shaking.

Exercise # 2

Practice the previous exercise without stops (after each motion) and with the assistance of a metronome. Begin practice at a slow pace (50 BPM). Repeat 10 times. Stop and re-start the practice with gradually increased speed. Continue to increase speed until it is practicably impossible. Make sure that the moment of 'grabbing' the bottle coincides with the metronome beats.

Exercise # 3

Similar to previous exercise but with reversed speed - begin at a faster speed and then gradually decrease it. Repeat each pace at least 10 times.

Exercise # 4

Similar to the previous exercise, but with a gradual change in speed. Begin practice at a slow pace and then gradually increase the speed (without stopping). Reverse - start at a faster speed and then gradually slow down. Make sure that the moments of grabbing the bottle coincide with the metronomic beats.

Relax arm muscles by a gentle arm shaking after each practice.

After making progress in the practice of the suggested exercises, it will be useful to continue practicing with two bottles of different weights – for example, empty and full bottles, half-full and empty bottles, quarter-full and half-full bottles, etc. **Notice and assess the different muscular sensations occurring after lifting bottles of different weights at a steady pace and with various speeds.** Later, it will be practical to combine the exercises of contour of sound with exercises for breath control and active muscular relaxation (see Chapter: *Active Muscular Relaxation* [*Breath Control, Active Relaxation and the Contour of Sound*]).

If there is an opportunity, ask a colleague (especially for Exercise # 4) to play a note or chord during practice (instead of using a metronome [or along with it]). Practice first at a steady rhythm, and then with reasonable *accelerando* and *rallentando*. Perform all the motions as full-length upbeats (avoid uncontrolled arm jerking as a reflex on the ultimate drop of a heavy bottle) and coordinate the moment of bottle grabbing with the occurrence of sound.

It is necessary to mention that the suggested exercises are auxiliary tools to obtain the practical physical reflex in response to the touch of sound. These exercises may mainly have a practical significance for those conductors who have problems eliminating instrumental reflexes and obtaining the physical sensation of the contour of sound.

FUSING THE UPBEAT AND THE CONTOUR OF SOUND

Essentially, the ultimate practical appearance of the concept of rounded motion is an intuitive reflection of the interactive and communicative nature of conducting. There is evidence suggesting that some conductors of the past began to implement this technique in their practices (e.g., Arturo Toscanini's "simple 'circular movements'"[336] in his later years).

The intercommunicative transformation of the concept of the visual strike (ictus) as the intention of the manifestation of an impulse is accomplished if the upbeat is modified and performed in reference to the phenomenon of the vicinity (contour) of sound. Instead of a mechanistic and illustrative performance of the visual strike (which is presumed to coincide with the beginning of the sound), the modification of rounded motion performed in reference to the contour of sound has a conceptually formative effect (i.e., the formation of the concept of upcoming sound).

As was mentioned earlier, in Chapter 7: *Milieu of Communication* (*Rounded Motion*), the primary practical benefit of the utilization of rounded motion is that it naturally manifests continuity and facilitates the interactive connection of the metrical points (beats) throughout metrical schemes. The

---

[336] Ginzburg, 118.

intercommunicative application of the various accents inside rounded motion will prevent interruptions of the movements and, at the same time, fulfill the requirements of the musical texture. Another important aspect of the technique of rounded motion and its interactive modifications is that it is especially effective if it stays in an interactive connection with the contour of sound. Such connection brings a sense of steady merging with the orchestra's sound (instead of a spring off the sound after each strike).

Other important benefits of the properly established technique of rounded motion are the correlation of the intermediate beat within the metrical pattern and the sense of the fulfillment of the metrical unit (beat or measure), especially in scores with multi-layered textural orchestration.

INTERMEDIARY UPBEAT AND THE CONTOUR OF SOUND

The inside-of-scheme upbeat is a motion which precedes the beginning of each beat within the schemes of conducting. As was mentioned previously (in the subchapter: *Beat Connection [Intermediary Upbeat]*), the inside-of-metrical-scheme upbeat is responsible for preceding the beginning of each beat within the conducting scheme (a function similar to the preparatory), and also for managing the current beat.

The practical importance of the intermediate (inside-the-metrical-scheme) upbeat is evident. The intermediate upbeats are the most essential parts of the interactive manual mode. Correct execution of the inside-of-the-metrical-scheme upbeat revives the original diagrammatic conventional schemes and is vital for an artistically valuable performance. The innate transformation of the formal (illustrative) upbeat into a **meaningful sound manager** (motion-impulse) brings breath and essence into a rigid frame of schemes.

For the following exercises, you will need several half-empty plastic bottles (16-20 oz. or 0.25 liter).

Exercise # 1

>Place the bottle on a horizontal surface of the appropriate height (on the waistline). Hold the arm in the primary position next to the bottle. With a small preparatory motion (move the arm left just over the bottle, up and then down), take the bottle and drop it half-way up. The motion should be rounded and even in speed throughout (avoid stopping or jerking at any point of the motion).

Repeat 10 times

Exercise # 2

This exercise is similar to Exercise # 1 but more complex. Place two bottles on the horizontal surface for the 2nd and 3rd beat in a 4/4 pattern (or the 1st and 2nd beat in ¾). Hold the arm in the primary position between the bottles. First move to the left and, with the same small preparatory motion as in the previous exercise, lift the bottle and drop it almost immediately. Without any interruption transfer motion to the next bottle, lift it, and drop it. It is important that when lifting the bottles the arm does not stop the motion. The contour of the motion should resemble this figure - ∞. Make sure that the arm is aligned. Again, as in the previous exercises avoid uncontrolled arm jerking as a reflex on the ultimate drop of the bottle and coordinate the moment of bottle grabbing with the occurrence of metronome beats (or sound).

Repeat 15 times

For better results, use a metronome at slow tempos. The suggested exercises mainly assist in the practical acquiring of the inside-the-metrical-scheme upbeats for simple *legato* modes. The upbeats for more complex textural features will be discussed in the following Chapter. Notice that, in contrast with the forceful style, the sound is expected to appear on the way up (after the lowest turning point).

A principal **uniformity** in the performance of an inside-of-metrical-scheme (intermediate) upbeat (informative motion-impulse) is a method for converting redundant beat measuring into interactive conducting modes. As was mentioned earlier in Chapter 7, this contrasts with the striking methodology's inside-of-metrical-scheme upbeats: performance occurs with a striking motion for the downbeat and non-unified slammed execution of the 2nd and 3rd beats in a 3/4 scheme, or a striking downbeat and a smashed execution of the 2nd, 3rd, and 4th beat within a 4/4 scheme. The enforced performance of upbeats reveals the conditional character of this approach in which the conductor's action artificially superimposes the non-fractured flow of the music.

11

TYPES OF UPBEATS

SUSPENDED MODE[337]

The motions which are manifested with the intent to strike, to put (or place) upon, to pick up, or to lay down and, conversely, the gestures which pretend to lift, to pull up, to tear off, etc., are all performed with a visual (formal) resemblance to each other (from the top down). Therefore all these actions are divergent from their inner meanings and are launched by various artistic necessities which cause a conductor's physical and mental sensational diversity.

---

[337] Ilia Musin used the term "upbeat" for the description of various modified types of upbeats. However, it appears that the term 'mode' reflects the nature of the phenomenon more appropriately. The general description of Suspended, Converted and Suspended Converted Upbeats can be found in Musin's book, *Technique of Conducting*, 55-61.

The first type of gesture affects a musician's intellectual assessment as a set of **complete** or **finished off** gestures; the second type is perceived as a **continuous** or **prolonged** set of gestures.

As one may notice, some of the previous exercises consisted of motions which are similar to the gestures of the traditional forceful mode. A distinctive feature of this traditional method is the forceful strike as a presumed manifestation of an impulse (or ictus). As was mentioned earlier, such a direct implementation of an impulse was transferred from the instrumental practice and possessed a limited artistic value. Furthermore, the performance of metrical schemes with continuous manifestations of forceful 'smashes' are monotonous and aesthetically unappealing.

Despite the interactive shortcomings of the forceful mode, it is necessary to recognize the importance of the depiction of the **impulse** itself, though the performance of the impulse has to be modified in accordance with the specifics of communication and perception. The intercommunicative design of the suspended type of the upbeat **assists in overcoming the practical and aesthetical shortcomings of the force-coming modes, and at the same time refashions the performance of the visual impulse.**

The practical difference between performance of the suspended upbeat and the forceful strike is principal. The proper performance of a suspended upbeat is an example of a gesture designed in accordance with the interactive modes of conducting, and it is intended to solve the practical predicaments and difficulties of dynamic enforcement of the beat without temporal disruption (which is typical for movements with slow or moderate tempos). A suspended upbeat also can be useful in fast tempos for the 'enforcement' of dynamics - in contrast with the performance of the upbeat suggested by the predominant methodology when the impulse fades as the lifting (rebound) passively slows towards the upper breaking point.

To avoid weakness and to focus the impulse, the 'lifting' section of the suspended upbeat is performed with acceleration and consequent suspension at the turning point, after which the 'falling' section accelerates towards the downbeat. However, the importance of both 'lifting' and 'falling' is equal, though the arm's speed throughout the beat is varied.

Suspended Mode

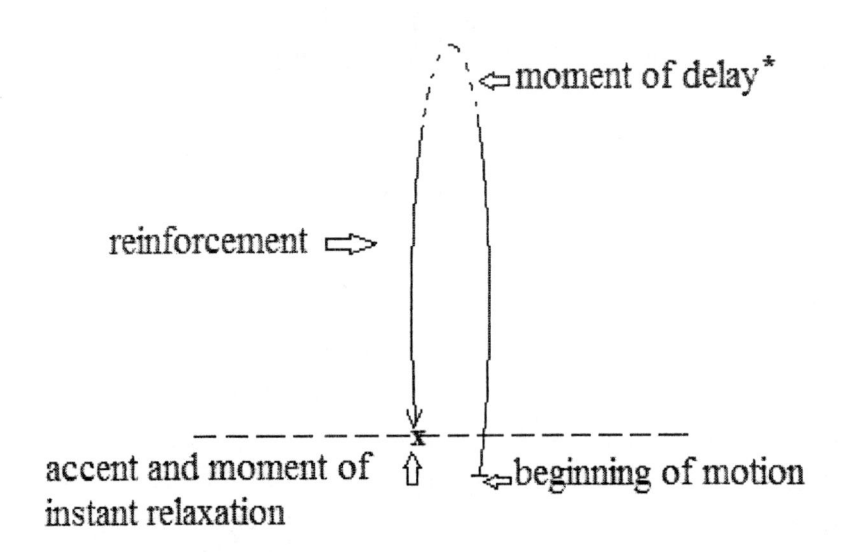

⇐ moment of delay*

reinforcement ⇨

accent and moment of ⇧ ⇐ beginning of motion
instant relaxation

* The moment of delay is the most challenging part of the suspended upbeat. At the beginning of practice, a common shortcoming is that the moment of delay at the turning upper part of the motion is either too long or too short, or is moving too quickly or too slowly towards the accent (a segment of time for compensatory reinforcement). For proper performance of the suspended upbeat, it is crucial to find a proper medium between the 'delayed' and 'reinforced' sections of the beat.

For better adaptation and feasible results, the exercises on suspended upbeats can be divided into two simple motions –

'lifting' and 'falling'. The wrist has to lead the motions during all exercises.

Exercise - **Lifting**

Place the right arm in the downbeat position. Lift the arm with an **accelerated speed** (in an active mode) and stop (with instant muscular relaxation!) at the upper (turning) point. From the upper point, move the arm slowly down (back to the starting point).

Repeat 10 times

Exercises - **Falling**

1. Place the right arm at the upper (turning) point. Make sure that the wrist and fore-arm are in a relaxed mode. With an abrupt relaxation of the shoulders (and part of the back), let the arm fall down with a natural acceleration towards the lowest point. It is important to perform the motion as weightless 'falling' (to feel the natural enforcement of gravity).

Repeat 10 times

2. Place the right arm at the upper (turning) point. At the end of the 'falling' motion, instantly stop the arm at the downbeat (plane of conducting) with immediate muscular relaxation[338] (similar to the arm abruptly encountering an obstacle). Initially, for better results, use an appropriate surface (table, counter, piano lid, etc.).

Repeat 10 times

3. Place the right arm at the upper (turning) point. The 'falling' segment is similar to the previous exercise, but at the starting point the arm has to overcome (struggle through) some virtual obstacle (as if someone suddenly grabs the arm for a moment) before reaching the downbeat with a consequent abrupt relaxation.

Repeat 10 times

Exercise - **Suspended Mode**

Place the right arm in the downbeat position. Lift the arm with an **accelerated speed.** Stop at the turn (from up to down) if the arm somewhat hangs up for a moment. The 'falling' part **brings force** and **acceleration** (simultaneously) toward the downbeat. The arm abruptly

---

[338] The techniques of interactive relaxation are discussed in Chapter 12: *Active Muscular Relaxation.*

stops with an instant relaxation at the downbeat.

Repeat 10 times

The use of a metronome (in slow tempos) will assist. Note that the arm's instant relaxation at the downbeat during these exercises is proof of the suspended upbeat's proper performance.

In the beginning, practice the exercise by stopping the motion; later, achieve more advanced types with a simultaneously **rounded** and **slowed** motion at the turning point (but not stopped). Both types of gestures, however, are practical.

A monitoring of the *rebound* has been vital since the *rebound* and *lift* became inseparable. The main challenge in the performance of the suspended upbeat is **to blend the arm's various speeds with the metrical value of the beat** (thus the metrical value of the beat will not change).

CONVERTED MODE

Given the necessity for the implementation of distinctive enforced modes during the performance of various accents within and throughout metrical schemes commonly required by a musical texture, a specific technical tool described as a "converted upbeat"[339] has been developed. The appropriate conversion of beats' accentuated application along the flow of a musical line (or inside metrical schemes) brings certain dynamism into conducting. However, that vitality is conditioned and even deceptive because it consists of a repetitive forcible placement of beats. This simultaneously weakens the intensity of the beat as a result of the necessary subsequent rebound after their vertical application from the top down. The striking monotony of gestures, though, can be softened or leveled (transformed) appropriately without damaging the overall musical concept. It is especially notable that the negative peculiarities of the direct enforcement of striking modes manifest themselves throughout slow movements with long unbreakable *legatos*.

The practical value of the converted suspended upbeat is particularly obvious in movements with slow or moderate tempos where the manifestation of beats and their junctions should be actively combined. Thus conventional striking is adopted by the beat connecting interactive mode.

---

[339] Terminology suggested by Ilia Musin.

The skilled application of converted upbeats assists in obtaining a distinctive 'presence' of sound in the conductor's hand, that is to say, **a feeling of the 'significance' of sound - the most important interactive mode of performance.** *In accordance with the needs of performance, a conductor is able 'to operate' tones as somewhat of a mass of sound - pull, form, squeeze or on the contrary make it weightless, airy, etc.*[340]

Exercise

At first, practice the converted upbeat in one beat without performance of metrical schemes. Place the right arm in the downbeat position and slightly to the right side of the beat at the provisional middle point of the full motion contour. Start the motion (upbeat) from this point (from this point the second [lower] part of the rounded motion goes under the plane of conducting). Conditionally, the plane of conducting divides the motion into two parts (the contour of complete motion resembles a squeezed letter O [the upper and lower ends are stretched]). After the arm makes a complete round it 'meets' the sound at the upper point of crossing the flatness of conducting (conditionally after performance of 1.5 [lower half plus full 'round'] of the motion at the left middle point of the full motion contour); see graphic below.

---

[340] Musin, 84. (Emphasis added)

Converted Mode

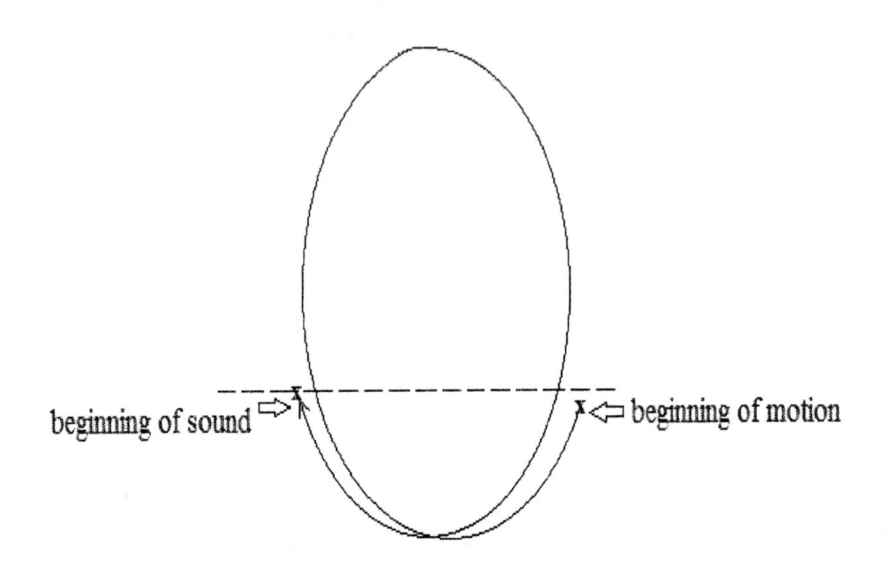

beginning of sound ⇨　　　　　⇦ beginning of motion

CONVERTED SUSPENDED MODE

A converted suspended upbeat is implemented for the performance of forceful dynamics, **and it is especially useful for the indication of accents**. In contrast with the suspended upbeat, the *lifting* and *falling* sections of the converted suspended upbeat are performed as a single 'steady' motion with a suspension next to the downbeat. The motion and suspension are temporally equal.

The functional application of the converted suspended upbeat is more specific than a suspended upbeat. At the beginning of the practical application of the converted suspended upbeat, the early arrival to the downbeat is a common error, which may result in a premature sound occurrence (in this instance the converted suspended upbeat will be perceived as a confusing unexpected acceleration of tempo). Thus the practical accommodation of the converted suspended upbeat should begin after an appropriate performance of the suspended upbeat has been obtained.

Though the external contour of the converted suspended upbeat is similar to the striking motion, the 'internal' intentions of these actions are different.

> *Compare the motion of the arm executing a strike on any object with the motion of the arm intended to catch a falling object.*[341]

---

[341] Musin, 67.

Converted Suspended Mode

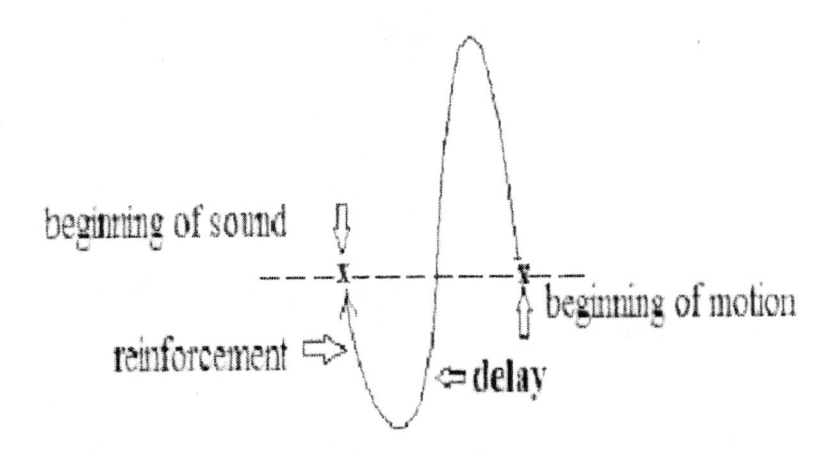

beginning of sound

reinforcement ⇨

⇦ delay

beginning of motion

For better practical results the exercises for converted suspended upbeats can be divided into simplified motions.

Exercise # 1 **'Grabbing'**

For this exercise, you will need some light object (tennis ball, half empty 16-20 oz bottle, etc.) and a light wooden or metal stick or cane.

A. Place the object on any surface at the level of the downbeat (at the same level as the plane of conducting). Place the right arm at the upper (turning) point. At the downbeat point, grab and hold the object. After the moment of 'grabbing' instantly rest the arm's muscles.

Repeat 10 times

B. Grab and hold the upper end of the stick. With a quick downward (catching) motion grasp the bottom end.

Repeat 10 times

After performing these exercises, compare the 'catching' downward motion with the striking gesture. Despite the visual resemblance, the inner meaning and, consequently, the arm's muscular sensation are different.

Exercise # 2 **Converted Suspended Mode**

A. Place the light object at the downbeat position. Place the right arm on the right side of the object (downbeat). The *lifting* (directed slightly to the left, up and outward) and *falling* (inward and down [back to downbeat]) sections are performed with an **active speed** (as in the *lifting* section of the suspended upbeat) and a **rounded turn** (with a curvature) as a 'purposeful' goal-oriented motion. At the downbeat point, grab the object for a short moment and then release it. Assess the arm's muscular sensation at the moment of grab and release. Continue practice with minimal breaks between the motions.

Repeat 10 times

It is important to accomplish a steady, solid and unbroken (uninterrupted) motion. With a metronome, the temporal lengths of the motion and the delay at the downbeat (suspension) should be equal. Coincide the moment of grabbing with the metronome beat. At first, practice with slow and moderate tempos.

B. Similar to the previous exercise, but the *falling* section at the beginning is continued at the same speed as the *lifting* and then is slowed (inhibited) just before the arrival at the beat. After an adequate moment of **suspension** it **accelerates** toward the beat. At the moment of the downbeat, instead of grasping the object, slightly hit it with consequent instant relaxation.*

*This exercise is more complex, and is recommended only when proper performance of the previous type of the converted suspended upbeat has been obtained. As in the suspended upbeat exercises, at first, practice with a stopping motion. Later practice with a more difficult continuous approach with the application of the impulse after a slight inhibition before the beat.

As was mentioned earlier, monitoring of the *rebound* has been vital ever since the *rebound* and *lifting* motions became inseparable (the functions of the rebound are discussed in the following subchapter). **The fingertips have to lead the motions during all exercises**. Despite challenges in performing the suggested exercises, it is important to practice with preservation of a linear (communicative) manifestation of the arm.

> *After obtaining all sorts of upbeats and gestures, a conductor will find the method for their best practical application in accordance with the expressiveness of musical material.*[342]

For all modes of suspended upbeats, body posture and facial expression play important roles in the actions and must express a certain confidence. However, the appropriate perception of the suspended upbeats must be launched **by the innate meaning of**

---

[342] Musin, 85.

the gesture and not by the elaboration of excessive muscular tension. Practical application of suspended modes of upbeats is only recommended after an appropriate performance of the simpler modes of upbeats and a familiarity with the techniques of the instant interchange of the arm's various muscular tensions and relaxations have been obtained.

It is important to mention certain challenge in the performance of all types of intercommunicative modifications of upbeats. Even the smallest inaccuracy in the performance of the suspended upbeat and the converted suspended upbeat will influence the accuracy of the ensemble. Later, the more advanced practical multi-dimensional applications of various types of modified upbeats can be implemented in complex interactive correspondence with the numerous combinations of the rounded motion. Also, it is important to mention again that all of the previous exercises have intensified practical efficiency only in direct reference to the phenomenon of the *Contour of Sound*.

The various modes of the upbeat/motion impulse are innumerable. However, for a schematic description of the intercommunicative modes of the upbeat it is necessary to use a certain traditional terminology. It is important to emphasize that the use of such terms as "preparatory," "intermediary," "delayed," "suspended," "converted" is an effort to expand further the multifunctional descriptions of the conceptual motion, which was originally known as an "upbeat."

As was mentioned earlier in Chapter 5: subchapter *Conceptual*

Motions, the quasi-linguistic principle of spontaneous involuntary functioning of the conductor's apparatus requires a revision of the traditional view on the conductor's gesture. In practice, the intellectual superimposition of the traditional concept of the upbeat may enforce certain pragmatic unproductive limits over the motion's performance and, consequently, the further development of the conductor's apparatus.

REBOUND

It is necessary to mention that the intercommunicative function of the rebound is an indivisible part of the upbeat and is crucial, especially for an orchestra's entrance on an incomplete beat (e.g., the beginning of G. Rossini's "Barber of Seville" Overture), as well as for rhythmical, dynamic and temporal management of inside-the-metrical-scheme metrical points. In general, the intercommunicative conceptual function of the rebound is equally important to the intercommunicative role of the upbeat, especially in scores in which the beat as a one-pattern unit with a complex melodic and metrical structure enfolds the entire measure (e.g., L. Beethoven, "Egmont" Overture, *Allegro*).[343]

There are two types of the rebound:[344]

---

[343] The separation of the upbeat and the rebound is conditioned by the methodological purposes. Practically, they are inseparable segments of the complex informative motion.

[344] A detailed description of various features of the rebound can be found in Musin's *Technique of Conducting*, 129-151.

1. **Non- rhythmically-contingent rebound**

   The performance of this rebound is equal in length and time to the beat (just simply mirroring the beat).

2. **The rhythmically-contingent rebound** with the various temporal delays of performance.

The performance of the rhythmically-contingent rebound with various temporal delays divides into several categories:

1. **Non-accentuated rhythmically-contingent rebound**

   This type of the rebound is typical for the emphasis of the dotted rhythm in slow tempos.

2. **Accentuated rhythmically-contingent rebound** is used:

   A. For indication of the incomplete preparatory upbeat with accent and with or without accent in the dynamic of *forte*.

   B. For accent of the inside-the-scheme beat

(e.g., the indication of the sixteenth note with accent at the end of the 2nd beat in 3/4 meter).

3. Doubled non-suspended rhythmically-contingent rebound

This type of the rebound is useful for the emphasis of the rhythmical pulsation of the inside-the-scheme beat and its textural fulfillment within the doubled meter.

This technique is particularly useful for slow and moderate tempos.

4. Double-meter suspended rhythmically-contingent rebound

This type of the rebound is useful for a metrical subdivision of the inside-the-scheme beat to accentuate the dotted rhythm.

A double-meter suspended rhythmically-contingent rebound is performed by a specific suspension at the beginning of the beat, with consequent, compensatory rebounds of various speeds after the suspension.

5. Tripled non-suspended rhythmically-contingent rebound

This type of the rebound is useful for the emphasis of a tripled meter's rhythmical pulsation (rhythmical characteristics) of the beat and its textural fulfillment.

6. Tripled suspended rhythmically-contingent rebound

This type of the rebound is used for a metrical subdivision of the beat to accentuate the dotted rhythm.

Notice that the performance of tripled-meter non-suspended and suspended rhythmically-contingent rebounds is different from the doubled-meter suspended rhythmically-contingent rebound, which is achieved (similar to the doubled) by a specific suspension at the beginning of the beat and followed by a compensatory rebound of various speeds after the suspension, but as a rule **within the rounded motion** (see performance of the *Triple-Meter Upbeat*).

Suggested exercises:

Practice the various types of rebound for the preparatory.

    1. The rhythmically-contingent rebound for an accentuated incomplete preparatory upbeat.

Place the arm in the downbeat position. From the lowest point of the beat, begin the arm's motion slowly (as if it is struggling to get through a muddy substance), and with consequent rapid acceleration (to the upper left corner). Practice rebounds for incomplete preparatory upbeats of various durations.

A.

  1.   2.

B.

  1.   2.

2. This is similar to the previous exercise, but with the rhythmically-contingent rebound for a non-accentuated preparatory incomplete upbeat.

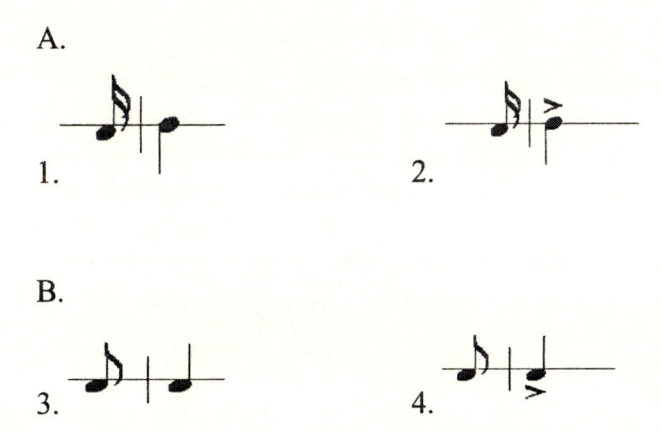

A.

1.   2.

B.

3.   4.

3. Rebound for an accentuated incomplete upbeat within the scheme of conducting: incomplete upbeat of various duration 16, 8 doubled, and 8 tripled with accent for different meters: 2/4, 3/4 and 4/4 (see graphic below).

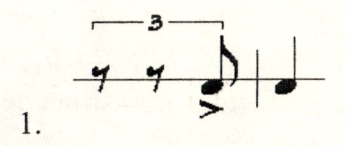

1.

2.

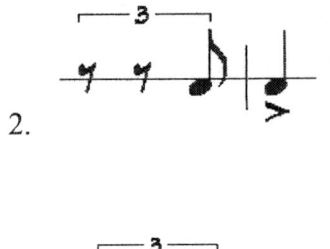

3.

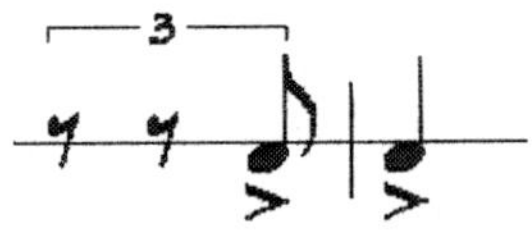

For 4/4 meter, practice varied types of the rhythmically-contingent rebound for each beat (i.e., 16 and 8 tripled, and 8 doubled). Then practice the rhythmically-contingent rebound in different order.

4. This is similar to the previous exercise. However, in this instance practice the rebound for a non-accentuated incomplete upbeat.

At the beginning, practice the rhythmically-contingent rebound for a single beat and then within the various schemes (2/4, 3/4 and 4/4). Next, practice more complex metrical schemes: 6/8 (in two but with fulfillment of the various tripled metrical figures of 6/8.

1.

2.

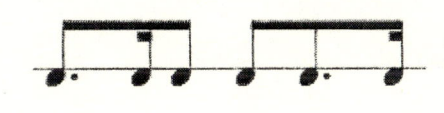

For better results, use a metronome for all suggested exercises. Notice, however, that the indication of non-accentuated rhythmically-contingent rebounds for textural and rhythmical fulfillment of the inside-the-scheme beat is practical for slow and moderate tempos.

The non-accentuated mode of the rhythmically-contingent rebound is very useful, specifically in slow tempos. This approach allows control not only of the "inner" space of the beat, but also controls the "mass" of the sound.[345]

Suggested musical material:

---

[345] Musin, 68.

1. Mozart, *Magic Flute.* Overture – Beginning to *Allegro* (first 18 measures)

2. Beethoven, Symphony # 7, movement I – 21 measures before *Vivace* to the end of the Exposition

3. Brahms, Symphony # 3, movement I

4. Tchaikovsky, Serenade for Strings, movement I – from A to H

5. Rimsky-Korsakov - Scheherazade, movement IV – *Vivo* (23 measures before A to K)

6. Shostakovich, Symphony # 5, movement I, beginning – first 4 measures

PENDULUM

The interactive techniques of conducting are techniques which incorporate the natural forces of motion: centrifugal, centripetal,[346] delaying, suspending, accelerating, etc. The motion which resembles the swing of a pendulum is another type of the interactive modes of conducting technique.[347] When designed appropriately, this technique incorporates the internal and external forces of Nature within the arm's motion. The proper implication of the pendulum-like motion is especially useful in movements with slow and moderate tempos (andante, moderato, etc.), which is characteristic of slower movements of symphonies (mainly in even meters – 2/4, 6/8). It is also useful in movements with faster tempos (for example, when a 3/4 meter needs to be conducted in single beat [waltzes]).

It is suggested that one start the practice of the pendulum-like motion once a substantial amount of progress on the other interactive modes of the upbeat has been reached. The pendulum-like motion can be performed with one hand or two

---

[346] Erzhemsky, 110.

[347] Other examples of the interactive mode of conducting, such as the "sling," can be found in Musin's book, *Technique of Conducting*, 210-211.

(more complex).

The proper performance of the pendulum mode as a principle is based on the proper amount of delay and the impulse being transferred from one arm to the other at the conjuctional lower spot.

Exercise # 1

> Place the right arm in the downbeat position. The motion starts from the downbeat position (moving slowly at the starting point and then becoming faster), then progresses to the right side and up. After a slight delay (suspension) at the turning point (motion resembles a stretched number 9), it falls down in a relaxed mode through the starting point and to the left upper point (the line's motion should resemble a curve with rounded upper corners [mirrored number 9]). Practice on count 3 for both sides (left and right) with the downbeat located at the lower point of the motion (the first count is at the moment when the arm returns to the down beat).

In the beginning, it is easier to practice with the palm facing the left side; later the palm can be in various positions.

Exercise # 2

This exercise is more complex than the first. Practice this only after achieving adequate progress in the previous exercise. This is similar to the first exercise, however, in addition to the motions to the right and left upper corners, at the same time the arm moves slightly forward, pushing the corners outward with an appropriate curve at the corner.

Exercise # 3

Place both hands in the downbeat position and then move them next to each other. The right hand starts from the downbeat position (moving slowly at the starting point and then faster), progressing to the right side and up. After a slight delay at the turning point, it falls down in a relaxed mode to the starting point with a slight inhibition before reaching the starting point (the line of the motion should resemble the curvature of the letter J). The left hand starts moving (with gradual acceleration) slightly before the right arm reaches the down beat, and it mirrors the right hand's motion. The pendulum effect comes at the moment when one hand transfers the impulse to the other hand at the lowest point of the motion.

At first, it is easier to practice with both palms facing up; later, both palms can be in various positions. Practice first with hands softly striking each other at the downbeat. Later, it can be performed with a soft strike or without.

Exercise # 4

This is similar to the previous exercise, but, as suggested in Exercise # 2, the motions to the right and left upper corners simultaneously move slightly forward, pushing the corners outward with an appropriate curvature at the corner. In contrast with exercises #'s 1 and 2, in exercices #'s 3 and 4 the performance of the curve and the outward motion at the corners is lessened and is not as important as the proper transfusion of speed (acceleration and exchange of impulses) in between the motions of the arms.

Suggested material:

1. L. Beethoven, Symphony # 7, movement II

2. P. Tchaikovsky, Serenade for Strings, movement II

3. J. Strauss, *Blue Danube* Waltz

For a simple meter such as 2/4, the pendulum is performed by way of a simple curvature. For more complex meters (6/8 in two or 3/4 as a single beat), the motions become more complex and include a rounded motion typical of the tripled upbeat. This could vary from the simple approach: from the right upper side (down) to the left upper side; to a more complex approach: from the right upper side moving outward and down, and then straight to the upper left (without moving outward), or vise versa; or a more complex combination within a measure or measures (depending on the texture, orchestration, dynamics or speed changes). In accordance with dynamics (e.g., at *subito p* or *subito f*), the strength of the manifestation of the impluse could be varied from softest to strongest.

Again, it is important to emphasize that all suggested exercises will have a practical efficiency only in direct reference to the phenomenon of the *Contour of Sound*.

12

ACTIVE MUSCULAR RELAXATION

As mentioned earlier in Chapter 6: *Interactive Techniques* (*Relaxation*), to instantly establishing a productive interaction with an orchestra, it is crucial for a conductor to possess a technique of effective muscular relaxation.

> *The body functions with maximum efficiency when all parts are in **dynamic balance** with one another. When excess tension is released, it is as if a heavy weight is lifted off the body; there is often a sense of relief and of wonder at how much easier movement can be.*[348]

---

[348] Leibowitz and Connington, xvii. (Emphasis added)

However, the muscular relaxation in and of itself is not an isolated phenomenon. It is part of a complex mental and physical action which includes mental control of breathing and action. Finding a proper balance between the complex interactions of the body and the mind is a crucial requirement of successful conducting. Possession of the technique of active muscular relaxation of various parts of the body is one of the basic skills in a conductor's apparatus. The ability to supervise and effectively manipulate muscular activity during conducting amplifies the conductor's intellectual and physical abilities. In addition to the practical advantages, the exercises on active muscular relaxation help in sensing and comprehending the innate means of conducting more distinctly through a conductor's own physical and mental performance.

Here are some suggested exercises for the development of the technique in active muscular relaxation.

Exercise # 1

1. The body is in the *Primary Posture* - a relatively relaxed body posture with an outward active manifestation of the head, shoulders, chest and overall posture. Place both arms in the downbeat position with forearms horizontally aligned. Slightly shake both hands to check that the arms' muscles are comfortably relaxed. Along with a wrist motion resembling "catching a tennis ball," instantly tense the right arm for several seconds and then

relax it. Ensure that exercise with the right hand does not provoke the simultaneous appearance of tension in the left hand. Maintain a steady and comfortable breathing rhythm.

Repeat 4-5 times

2. Do the same *catching* motion with the left hand. Before practice slightly shake the right hand to release residual tension.

Repeat 4-5 times

3. Exchange *catching* between the right and left wrists with a simultaneous instant relaxation of the opposite hand. Before switching hands from the relaxed to tense mode, make sure that the non-tense arm is as relaxed as possible. At first, practice at a slow pace, and then try at a moderate speed. It may take some practice to perform this exercise at a fast speed.

Suggested practice time: 5-10 minutes

Exercise # 2

The body is in the *Primary Posture*. Place both arms in the downbeat position with forearms parallel to the floor (similar to the previous exercise). At this time, 'concentrate' tension on the right wrist while, at the same time, preserving the right shoulder in a relaxed mode. Do not switch hands until a controlled relaxation in the right shoulder is reached. Practice an instant switch of tension between wrists. Notice that the moment of exchange of muscular tension and relaxation affects the pace of breathing. During practice, at slow and then in faster speeds, **maintain a steady breathing rate**.

Suggested practice time: 5-10 minutes

Exercise # 3

The body is in the *Primary Posture*. Place both arms in the downbeat position with forearms parallel to the floor (similar to Exercise # 1). While keeping both wrists in a relaxed mode, switch tension between the shoulders. Throughout the exercise, maintain a conditionally relaxed mode in both wrists and instant relaxation for the non-tense shoulder. Be aware of a steady pace of breathing.

Suggested practice time: 5 minutes

Exercise # 4

> While practicing Exercises #'s 1, 2 or 3, tense the abdomen (diaphragm) for 5-10 seconds at the beginning and then prolong for 30-45 seconds. After 2-3 times, stop the exercise and relax. Notice how the presence of tension in the diaphragm affects the arms' performance as well as the pace of breathing.

Exercise # 5

> While practicing Exercises #'s 1, 2 or 3, hold the buttocks tense. Make sure that the surrounding areas such as the legs, back and abdomen are not affected by the buttocks muscles tension. Notice how the presence of tension in the buttocks affects the arms' performance as well as the pace of breathing.

Exercise # 6

> While practicing Exercises #'s 1, 2 or 3, instantly exchange

tension between the abdomen and buttocks.

Exercise # 7

During this exercise instantly exchange tension between the arms and feet. At first tense the arm and foot of the same side, then the opposite (left arm – right foot, etc.).

Exercise # 8

Combine all the previous exercises in an interactive exchange. Add more complexity to the exercises. While practicing exercises, perform a rounded motion with a relaxed hand. Perform rounded motions in various directions – from right to left, left to right, inward – outward, outward – inward, etc. Make sure that after each exercise, after coming back to the *Primary Posture*, all residual muscular tension is eliminated. Gradually gain control over the amount of tension, down to the necessary practical minimum. Make sure that the speed of the exchange of modes of tension and relaxation does not affect the steady pace of breathing.

As was mentioned before in Chapter 6: *Interactive Techniques* (*Relaxation*), conductors with well-developed musculature (naturally inherited or developed through certain physical exercises) may struggle with making certain progress in techniques of active muscular relaxation. The perpetual presence of augmented muscular tonus may be an obstacle on the way to achieving complete muscular relaxation. In this instance, it is beneficial at the beginning to achieve relaxation in smaller segments of the body (e.g., right wrist [or just fingers] and shoulder) and then expand practice to larger parts of the body - arm, arm and shoulder, back, etc.

BREATH CONTROL, ACTIVE RELAXATION AND THE CONTOUR OF SOUND

The following exercises develop one's breath control, management of the active muscular relaxation and sensation of the contour of sound and the ultimate psycho-physical clustering.

To inhale is to concentrate, to exhale is to release.[349]

---

[349] Scherchen, 29.

Exercise # 1

Place the arms along the body. With a gentle shake, check that they are both as relaxed as possible. Exhale deeply. At a steady speed, move the right hand up and stop it on the same level as the shoulder (the wrist is in a relaxed [slacked] position). Make sure that the arm is aligned and not bent at the point of the elbow. Simultaneously let the arm fall down and quickly inhale. Make sure to stop inhaling at the moment when the arm reaches the lowest point. Slightly pause at the lower point and hold your breath for a moment. Check to see if the arm's muscles are relaxed while holding your breath. Simultaneously move the right hand back to the upper point (at the same level with the shoulder) and exhale. Stop the arm and breathe at the same time. Check that the arm's muscles are relaxed (with a loose wrist). It is important to reach complete muscular relaxation at each point (upper and lower) when holding your breath.

Suggested practice time: 5 minutes

Exercise # 2

This is similar to the previous exercise, but with the exhalation on the arm's way down and inhalation on the way up. **Notice the difference of muscular reaction**

with this change.

During the practice, assess the different muscular sensations for performance of similar motions while *inhaling* and then *exhaling*.

Suggested practice time: 5 minutes

Exercise # 3

> Place the right hand in the primary downbeat position. Fully exhale and hold the breathing for a moment. With relaxed arm muscles (the arm is aligned), start a rounded motion (to the right side and up). When the arm turns down after the upper point, inhale. Exhale after the arm turns up again. **Notice the hand muscles' 'natural' relaxation at the lower turning point (from down to up).**

Suggested practice time: 5-10 minutes

If there is an opportunity, ask a colleague to play a single note (or a chord) and match the beginning of the sound with your hand muscles' natural relaxation at the lower turning point. Additionally, try this with various instruments and groups of instruments. Notice the difference at the appearance of sound for instruments of different types (e.g., for a single stringed, woodwind, brass or percussion instrument, and for groups of strings, etc.) **Note the necessary speed adjustments at the lower turning point throughout the performance of the upbeat for the appearance of sound in different instruments or groups of instruments.**

Exercise # 4

> This is similar to the previous exercise, but with the exhalation on the arm's way up and the inhalation on the way down. Notice the difference in muscular reaction with this change.

Again, similarly to the previous exercises, during practice assess the different muscular sensations for the performance of similar motions while *inhaling* and then *exhaling*.

Suggested practice time: 5-10 minutes

Exercise # 5

> This exercise is more complex, but is still similar to the previous two (Exercises #'s 3 and 4). Place four or five 8 oz bottles with various amounts of water (empty, one

quarter full, half full, three quarters full and full) on the same level as an appropriately raised music stand, high table, on the top of the piano lid, etc. Combine breathing (exhale) before the moment of grabbing a bottle. Start the exercise by grabbing the empty bottle at the lower point and drop it on the way up, then continue practice with bottles of different amounts of weight: empty - full, one quarter full - full, etc.

Suggested practice time: 10-15 minutes

Exercise # 6

This is similar to the previous exercise, but with inhalation before the moment of *grabbing*. Notice the difference in muscular reaction with this change.

During practice, assess the different muscular sensations for the performance of similar motions with *inhalations* and then *exhalations*.

Suggested practice time: 10-15 minutes

It is very important to maintain a steady rhythm throughout all suggested exercises. Start practice slowly (30-40 beats per second on a metronome), gradually increasing speed. Achieve full control over the hand muscles' performance: make an effort to avoid any jerking on the way up (after the exchange of bottles of various weight [especially full - empty]) or uncontrolled acceleration (on the way down). Be sure that after each exercise there is no presence of excessive muscular tension. Check your arm relaxation with a gentle shake of both hands.

Breathing exercises assist in setting a useful **reflex of sound taking**, which can help to establish the arm's (and consequently the mind's) tied connection with the sound and eliminate the dynamic *bouncing* reflex. The development of the *taking* reflex eventually can bring a vibrant *breath* into the upbeats/motion-impulses.[350] It is especially vital in the establishment of appropriate inner (intermediate) upbeats (within the metrical scheme of conducting). Wind players in general, and low brass players in particular, have a natural (and practically non-intentional) routine of taking their breaths **during the arm's downward portion of the upbeat**. This phenomenon is especially obvious in orchestras with a tradition of considerable

---

[350] It is important to mention that, from my teaching experience, I have noticed that the development of the sound's *taking* reflex is easier for novice conductors, and needs a complete mental reorientation for conductors with the developed dynamic (forceful) manner. For some colleagues, such mental adjustment seemed to be so radical and 'unconventional' (mainly because it mentally converts the entire approach to the management of the sound) that they were not willing to proceed with the practice and preferred to stay with the conventional dynamic approach.

time-lag before the appearance of the sound (e.g., Berlin Philharmonic, St. Petersburg Philharmonic, etc.). In general, however, such an occurrence is more or less characteristic of any orchestra.

The continuous development of interactive (communicative) gesturing is an essential part of the conductor's professional progress. As was mentioned earlier, all suggested exercises assist in the transformation of motion from a formal operational gesture/upbeat into an informational motion-impulse.

The practical refinement of the motion's informational weight never stops, and there is always an opportunity to add another conceptual (informational) layer into the motion. **As a rule, the conductor's mental/physical apparatus has to be under constant transformation into more informative complex techniques.** The conductor's vivid musical images, which evoke valuable inner artistic intentions, along with projections of strong (immutable) creative impulses will fertilize and perpetuate a conceptual sustenance of the motion-impulse.

13

INNER TECHNIQUES

As was discussed earlier in Chapters 5 and 6, a development of the inner (intangible) techniques is the most essential part of the conductor's apparatus. Despite the common (traditional) methodological practice, which focuses mainly on the external (pictorial) side of conducting, from the very beginning the development of inner techniques should not be given less attention than the study of the arms' motions. Despite the fact of being 'intangible,' the inner techniques actually determine the quality of the conductor's performance. From a practical and, most importantly, an artistic view, the inner techniques are the core of the conductor's apparatus. In reality, the full complexity of the conductor's apparatus cannot be reached without the organic unity of its appearance (the external features) and content (inner techniques).

For practical purposes, the complexity of inner techniques can be conditionally separated into three components:

    Creative Will (Inner Impulse)

    Inner Vocalization (Auditory Differentiation)

    Technique of Mental Anticipation of Texture

INNER IMPULSE

Psychologically, it is important to adequately manage superimposed musical ideas of a piece. As was mentioned earlier in Chapter 5: *Inner Mechanisms* (*Conceptual Motion, Inner Will*), the proper formal (mechanistic) performance of an upbeat will most likely not evoke an effective sound. Suitable inner programming (psychological and emotional) will direct and ultimately justify all of a conductor's interactive motions.

The strong anticipated manifestation of such an inner (psychological and emotional) state (or inner impulse) is an innate engine of productive performance.

The conductor manifests an artistically valuable *upbeat-impulse* **before receiving the orchestral sound in response**. The quality of the orchestra's response depends **only** on the quality (the strength and artistic striving) of the conductor's **inner impulse**.

For practice, take as an example some sections from two contrasting movements – the First movement of Beethoven's Symphony # 3, and the Finale from Tchaikovsky's Symphony # 6. Please be advised that the practice of the inner impulse should be done as a part of more complex score study - its structure, form, harmony, orchestration, overall musical content, etc. For better practical results, it is useful to memorize the score: either an entire piece or movement (or at least a part of a movement [e.g., exposition]).

1. When beginning to practice, notice the character and emotional state of each suggested movement as if a performance of the movement would last only a few seconds. Such practice helps in understanding the general character of the movement: the inner emotional 'color' as heroic, lyric, dramatic, pastoral, energetic, etc., or as a combination of various characters.

2. Next, practice different fragments or sections of the movement – for example 'snap-shots' of the first two chords, dynamic pulsation of the main theme or 'lamentation' of the second theme at the beginning of "Eroica," or lamenting in (sighs-like) strings' entrance at the beginning of the Finale of Tchaikovsky's 6th Symphony. Based on musical content and orchestration, form a 'clear' and uncompromised personal concept of the orchestral sound, its color (timbre[s]) and intensity (dynamic) for each fragment or section.

3. When the appropriate psychological and emotional states are achieved, practice a switch between fragments of contrasting characters within each movement. It is important that different psychological and emotional characters for contrasting sections of the movement should change instantly and, most importantly, with appropriate mental anticipation. Later, after achieving a certain level of comfort in managing the anticipated inner impulse, continue to practice in the primary posture with an active but relaxed external manifestation of posture (without arm movements). **While practicing without arm movements, preserve a physical relaxation as strictly as possible, and note the manner in which this mental exercise affects the body's physical (muscular) activity.** Also, analyze how the body responds to such practice. Make sure that none of the body parts develop unwilling tension, especially in the neck, shoulders, back, buttocks or any other part of the body. Also, notice how the advanced projection of

the inner impulse affects the pace of breathing.

4. This is similar to Exercise # 3. However, this time, practice with arm motions in a simplified and non-forcible measuring, though with a linear (communicative) performance of the arms. Conduct without the assistance of a recording. Make sure that the performance of the inner impulse constantly **precedes** the arm motions. While practicing, analyze how the arms respond to such exercises. Make sure, though, that none of the arm's parts develop uncontrolled tension. Preserve the active but relaxed manifestation of the posture. Do not bend. Ensure that the anticipated manifestation of the 'inner' impulse does not negatively affect the upbeats (i.e., in the form of uncontrolled arm jerking).

5. Practice with a complete application of all technical skills. Make sure that the physical apparatus follows the mental anticipation of the innate impulse. Note if these exercises change your physical and mental sensations. Make sure that both the active appearance and relaxed mode of the posture are sustained. Similarly to previous exercises in *Active Muscular Relaxation*, make sure that the exercises for the inner impulse do not affect the steady pace of breathing.

Again, for better practical results, it is useful to practice without the score. If memorizing a large section is problematic, use a smaller segment (8-16 measures) for each contracting fragment.

At first, practice the technique of the constant (non-fractured) advanced performance of the impulse throughout the small section of the movement (e.g., introduction, 1st theme, etc.). Later, after a certain comfort level in performance of the impulse has been reached in the small section, practice the larger section of the movement. Then move on throughout the entire movement. Also, the character of the inner impulse can vary for different parts of the movement (i.e., stronger for the entrance of the large section, or loud dynamic and softer for a single instrument, or soft nuance).

Obtaining the appropriate inner psychological and emotional impulse helps to organize the external apparatus with adequate upbeats. Paradoxically, a strong inner impulse and its properly anticipated manifestation will help the arms to find an appropriate gesture or suitable upbeat mode on their own.

INNER VOCALIZATION
(AUDITORY DIFFERENTIATION)

The development of the inner hearing of multiple timbres, or the textural inner vocalization (the "inner" ear) of a score is an important part of the inner technique. The advanced inner anticipation of various timbres and colors of sound of different instruments or groups of instruments and expectation of certain qualities of articulation at the beginning of a phrase or passage, will affect the collection of actions included in the external apparatus. A common shortcoming is a perception of orchestral sound as a middling unified tone. This deficiency is especially frequent for novice conductors whose previous orchestral experience is limited primarily by piano instrumental background or choral conducting.

The technique of inner vocalization is beneficial in establishing the ability of multi-layered textural hearing in an orchestral performance. Constant inner vocalization assists in the monitoring of intonation and balance of orchestral sound, especially during the performance of a piece scored with multi-ranged thematic developments, or when there is a need to pull out or mute some sections or instruments of the orchestra. For successful professional practice, it is important to develop a multi-timbered and multi-colored inner vocalization of a musical score. The practical implementation of an expanded inner vocalization, directly (consciously) or indirectly (subconsciously), affects a conductor's actions with the emergence of an essential inner flexibility and elasticity of apparatus. This results in an aesthetically efficient external performance. Such an inner technique enables a conductor to feel and sense how the different parts of the hand simultaneously may control the management of different layers of texture (especially in slow movements). For example, in J. Brahms's First Symphony, 2nd movement, measures 40-50, the forearm leads the oboe and then the clarinet solos, while the wrist is responsible for the fulfillment of the syncopated rhythm played by the strings.

ANTICIPATION OF MUSICAL TEXTURE

An anticipation of musical texture is one of the most important tasks of conducting. Possession of this mental technique provides confidence in conducting a score. The practice of anticipation of texture is useful in combination with the exercises for the development of the inner impulse.

Here are some suggested inner practices for establishing mental anticipation during the study of a score.

1. Small 8-16 measures fragments from the Classical and early Romantic repertoire are suggested for initial practice. Without the assistance of a recording or instrument, mentally conduct an inner (imaginary) orchestra and foresee the musical texture of every upcoming measure - dynamics, instrument entrances, and harmonies.

   Suggested material:

   W. A. Mozart, Symphony # 41, movement I

   F. Schubert, Symphony # 5, movement I

2. Complicate the task of practice with anticipation not only of a musical texture but with imagining the timbre of the upcoming instrumental sound.

3. Segments of the score can then be enlarged to sections – for example: the Introduction, Exposition or Development.

Practicing the score by memorizing as much of it as possible is another important aspect of a conductor's mental training in developing advanced inner techniques.

1. It is practical to begin by memorizing smaller segments of a movement and then mentally anticipating the entrance of each instrument or section (e.g., the first 33 measures of the introduction of the first movement of Beethoven's Symphony # 7). It is important to practice an **anticipated** inner vocalization of each entrance – to have an inner **ideal model** of the instrumental or orchestral sound (i.e., specific bow strokes for strings - short (*staccato*) or long (*sostenuto*), different types of *attaccas* for woodwinds and brass, etc.). Then continue further practice with more complex (textural) fragments of the piece.

2. Practice *hearing* the character of the introduction of the first movement and preserve an adequate emotional state.

3. From the very first measure, mentally anticipate dynamic changes and entrance of the instruments. This approach is especially important for beginners in establishing a technique of constant inner anticipation.

Later, practicing with an alternation of the psychological exercises with the inner imaginary orchestra, and the limited assistance of recordings or the assistance of an instrument (piano or other instruments) could have a positive practical impact.

MULTI-LEVELED MANIFESTATION OF THE ARMS

The use of both hands on the same (horizontal) level is inexpressive (the manner in which both hands continuously mirror each other). The artistic value of such conducting is minimal. The presence of two spots of "attention gathering" on the same visual level, which are constantly moving against one another, confuses the perceptions of orchestral players.

It is more practical and artistically useful if both hands are not present on the same level of conducting.

The right hand is traditionally treated as being responsible for the measuring and manifestation of metrical schemes, while the left hand is artistically expressive. However, such a conditional division of the hands' duties is inappropriate since the hands by definition cannot act independently. In reality, both hands bear a mutual indivisible task. What is reasonable, however, for intercommunicative practical purposes, is the separate use of the hands throughout the different levels of conducting.

Exercise:

1. With the right hand is conducting measures, start practice with a simple 2/4 meter and later add 3/4 and 4/4 or more complex meters. Place the left hand above the level of the pattern and start a rounded motion from left to right, then, without rhythmical interruption, switch the motion from right to left; then from inward to outward, and from outward to inward.

2. Elevate the level of the right hand measuring. Practice similar exercises for the left hand, but beneath the level (plane) of conducting.

It is useful to perform this exercise for both hands (with the left hand conducting measures) as well as switching levels - start with the left hand above, then exchange hands and so on. Also, it is important to achieve a rhythmically even performance of rounded motions, though the hand (or wrist, or wrist and forearm) which is measuring can perform various motions - rounded, striking, tossing, etc. The performance of the different strokes of one hand, however, should not influence the smoothness of the other hand's rounded motions.

THE METHOD OF JUXTAPOSITION AND COMPARISON

The development of an expressive palette of informative gesture-actions (with profound semantic meaning) is challenging, but at the same time it is the most interesting and creative part of a conductor's homework. Earlier in this Chapter, it was suggested to use the method of comparison to find an appropriate position for the body and arms. The implementation of a method of juxtaposition is a practical tool for the development of the techniques of a conductor's complex concept-formative actions. The practice of this method is valuable for obtaining a meaningful array of gesture-actions in connection with the musical images of a piece. This method was described in detail in Ilia Aleksandrovich Musin's book, *Technique of Conducting*, and in his unpublished manuscript, *Vado Mecum*.

The search for an expressive tool of gestures for depiction of the expressive characters of music is the most difficult goal during the study of conducting. It is impossible to describe verbally (and moreover to illustrate) the specifics of a gesture depicting one or

> another character of music. It is possible, however, to explain how a gesture depicting staccato differs from one expressing legato or how a gesture illustrating forte differs from one expressing piano. However, words cannot provide a sufficient conception of gestures expressing a majestic or lyrical character of music transferring different nuances of mood – happiness or sadness.... It is necessary to take into account that every conductor, for the depiction of musical images and emotions, will find gestures which match his personality, temperament, and individual motivation.[351]

In actuality, the search for the expressive semantics of gesture-actions never ends. This is why a method of juxtaposition is useful not just for the novice but for experienced conductors, as well.

Initially, practice several opening measures from any piece from the late Classical or Romantic Symphonic repertoire. As a suggested example, take the opening measures from the first movement of Tchaikovsky's Symphony No. 4.

Exercise # 1

> The body is in the Primary Posture (a relaxed position with an outward active manifestation). Mentally (without

---
[351] Musin, 241.

actually conducting), practice the four opening measures, the first time in *ppp* and then the same excerpt in *fff*. Compare the emotional state of both contrasting dynamics. Continue with the juxtaposition of various dynamics - *p* and *f*, *pp* and *ff*, *pp* and *mf*, etc. Anticipate which emotional state best would correspond with the character of the music.

Exercise # 2

The body is in the Primary Posture. With the preservation of the appropriate mental and emotional state taken from the previous exercise, practice conducting with the juxtaposition of two contrasting techniques:

1. In a straightforward striking manner

2. With the implementation of advanced modes - suspended and converted suspended upbeats

Notice which technical approach is more appropriate in revealing the fanfare like (*ff*) character of the music – especially in emphasizing the rhythmical figure:

Exercise # 3

The body is in the Primary Posture. With an appropriate mental and emotional state, practice both manners from Exercise # 2 with and without a reference to the Vicinity of Sound. During practice, compare both approaches and recognize the difference in the physical and mental states of the conducting apparatus. Anticipate which technical approach would correspond best with the character of the music.

14

BATON

A description of the conductor's apparatus will not be complete without mentioning the baton. The baton underwent a significant transformation from an original heavy staff (battuta), paper roll, or long, thick stick to the light and short baton of modern times. The baton's technique must be so clear as to become the live element of the rest of the arm. Only under such conditions will the baton become the genuine transformer of a conductor's finest intentions.[352]

---

[352] Here it is necessary to mention, however, that G. Erzhemsky suggests that the time of the baton is gone. If the conductor's apparatus has developed properly (in advanced and interactive modes), there is no need for the baton to establish instant and productive communication with the orchestra. In Erzhemsky's assumption, conducting without a baton gives the arms an opportunity to instantly and genuinely connect with the sound. Erzhemsky,

> The role of the baton in conducting is crucially important. It is needed for making the wrist motions more visible as well as to serve as an "amplifier" of the expressiveness of the gesture. The intelligent and skillful use of the baton during conducting may provide such an expressiveness, which cannot be achieved by other means.[353]

Some methodologies suggest finding an individual way to hold the baton. Without a proper guide, it is difficult to situate the baton properly and, often, the baton's initial implementation is rather confusing. Here are several suggestions for the baton's position:

A. The baton should not constrain the wrist's mobility.

B. The baton must be situated in a mode conducive to expressive conducting and corresponding with the musical image.

Dirijeru 21 Veka [To the Conductor of the 21st Century], 63-4. As a compromise, the baton can be employed primarily during rehearsals and performances conducted without it. Also, using the baton is advised for conducting ballets and operas.

[353] Musin, 19.

For example, the method of holding the baton with squeezed fingers is less likely to match a light and airy character of some music. On the contrary, holding the baton with two or three fingers will not work well with music utilizing loud dynamics, high energy and strong rhythmical figures.

The position of the baton in the hand should be flexible. The baton in the conductor's hand should "touch the sound". The performance of this technique will emanate the concept of the sound. In one instance the baton "touches the sound" just by its end; in others, by "its entire surface."[354]

1. Place the baton between the first and second joints of the index finger and then place the thumb on top of it (Picture # 1).

2. The short (thicker) end of the baton should touch the palm. Gently wrap the pinky, ring, and middle fingers around the thicker end of the baton (Picture # 2). Put the arm in the downbeat position.

3. Turn the wrist over so that the baton's long end is directed to the left. The wrist and arm should form a

---

[354] Musin, 19 - 21.

line. Tilt the hand up slightly, bending at the wrist. This assists the manifestation of an active arm position. All four fingers should gently cover the thicker end of the baton (Picture # 3).

4. For this position, the end of the baton should touch the lower middle end of the palm. Hold the baton between the tips of the index and middle fingers (without exceeding the first and second joints). The ring finger and pinky are slightly drawn inside, towards the palm, and the thumb is in a straight position along the baton. The ring finger and thumb should slightly support the underside of the baton. The baton is in position when its tip is directed straight forward and is pointed up slightly, making the line of the arm longer and widening the amplitude of the wrist's motion. In this position, the wrist should not help the baton to reach a geometrically perfect line. On the contrary, the wrist must remain in the primary position. Avoid a position in which the wrist moves to the left - it will cause excessive tension (Pictures # 4 and 5).

This position provides an opportunity to depict the gentle nuances of the performance as soon as the baton touches the sound at its end. The advantage of this position is that the wrist can move in isolation from the other parts of the arm and can be used for rounded motions of any sort during the performance of waltzes or triple rhythms. This position also helps to connect one-pattern motions and beats within schemes (e.g., one-pattern 3/4, or 3/4 and 4/4 meters).

5. This position is more difficult: it is better to work on such a position after a certain comfort with the previous positions has been reached. The range for the implementation of expressive gestures is more variable. Hold the baton similarly to the first position, without gripping the baton with the middle, ring, and pinky fingers. The wrist is on its side with the thumb up. This position is comfortable for facilitating left, right, and circular motions supported by the middle and ring fingers. The baton's rounded motion is often used for scherzos (Picture # 6). A similar position also assists in expressing a heroic and majestic character of music (Picture # 7).

Picture # 1

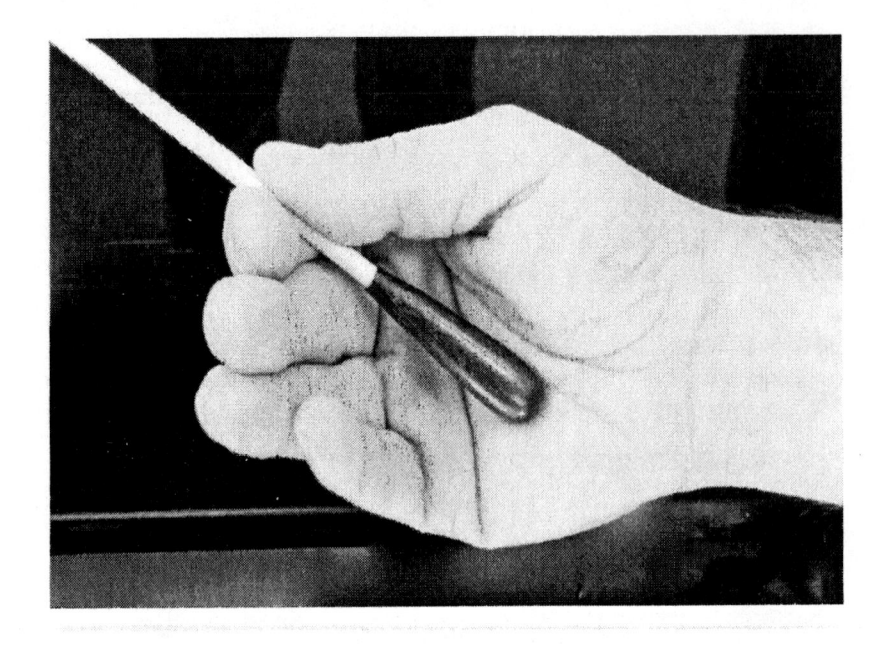

Picture # 2

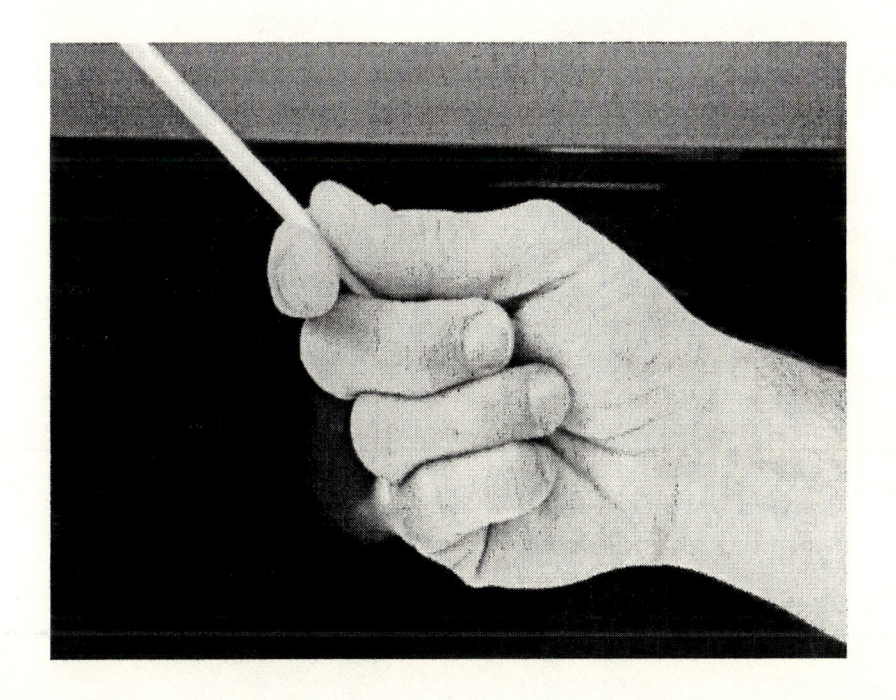

Picture # 3

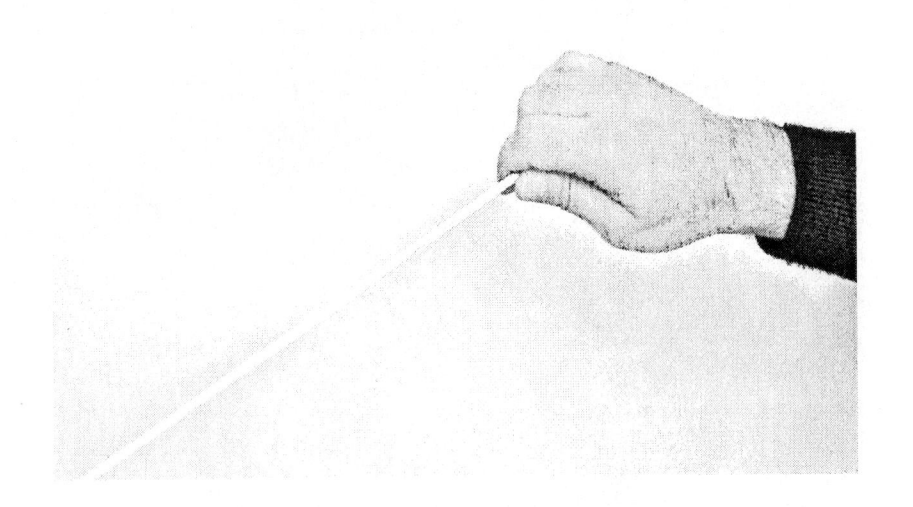

Picture # 4

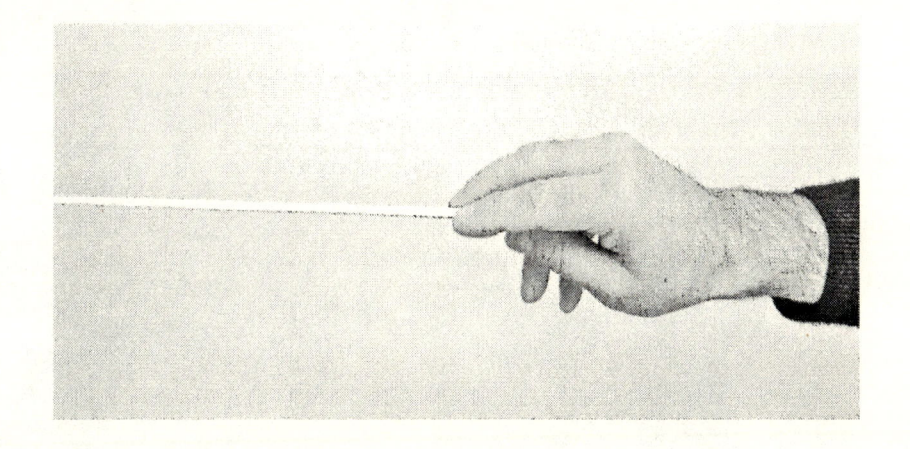

Picture # 5

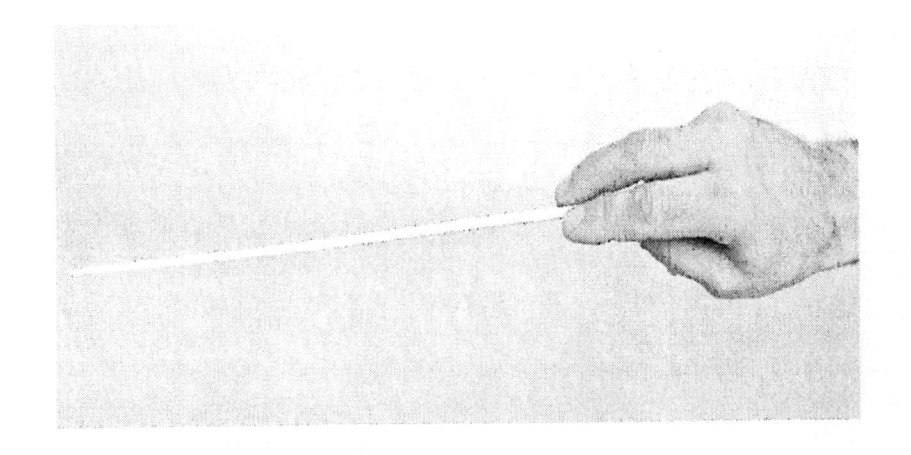

Picture # 6

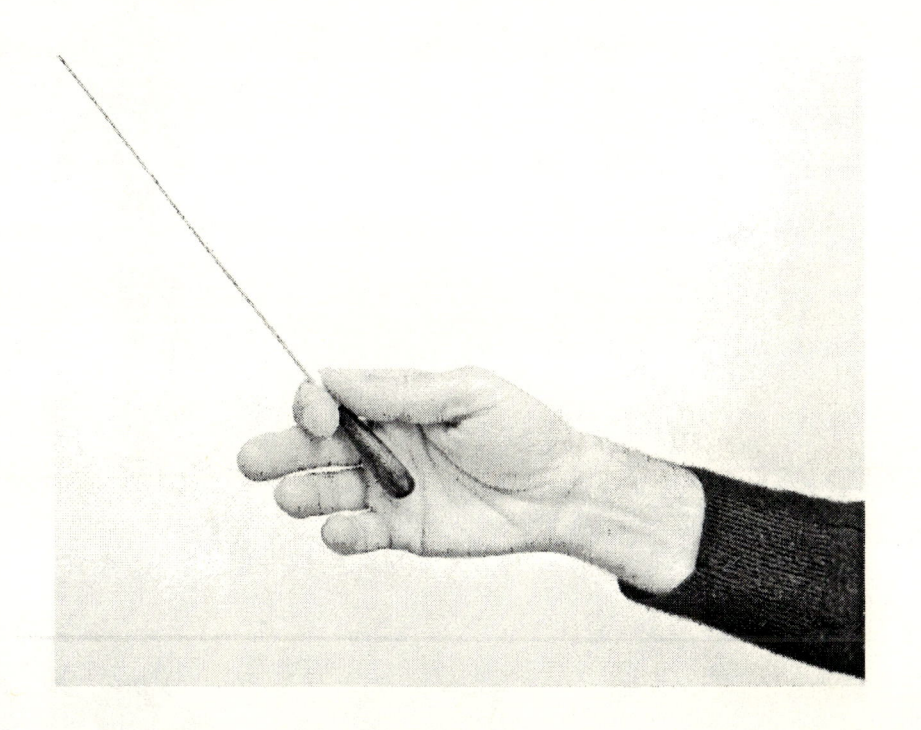

Picture # 7

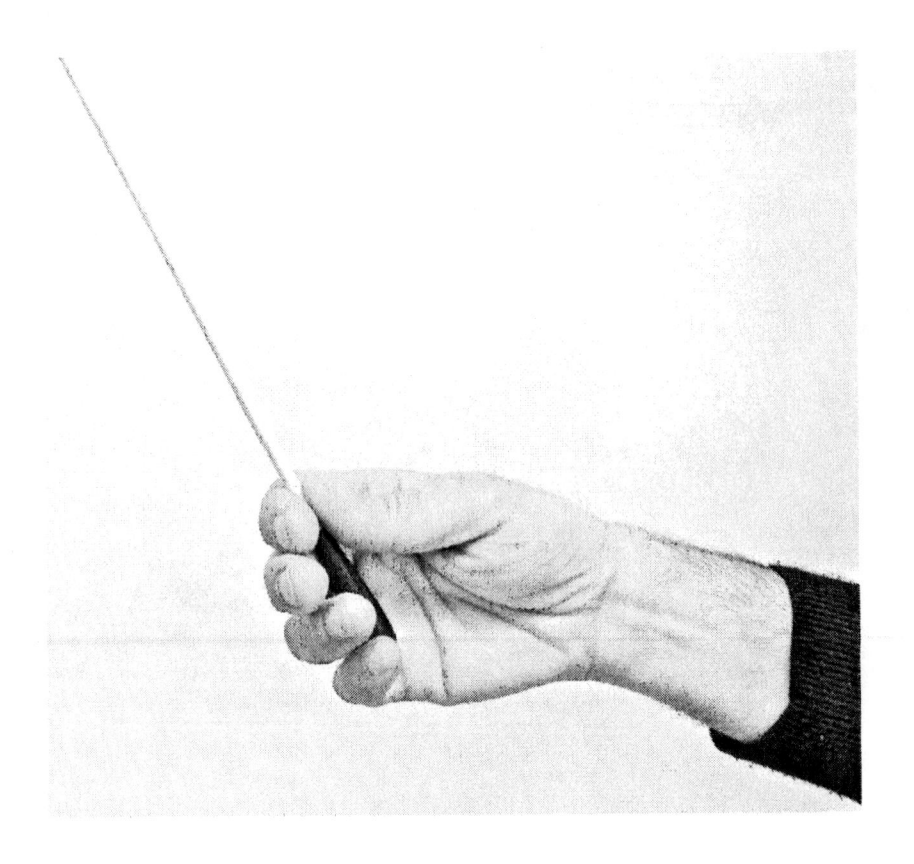

AFTERWORD

From the moment conducting was defined as an independent discipline, the art form has been challenged by questions of balance between clear (a definition that generally assumes the predominance of a mechanistic [schematic] type of conducting) and expressive styles of conducting. Since the days of Berlioz, Liszt, Wagner, Nikish, and Mahler, a clear definition of the balance and unity of clear and expressive manners in the conducting methodology has seemed to be beyond reach. Should the conducting technique be manifested as a beat-striking or in an anticipatory mode with a delayed appearance of sound? Which approach has more advantages? And which way will make conducting a more attractive artistic experience for the audience? Such questions still generate controversy among scholars and conductors, mainly because most of the conducting technique lies beyond empiricism. Common sense dictates that the simple recognition of evident (external) features is not equivalent to the inner substances of the phenomenon.

Even though it was largely customary throughout the nineteenth and the beginning of the twentieth centuries, the modern forceful approach emasculates the essence of conducting itself.

More over, due to rapid social and cultural changes, it deteriorates the whole business of live public orchestral performance. This leads to exhausting orchestral auditions in which musicians must perform a great deal of orchestral excerpts in certain premeditated unified styles, sacrificing individuality for clear rhythms and specific non-selective tones. What is it, if not an attempt to protect orchestral performance from a conductor's (music director's, assistant's or guest conductor's) apparent shortcomings in establishing productive communication? The forceful approach formalized and eventually codified the formerly unique orchestral sound belonging to, and distinguishing, the Chicago Symphony from the Berlin Philharmonic, Cleveland from Los Angeles, New York or Philadelphia, etc. In modern times, all major orchestras have more or less lost their individuality, and perform with similarly common sound.

As with any stagnated tradition, the forceful style is nothing but a well-preserved corpse which has poisoned the orchestral environment. Similar to stagnation in other aspects of human life (social or political), the postponed development of updated paradigms in conducting methods has brought a subtle corruption into the conducting community (and the present system of recruiting in general). In modern times, young conductors seek the career launcher rather than someone who can teach them the deep fundamentals of the profession. This is especially obvious when decisions of hiring and preliminary pre-audition selection are in the hands of 'competent' members of a board which relies upon recommendations of conductors with big names and, often, on non-musical aspects (such as: "I like him/her because he/she looks better on a podium than others", etc.). Unfortunately, such a system takes its toll, along with other problematic aspects of the orchestral business, in the form of a shrinking and aging audience. A conductor can (and only for a limited time) deceive musicians and board members. However, he/she cannot trick the audience for an extended period of time. Among other social and cultural issues, the conductor's physical inhuman use of himself/herself is another reason why orchestral audiences in our time are disappearing. Without the radical modernization of conducting techniques, the role of the conductor soon will be narrowed to that of the specialists in social relations, mainly for the entertainment of an aging audience and only for social communications with the orchestral board.

Refusing to update and accept changes in methods (as unconventional mannerisms), the elite of the conducing community (especially in the academic field) are mainly trying to preserve the *status quo* which once brought them luck (or because it is what they "believe in"). Practically, the main secret of this *status quo*'s preservation is that the illustrative principles of the dynamic generally accepted methodology of conducting (arm positions, schematic metrical motions, application of beats, performance of upbeats, etc.) could be explained by a tutor and learned by a student **within a short period of time** (several months, if not weeks or even days). With minimal effort, however, it can be 'stretched' to years of tutoring.

The conductor is the only performer who does not generate music by direct (physical) contact with an instrument. Therefore, revision of the modern conducting method **requires**

an interdisciplinary approach through the amalgamation of proven positive experience and the support of the scientific disciplines that are directly linked to conducting, such as psychology, social psychology, linguistics, and physiology. Modern professional conducting methods demand a knowledge of these disciplines that is not within the immediate circle of traditional musical training. This approach embodies certain functions that are not only connected with generating musical ideas and their visualizations through conducting techniques, but which are also connected to knowledge of the latest research in human intercommunication and social management. In the modern musical environment, the conductor and the orchestra are inseparable components of the creative intercommunicative process, and they are the basic elements of a unified group that evolved together for creative aspirations.

Over the last two centuries, the art of conducting has been transformed from an approach based upon primitive audible beating to a discipline that incorporates a growing complexity of mental and physical artistic activities. But despite increasing autonomy, most conducting methods still bear an indelible physical stigma inherited from the environment of instrumental performance which reflects a developmental imbalance between the progress of orchestral performance itself and the development of conducting methods. Modern orchestral conducting is primarily based upon non-verbal principles of communication and creative interaction between the conductor and a group of musicians. The practical notion that shapes the specific psychological intercommunicative apparatus supporting the conductor's creative intention is crucial for establishing productive contact between a conductor and an orchestra. This is in addition to the acknowledgment of the principal differences between instrumental and conducting practices, their interdependencies and interactions.

In reality, all of the above suggested methods and techniques are not as complex as they may appear at first. Thus, deeply learning advanced conducting techniques, such as a communicative manifestation of the apparatus, mental anticipation, a sense of the contour of sound, active muscular relaxation, etc., requires time and practice (not to mention score analyses, musicological and theoretical training). All the suggested practical and methodological approaches are intended to contribute to the natural essence of the complex phenomenon of conducting. Essentially, this book is an effort to reevaluate the existing generally accepted methodology and to explain some recent developments in conducting skills.

TRANSLATED EXCERPTS

[Законы речевой деятельности, строящиеся на фундаменте психомоторики, абсолютно едины для всех видов межличностных коммуникаций, в том числе для общения дирижера и оркестра.] G. Erzhemsky, *Dirijeru 21 Veka* [To the Conductor of the 21st Century], p. 67 (131; Footnote 220).

[...основная задача координации движений - преодоление избыточного числа степеней свободы, то есть уменьшение числа независимых переменных, управляющих движением.] Alexei Alexeevich Leontiev, *Deyatel'nii Um. Deyatel'nost'. Znak. Lichnost'* [The Active Mind. Activity. Sign. Personality] p. 123 (162; Footnote 271).

[Смысл, извлекаемый реципиентом из произведения искусства - это всегда его собственный смысл, обусловленный контекстом его собственной жизни и его личности, а не смысл, "заложенный" художником в структуре произведения; вместе с тем, структура произведения строится художником - осознание или неосознание - таким образом, чтобы передать или, точнее, подсказать людям совершенно определенный смысл. В силу наличия общих для многих людей условий жизнедеятельности и, тем самым, общих задач на смысл, о чем говорилось выше, оказывается возможной сравнительно адекватная передача смысла. Тезис о коммуницируемости личностных смыслов можно признать правомерным с учетом этих оговорок.] Dmitri Alekseyevich Leontiev, *Vvedenie v Psihologiyu Iskusstva* [Introduction of the Psychology of Art], pp. 15-16 (81; Footnote 147).

["Художник обращается к эмоционально-акустическим и эмоционально-визуальным единицам своеобразного кода, языка, в котором закреплены определенные смыслы и значения. Так, высокие тона однозначно воспринимаются как светлые, острые, тонкие, а низкие - как темные, массивные, толстые...; симметрия вызывает ощущение покоя, асимметрия - беспокойства; прямая вертикаль - стремление вверх; горизонталь - пассивна, диагональ - активна"] G. *Prazdnikov, Napravlennost' Hudojestvennoi Formi//Hudojnik i Publika* [The Purposefulness of the Artistic Form//The Artist and Audience] p. 51, quoted in Dmitri Leontiev, *Vvedenie v Psihologiyu Iskusstva* [Introduction of the Psychology of Art], p. 17 (121; Footnote 202).

[Если мы рассмотрим технику игры на музыкальных инструментах, то увидим, что она состоит из ряда технических движений, которые следует изучить как можно более тщательно. Однако освоенный инструменталистом двигательный прием в дальнейшем, связываясь со звуковым результатом, перестает им замечаться как некое движение.

Исполнитель мыслит музыкальными образами, и пальцы его послушно выполняют все те движенния, которые необходимы для адекватного воплощения его музыкальных мыслей. Музыкант вовсе не думает о самих движениях, он оперирует главным образом ощущениями от движений. Именно они позволяют ему извлекать звуки определённой силы, колорита, помогают связывать звуки в музыкальные фразы и т.д. Музыкант "говорит" руками то, о чем думает, он мыслит звуками. Точно так же, говоря вслух, излагая свои мысли, мы не думаем о необходимых для этого движениях губ, языка, гортани.] Musin, Ilia *Tehnika Dirijirovaniya* [The Technique of Conducting], p. 4-5 (37; Footnote 70).

[Общеизвестно, что любое действие, выполняемое совместно несколькими лицами, может быть начато строго одновременно лишь по сигналу звуковому (слово, стук, пение и т.п.) или двигательному (взмах руки). Но никакой единичный звук или движение руки не станет сигналом, ибо будет воспринят как неожиданный. Чтобы сигнал ответил своему назначению, он должен подготовить сознание участвующих к совместному действию, создать у них одинаковую ритмическую настройку.] Musin, Ilia *Tehnika Dirijirovaniya* [The Technique of Conducting], p. 56 (75; Footnote 130).

[Для отображения в жесте дирижера силы, энергии необходимо не мышечное напряжение, а действие, дающее представление об этой энергии.] Musin, Ilia *Tehnika Dirijirovaniya* [The Technique of Conducting], p. 109 (85;

Footnote 156).

[Пальцами руки дирижер получает специфическое ощущение соприкосновения со звуком, от чего зависит, в частности, дирижерское туше.] Musin, Ilia *Tehnika Dirijirovaniya* [The Technique of Conducting], p. 17 (89; Footnote 165).

[Действие дирижера воспринимается исполнителями в связи с определенной ситуацией, создаваемой процессом исполнения. Однако дирижер должен учитывать, что у музыкантов не возникает нужных ассоциаций, если в жестах не будет содержаться ничего из тех движений, которыми мы обычно пользуемся в повседневной деятельности.] Musin, Ilia *Tehnika Dirijirovaniya* [The Technique of Conducting], p. 210 (123; Footnote 205).

[У дирижера подобное соотвествие между движением и его результатом (за исключением определения темпа) практически существовать не может. Одно и то же движение дирижера может вызвать различный результат, и наоборот, один и тот же результат может быть достигнут разными способами.] Musin, Ilia *Tehnika Dirijirovaniya* [The Technique of Conducting], p. 290 (144; Footnote 242).

["… когда дирижировал Вагнер, уоркестрантов совершенно не было ощушения что ими кто-то управляет. Каждому казалось, что он руководится лишь собственным музыкальным чутьем и, однако, получался великопепный ансамбль. То была могучая воля Вагнера, которая бессознательно, но упорно овладевала волей каждого оркестранта, и каждый исполнитель, чувствуя себя свободным, на самом деле лишь следовал указаниям руководителя."] Weingartner, Felix, *O Dirijirovanii* [About Conducting], стр. 15, quoted in Musin, *Tehnika Dirijirovaniya* [The Technique of Conducting], p. 152 (154; Footnote 262).

[Вместо отображения логически связанных построений дирижер тактированием механически расчленяет музыкальную ткань. Подчеркнутое ударом ауфтакта обозначение каждой доли обособляет ее, чему способствует также и показ каждой доли в разные стороны. Метрические схемы приводят к тому, что метротакт приобретает нсизменную структуру с постоянством сильных и слабых долей. Таким образом, в жестовом отображении тактирование состоит из ряда повторяющихся циклических движений, отделяющих одну долю от другой. Дирижер словно повторяет одно и то же движение, только направляя его в разные, не связанные друг с другом точки. В музыке же звуки взаимосвязаны, образуют целостные музыкальные построения.] Musin, Ilia *Tehnika Dirijirovaniya* [The Technique of Conducting], p. 189 (180; Footnote 287).

[Под этим будем подразумевать типовые движения рук, являющиеся основой всех приемов дирижерской техники. Постановка заключается в выработке таких форм движений, которые наиболее рациональны, естественны и базируются на внутренней (мышечной) свободе. Аппаратом, с помощью которого дирижер управляет оркестром, являются его руки, их многообразные движения, сведенные в стройную систему дирижирования. Однако для дирижера далеко не безразличны мимика, положение корпуса, головы и даже ног.] Musin, Ilia *Tehnika Dirijirovaniya* [The Technique of Conducting], p. 15 (216; Footnote 315).

[Одна нога иногда несколько выставляется вперед. Если дирижеру во время исполнения приходится обращаться преимущественно в левую сторону, то вперед выставляется правая нога, при обращении в правую - левая. Перемены положения ног делаются незаметно.] Musin, Ilia *Tehnika Dirijirovaniya* [The Technique of Conducting], p. 16 (219. Footnote 317).

[Общеизвестно, что внешний вид, осанка человека свидетельствуют о его душевных свойствах, эмоциональном состоянии, темпераменте. Внешний вид дирижера должен показывать наличие воли, активности, решительности и энергии.] Musin, Ilia *Tehnika Dirijirovaniya* [The Technique of Conducting], p. 15 (222; Footnote 318).

[Большое значение в выработке типовых дирижерских движений имеет основное положений рук во время дирижирования. От этого во многом зависит свобода, естественность и характер движений.] Musin, Ilia *Tehnika Dirijirovaniya* [The Technique of Conducting], p. 16 (223; Footnote 319).

[В начале обучения развитию технических навыков должно быть уделено достаточное внимание. Следует иметь в виду, что многие из начинающих дирижеров приходя в класс, уже имея некоторые навыки, обычно в виде знакомства с элементарными приемами тактирования; приобретенные самостояельно, они, как правило, очень несовершенны и потому не могут служить базой дальнейшего обучения. Недостаточно отработанные движения не только не позволяют совершенствовать технику дирижирования, но и не дают возможности избавиться от имеющихся дефектов. Чаще всего они проявляются в хаотичности и некоординированности движений, приводящих к неясности схем тактирования, скованности, напряженности жестов, делающих их маловыразительными.

Другая крайность педагогического метода состоит в том, что обучающийся долгое время осваивает движения и приемы изолированно от музыки. Если учащийся не связывает свой жест с определенной целью управления исполнением, то такой жест теряет свой смысл и грозит превратиться в отвлеченную гимнастику. Истина, на наш взгляд, находится где-то посередине. Постановку рук дирижера, изучение основных движений и приемов тактирования целесообразно проводить на специальных упражнениях вне музыки.] Musin, Ilia *Tehnika Dirijirovaniya* [The Technique of Conducting], p. 14 (224; Footnote 321).

[Положение рук должно быть срединным, предоставляющим возможность делать движения в любую сторону- вверх, вниз, к себе, от себя.] Musin, Ilia *Tehnika Dirijirovaniya* [The Technique of Conducting], p. 16 (225; Footnote 322).

[В функции ауфтакта входит: а) определение начального момента исполнения (подготовка совместного действия, дыхания) и начала каждой доли в такте; б) определение темпа; в) определение ритма доли как дуольной или триольной; г) определение динамики; д) определение характера атаки звука (степени его остроты или протяженности); е) определения образного содержания музыки.] Musin, Ilia *Tehnika Dirijirovaniya* [The Technique of Conducting], p. 55 (238; Footnote 325).

[Наиболее простой вид триольной доли - три звука - это вальсы, многие скерцо. Сложнее для дирижирования счетные доли, содержащие шесть звуков (Шуберт. Седьмая симфония, Скерцо). И, наконец, наибольшего внимания требует триольная счетная доля, содержащая синкопированный ритм (Глинка. " Князь Холмский", Увертюра; Брамс. Третья симфония).] Musin, Ilia *Tehnika Dirijirovaniya* [The Technique of Conducting], p. 59 (248; Footnote 331).

[Часто молодой дирижер при переходе с дуольного ритма на триольный и обратно не только не помогает исполнителю, но и мешает ему. Приноровив свой жест к дуольному ритму, он в момент перехода на триоли не изменяет его и тем самым дезорганизует исполнение. Затруднения увеличиваются, если смены ритма следуют одна за другой и сочетаются с изменением темпа.] Musin, Ilia *Tehnika Dirijirovaniya* [The Technique of Conducting], p. 59 (249-250; Footnote 333).

[Во время дирижирования рука дирижера действует как слаженный аппарат, части которого взаимодействует друг с другом. Любое движение той или иной части руки не может совершаться без участия остальных ее частей. Самому изолированному, казалось бы, движению кисти помогает предплечье и плечо. Поэтому, когда говориться о самостоятельных движениях кисти или предплечья, то под этим подразумевается их доминирующее значение в жесте. Каждая из частей руки имеет вместе с тем свои выразительные особенности и выполняет специфические функции.] Musin, Ilia *Tehnika Dirijirovaniya* [The Technique of Conducting], p. 17 (253-4; Footnote 334).

[Наиболее подвижная и гибкая часть руки - кисть - предназначена для выполнения тонких и разнообразнейших движений : ударных, бросковых, кругообразных, гладящих, отталкивающих, подбрасыбающих и пр. ... Кисть - передатчик всевозможных импульсов, тонких двигательных ощущений, на основе которых и возможна трансформация музыкальных представлений дирижера в выразительный жест.] Musin, Ilia *Tehnika Dirijirovaniya* [The Technique of Conducting], p. 17 (254; Footnote 335).

[Умелое применение обращенных ауфтактов помогает дирижеру почувствовать так называемое ощущение звука в руке, иначе говоря, ощущение «материальности» звучания - важнейшего выразительного средства управление исполнением. Соотвественно требованиям исполнения дирижер имеет возможность «оперировать» звуками как некой звуковой массой - вытягивать ее, уплотнять, сжимать или, наоборот, придавать ей легкость, воздушность и т.п.] Musin, Ilia *Tehnika Dirijirovaniya* [The Technique of Conducting], p. 84 (287; Footnote 340).

[Сравните, например, движение руки, производящей удар по какому-нибудь предмету, с движением, которым рука стремится подхватить падающий предмет. В первом случае активное участие мышц, направляющих руку вниз, не прекратится до момента удара; во втором, поскольку движение не направлено к удару, остановка руки произойдет не в результате толчка (соприкосновения с предметом, на который обращен удар), а вследствии мгновенного ее торможения.] Musin, Ilia *Tehnika Dirijirovaniya* [The Technique of Conducting], p. 67 (125, 289; Footnote 211, 341).

[Освоив все формы ауфтактов и движений тактирования, дирижер на практике найдет случаи наилучшего применения их соответственно задачам музыкальной выразительностию.] Musin, Ilia *Tehnika Dirijirovaniya* [The Technique of Conducting], p.85 (293; Footnote 342).

[Роль палочки в дирижировании исключительно велика. Она необходима для того, чтобы сделать более заметными движения кисти. Важнейшее ее назначение - служить средством усиления выразительности жеста. Разумное и умелое пользование палочкой дает дирижеру такие средства экспрессии, какие не могут быть достигнуты другими способами.] Musin, Ilia *Tehnika Dirijirovaniya* [The Technique of Conducting], p.19 (344; Footnote 353)

BIBLIOGRAPHY

BOOKS

Adler, Samuel. *The Study of Orchestration*. 2nd ed. New York: W. W. Norton and Company, 1989.

Alcantara, Pedro de. *Indirect Procedures. A Mucisian's Guide to the Alexander Technique*. Clarendon Press, Oxford, 1997.

Anokhin, Petr K. *Ocherki po Fisiologii Funktsionalnykh Sistem* [The Essays About Physiology of Functional System]. Moscow: Akademia Nauk, [Academy of Science], 1975.

_____. *APA Dictionary of Psychology*, VandenBos, Gary R., PhD, Editor in Chief. Washington, DC: American Psychological Association, 2007.

Applebaum, Samuel and Roth, Henry. *The Way They Play*. New York: Paganiniana Publications, Inc., 1981.

_____. *Baker's Biographical Dictionary of 20th Century Classical Musicians*, Slonimsky, Nicolas and Kuhn, Laura, Editors. New York: Schirmer Books, 1997.

_____. *Baker's Biographical Dictionary of Musicians*. Slonimsky, Nicolas, ed., 6th Edition. New York: Schirmer Books, 1978.

_____. *Baker's Biographical Dictionary of Musicians*. Slonimsky, Nicolas, ed., 8th Edition. New York: Schirmer Books, 1992.

Barenboim, Daniel. *A Life in Music*. New York: Charles Schribner's Sons, 1992.

Benson, Herbert, M.D. with Klipper, Miriam Z. *The Relaxation Response*. New York: HarperCollins Publishers Inc., 2001.

Berger, Nina Alexandrovna. *Garmonia Kak Prostranstvennaja Kategorija Muziki* [Harmony As a Dimensional Category of Music] *Dissertazija Na Soiskanie Uchenoi Stepeni Kandidata Iskusstvovedenija* [PhD Dissertation]. (Leningrad Conservatory of Music after Nikolai

Rimsky-Korsakov) Leningrad. 1979.

Bernstein, Nikolai A. *The Coordination and Regulation of Movements*. Oxford: Pergamon Press, 1967.

Bodegraven, Paul Van and Wilson, Robert Harry. *The School Music Conductor: Problems and Practices in Choral and Instrumental Conducting*. Chicago: Hall & McCreary Company, 1942.

_____. *The Body as a Medium of Expression*. Essays Based on a Course of Lectures Given at the Institute of Contemporary Arts, London, Edited by Benthall, Jonathan and Polhemus, Ted. New York: E. P. Dutton& Co., Inc., 1975.

Bolshakov, V. Yu. *Evolutionary Theory of Behavior.* St. Petersburg : St. Petersburg University Press, 2001.

Chesterman, Robert, ed. *Conversations with conductors*. London: Robson Books Ltd., 1977.

_____. *Collins Encyclopedia of Music*. Sir Jack Westrup and Harrison, F. L1, Editors. Revised by Conrad Wilson. London: Chancellor Press, 1984.

Coon, Dennis. *Essential of Psychology, Exploration and*

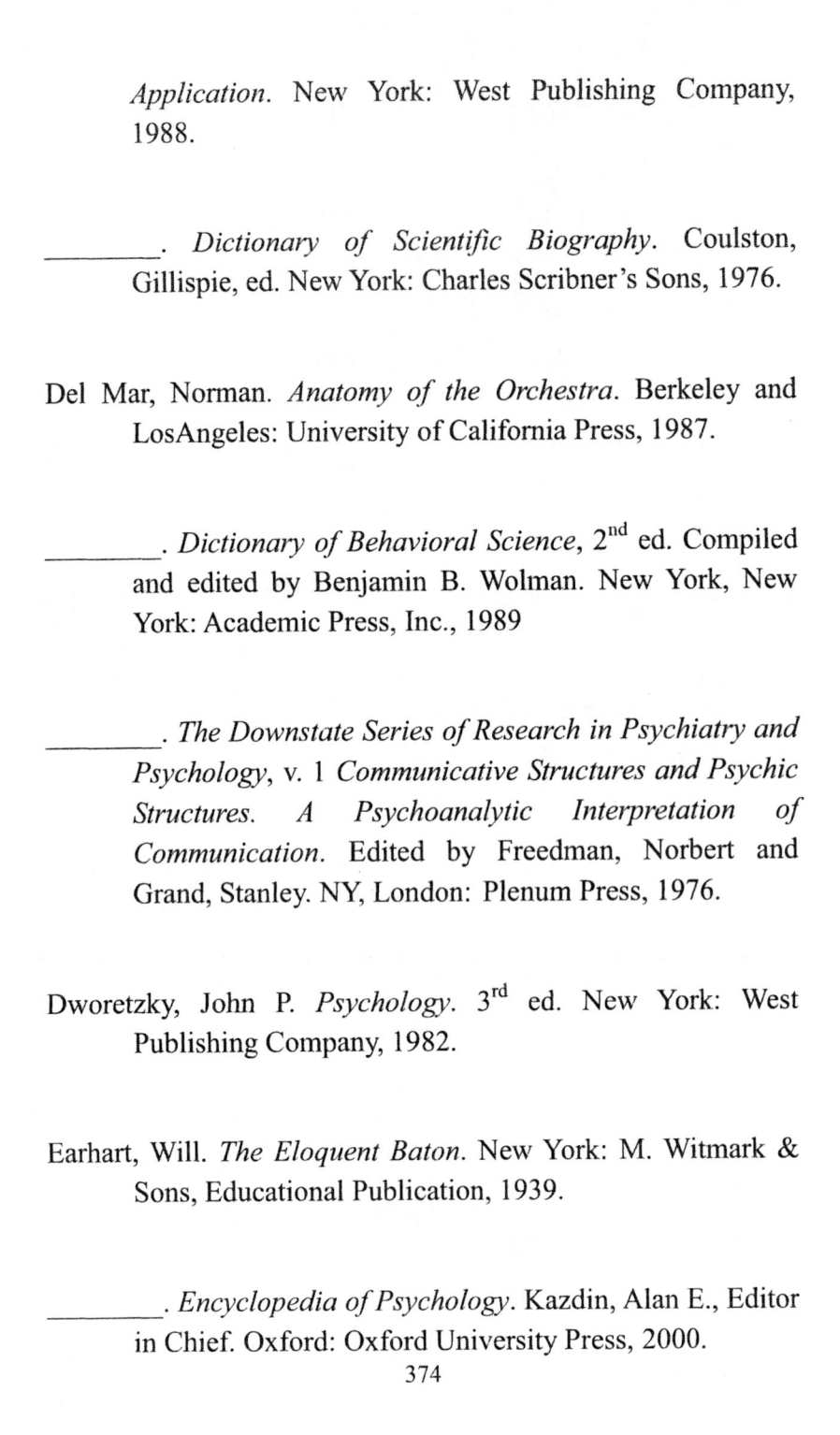

Application. New York: West Publishing Company, 1988.

_____. *Dictionary of Scientific Biography*. Coulston, Gillispie, ed. New York: Charles Scribner's Sons, 1976.

Del Mar, Norman. *Anatomy of the Orchestra*. Berkeley and LosAngeles: University of California Press, 1987.

_____. *Dictionary of Behavioral Science*, 2nd ed. Compiled and edited by Benjamin B. Wolman. New York, New York: Academic Press, Inc., 1989

_____. *The Downstate Series of Research in Psychiatry and Psychology*, v. 1 *Communicative Structures and Psychic Structures. A Psychoanalytic Interpretation of Communication*. Edited by Freedman, Norbert and Grand, Stanley. NY, London: Plenum Press, 1976.

Dworetzky, John P. *Psychology*. 3rd ed. New York: West Publishing Company, 1982.

Earhart, Will. *The Eloquent Baton*. New York: M. Witmark & Sons, Educational Publication, 1939.

_____. *Encyclopedia of Psychology*. Kazdin, Alan E., Editor in Chief. Oxford: Oxford University Press, 2000.

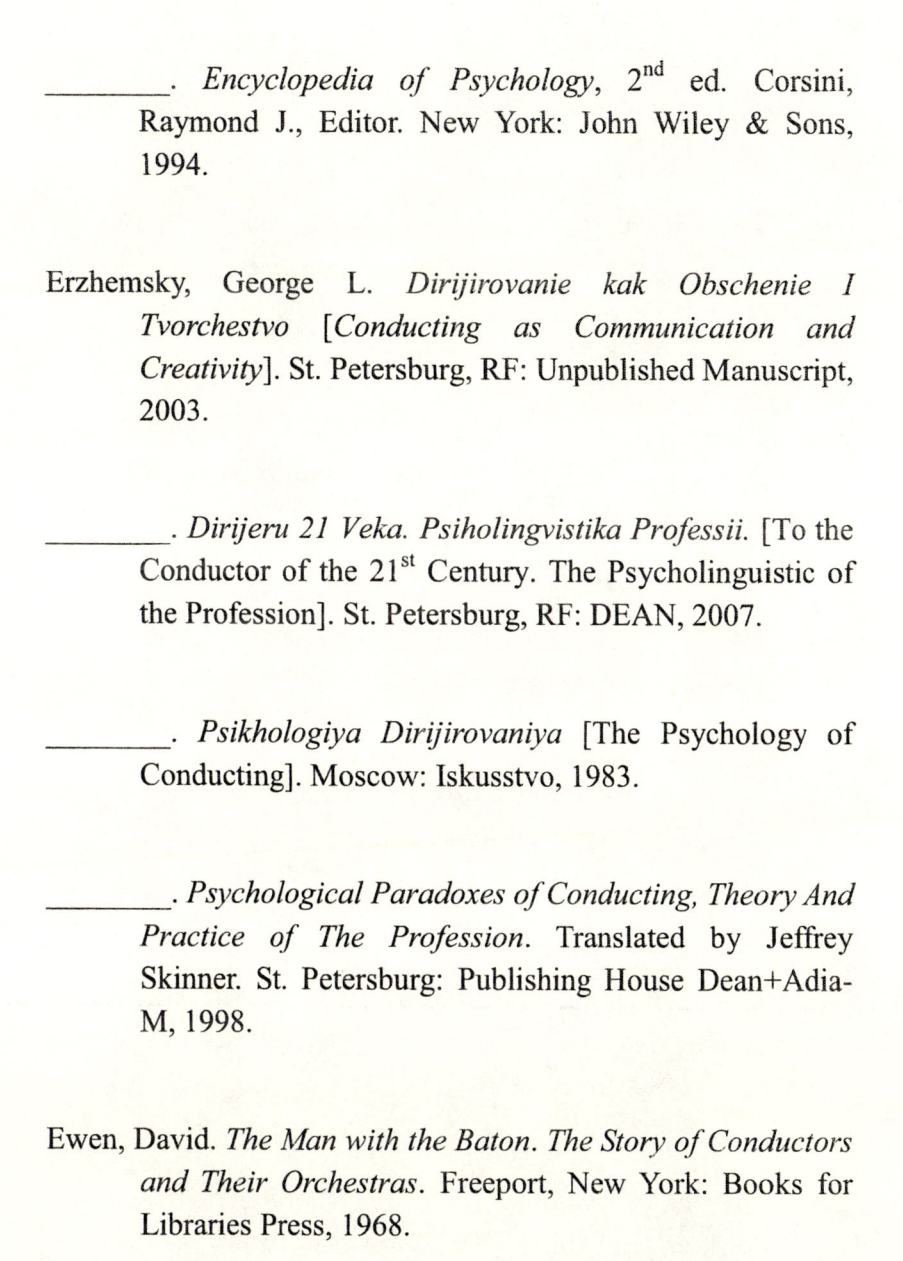

_____. *Encyclopedia of Psychology*, 2nd ed. Corsini, Raymond J., Editor. New York: John Wiley & Sons, 1994.

Erzhemsky, George L. *Dirijirovanie kak Obschenie I Tvorchestvo* [*Conducting as Communication and Creativity*]. St. Petersburg, RF: Unpublished Manuscript, 2003.

_____. *Dirijeru 21 Veka. Psiholingvistika Professii.* [To the Conductor of the 21st Century. The Psycholinguistic of the Profession]. St. Petersburg, RF: DEAN, 2007.

_____. *Psikhologiya Dirijirovaniya* [The Psychology of Conducting]. Moscow: Iskusstvo, 1983.

_____. *Psychological Paradoxes of Conducting, Theory And Practice of The Profession.* Translated by Jeffrey Skinner. St. Petersburg: Publishing House Dean+Adia-M, 1998.

Ewen, David. *The Man with the Baton. The Story of Conductors and Their Orchestras.* Freeport, New York: Books for Libraries Press, 1968.

Farberman, Harold. *The Art of Conducting Technique: A New Perspective.* Warner Brothers Publications, 1997.

Galamian, Ivan. *Principles of Violin Playing and Teaching*. London: Faber and Faber, 1964.

Galkin, Elliot W. *A History of Orchestral Conducting in Theory and Practice*. New York: Pendragon Press, Stuyvesant, 1988.

Gamble, Teri Kwal and Gamble, Michael. *Communication Works*. Third Edition. NY: McGraw-Hill Inc., 1990.

Ginzburg, Leo M., Editor. *Dirijerskoe Ispolnitel'stvo, Practika, Istoria. Estetica* [The Performance of Conducting, Practice. History. Aesthetic]. Moscow: Muzika, 1975.

Green, Elizabeth A. H. *The Modern Conductor*. Fourth Edition. Englewood Cliffs, New Jersey: Prentice-Hall, Inc., 1987.

Grosbayne, Benjamin. *Techniques of Modern Orchestral Conducting*. Cambridge, Massachusetts: Harvard University Press, 1956.

Guyton, Arthur. *Textbook of Medical Physiology*, 8th ed. New York: W. B. Saunders Co. & Harcourt Brace Jovanovich, Inc., 1991.

_____. *Hands, Words, and Mind: On the Structuralization of*

Body Movements During Discourse and the Capacity for Verbal Representation by Freedman, Norbert in The Downstate Series of Research in Psychiatry and Psychology, v. 1 *Communicative Structures and Psychic Structures. A Psychoanalytic Interpretation of Communication.* Edited by Freedman, Norbert and Grand, Stanley. NY, London: Plenum Press, 1976.

Holden, Raymond. *The Virtuoso Conductors. The Central European Tradition from Wagner to Karajan.* New York and London: Yale University Press, 2005.

Holmes, Malcolm H. *Conducting an Amateur Orchestra.* Cambridge, Massachusetts: Harvard University Press, 1951.

Hunsberger, Donald and Ernst, Roy, E. *The Art of Conducting, Second Edition.* New York, McGraw-Hill, Inc., 1983.

Jordan, James. *Evoking Sound, Fundamentals of Choral Conducting and Rehearsing.* Chicago: GIA Publications, Inc. 1996.

Kagan, Jerome and Havemann, Ernest. *Psychology: An Introduction*, 2nd ed. New York: Harcourt Brace Jovanovich Inc., 1972.

Kahn, Emil. *Elements of Conducting.* Second Edition. New York: Schirmer Books, A Division of Macmillan Publishing Co., Inc., London: Macmillan Publishing Co., 1965.

Kohut, Daniel, L. and Grant, Joe, W. *Learning to Conduct and Rehearse.* Englewood Cliffs, New Jersey, Prentice-Hall, Inc., 1990.

Kondrashin, Kirill. *Mir Dirijera* [The Conductor's World]. Leningrad: Muzika, 1976.

_____. *O Dirijerskom Iskusstve* [About the Art of Conducting]. Moscow: Muzika, 1970.

_____. *Vospominaniya* [Memoirs] (Moscow: Muzika, 1970).

_____. *Language Functions and Brain Organization.* Edited by Sidney J. Segalowitz. New York, London: Academic Press, 1983.

Laszlo, Judith I. *Perceptual-Motor Behavior, Developmental Assessment and Therapy.* New York: Praeger Publishers, 1985.

Leibowitz, Judith and Connington, Bill. *The Alexander*

Technique. New York: Harper and Row, Publishers, 1990.

Leinsdorf, Erich. *The Composer's Advocate: A Radical Orthodoxy for Musicians*. New Haven and London: Yale University Press, 1981.

Leontiev, Alexei Alexeevich. *Deyatel'nii Um. Deyatel'nost'. Znak. Lichnost'* [The Active Mind. Activity. Sign. Personality]. Moscow: Smisl, 2001.

Leontiev, Dmitri A. *Vvedenie v Psihologiyu Iskusstva* [Introduction of the Psychology of Art]. Moscow: Moscow University Press, 1996.

Losev, A. F. *Problema Simvola I Realisticheskoie Iskusstvo* [The Problem of Symbol and Realistic Art]. Moscow: Gosizdat, 1976.

Lumley, John and Springthorpe, Nigel. *The Art of Conducting. A Guide to Essential Skills*. London: Rhinegold Publishing Limited, 1989.

Malko, Nicolai A. *The Conductor and His Baton. The Fundamentals of the Technic of Conducting*. Copenhagen: Wilhelm Hansen, 1950.

_____. *Osnovi Techniki Dirijirovaniya* [The Fundamentals of the Technic of Conducting]. Moscow: Muzgiz, 1965.

_____. *Vospominaniya. Stat'i. Pis'ma.* [Memoirs. Articles. Letters]. Leningrad: Muzika, 1972.

Meier, Gustav. *The Score, The Orchestra, and The Conductor.* Oxford University Press, NY, NY 2009.

Musin, Iliya A. *Technique of Conducting.* [Tehnika Dirijirovaniya] St. Petersburg: Dean-Adia-M, 1995.

_____. *Vado Mecum.* Unpublished manuscript.

_____. *New Grove Dictionary of Music and Musicians.* Sadie, Stanley, Editor. London: Macmillan Publishers Limited, 1980.

_____. *New Grove Dictionary of Music and Musicians.* Sadie, Stanley, Editor. London: Macmillan Publishers Limited, 2001.

_____. *Non-Verbal Communication.* Hinde, R. A., Editor. Cambridge: University Press, 1972.

Pavlov, Ivan P. *Polnoe Sobranie Sochinenii* [Completed

Collection of Works]. 2nd ed. Moscow: Nauka, 1951.

Pickering, David, ed. *International Dictionary of Theatre - 3. Actors. Directors and Designers.* New York, London: St. James Press, 1996.

Piston, Walter. *Orchestration.* Ney York: W. W. Norton & Company Inc., 1955.

Prausnitz, Frederick. *Score and Podium.* New York, London: W. W. Norton & Company, 1983.

Prokhorov, A M. and Waxman, Maron, L., Editors. *Great Soviet Encyclopedia* [Bol'shaya Sovetskaya Entsiklopediia]. A Translation of the Third Edition, New York, London: Macmillan, Inc., Collier Macmillan Publishers, 1978.

Rhoades, Rodney A. and Tanner, George A. *Medical Physiology.* Second Edition. Philadelphia, Lippincott Williams & Wilkins, 2003.

Robinson, Paul. *Karajan.* Toronto: Lester and Orpen Limited, 1975.

Rudolf, Max. *The Grammar of Conducting.* New York: G. Schirmer, Inc., 1950.

Saito, Hideo. *The Saito Conducting Method by Hideo Saito*. Tokyo: Min-On Concert Association & Ongaku No Tomo Sha Corp., 1988.

Scherchen, Heinrich. *Handbook of Conducting*. London: Oxford University Press, 1935.

Schmid, Adolf. *The Language of the Baton*. New York: G. Schirmer, Inc., 1937.

Schonberg, Harold C. *The Great Conductor*. New York: Simon and Schuster, 1967.

_____. *Shorter Oxford English Dictionary. On Historical Principles*. 6th Edition. New York: Oxford University Press, 2007.

Schuller, Gunther. *The Complete Conductor*. New York: Oxford University Press, 1997.

Spitzer, John and Zaslaw, Neal. *The Birth of the Orchestra*. New York: Oxford University Press, 2004.

Stanislavsky, Konstantin S. *An Actor Prepares*. New York: Theatre Arts Books, 1965.

_____. *Polnoe Sobranie Sochnenii* [Complete Edition of Works]. Moscow: Iskusstvo, 1989.

_____. *Stedman's Medical Dictionary*. 25th ed. Basmajian, John B., ed. Baltimore: Williams and Wilkins Company, 1990.

_____. *Stedman's Medical Dictionary*. 28th edition, Illustrated in Color. Baltimore: Lippincott Williams and Wilkins, 2006.

Stoddard, Hope. *Symphony Conductors of the U.S.A.* New York: Thomas Y. Crowell Company, 1957.

Stoessel, Albert. *The Technic of the Baton*. New York: Carl Fisher, Inc., 1928.

_____. *Taber's Cyclopedic Medical Dictionary*. Thomas Clayton L., ed. Philadelphia: Davis Company, 1989.

Victor, Maurice and Ropper, Allan H. *Principal of Neurology*. 7th ed. New York: McGraw-Hill Medical Publishing Division, 2001.

Vygotsky, Lev S. *Iskusstvo i Mirovozzrenie* [The Art and Inner-Outlook]. 2nd ed. Moscow: Iskusstvo, 1968.

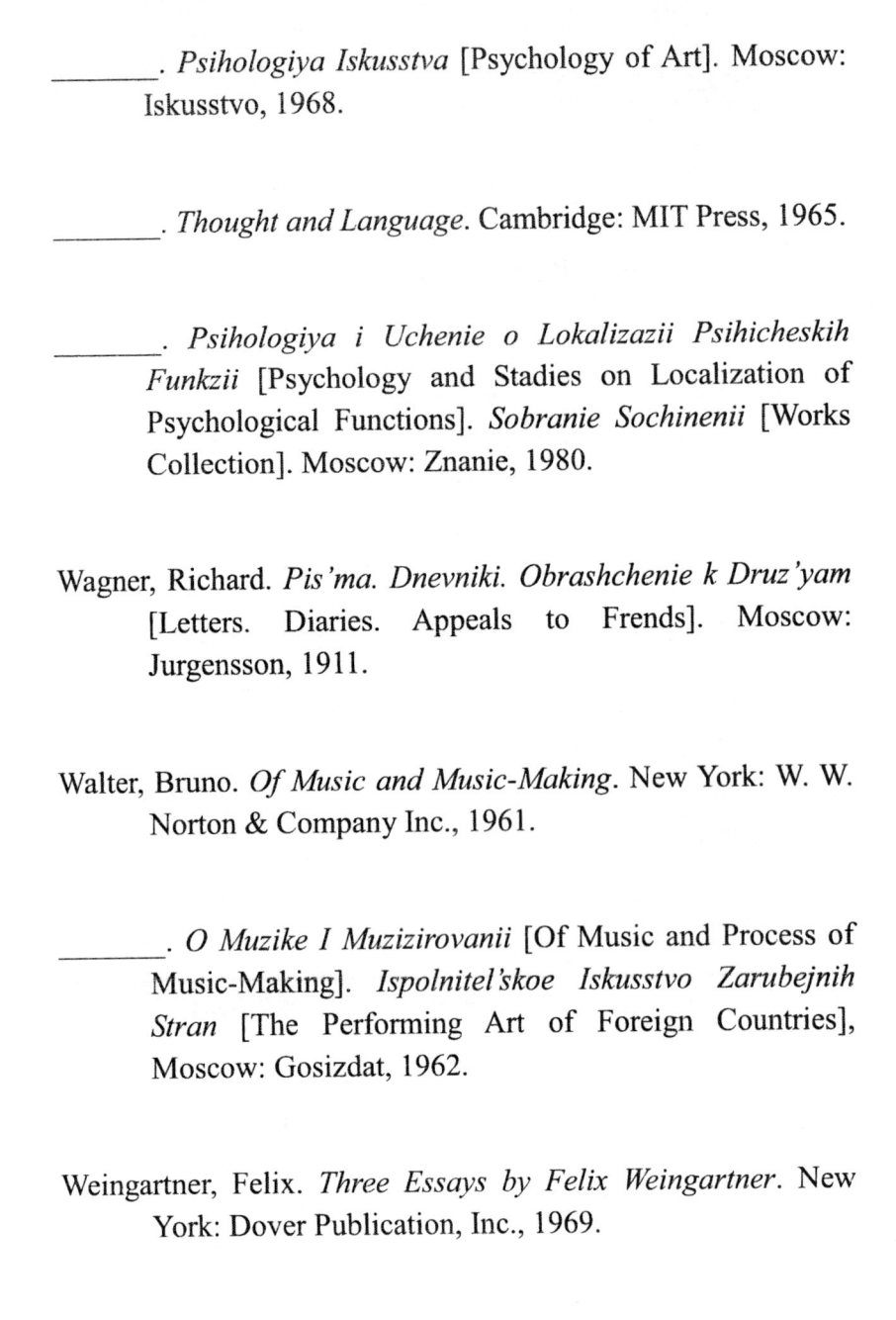

_____. *Psihologiya Iskusstva* [Psychology of Art]. Moscow: Iskusstvo, 1968.

_____. *Thought and Language*. Cambridge: MIT Press, 1965.

_____. *Psihologiya i Uchenie o Lokalizazii Psihicheskih Funkzii* [Psychology and Stadies on Localization of Psychological Functions]. *Sobranie Sochinenii* [Works Collection]. Moscow: Znanie, 1980.

Wagner, Richard. *Pis'ma. Dnevniki. Obrashchenie k Druz'yam* [Letters. Diaries. Appeals to Frends]. Moscow: Jurgensson, 1911.

Walter, Bruno. *Of Music and Music-Making*. New York: W. W. Norton & Company Inc., 1961.

_____. *O Muzike I Muzizirovanii* [Of Music and Process of Music-Making]. *Ispolnitel'skoe Iskusstvo Zarubejnih Stran* [The Performing Art of Foreign Countries], Moscow: Gosizdat, 1962.

Weingartner, Felix. *Three Essays by Felix Weingartner*. New York: Dover Publication, Inc., 1969.

Wiener, Norbert. *Cybernetic. Or Control and Communication in the Animal and the Machine*. New York: The

Technology Press, John Wiley & Sons, Inc., Paris: Herman et Cie, 1949.

Wiener, Norbert. *The Human Use of Human Beings, Cybernetics and Society*. Boston: Houghton Mifflin Company, 1950.

Younghusband, Jan. *Orchestra! Foreword by Sir Georg Solti & Dudley Moore*. North Pomfret, Vermont: Trafalgar Square Publishing, 1991.

Ziloti, Alexander I. *Vospominaniya I Pis'ma* [Memoirs and Letters]. Leningrad: Muzgiz, 1963

ARTICLES AND PERIODICALS

Bongaardt, Robert and Onno, Meijer G. "Bernstein's Theory of Movement Behavior: Historical Development and Contemporary Relevance." *Journal of Motor Behavior* 32, no. 1 (March 2000): 57-71.

Erzhemsky, George L. "Psychologicheskie Mechanizmy

Ispolnitel'skikh Deistvii Dirizhyora" [Psychological Mechanisms of Conductor's Performing Activities]. *Psihologicheskii Jurnal*, [Journal of Psychology], no. 2 (1983): 15-27.

Jacob, Evelyn. "Vygotsky and the Social Formation of Mind." *Anthropological Quarterly* 64, no. 2 (April 1991): 96-97.

Keller, Charles M., and Keller, Janet Dixon. "Imagery in Cultural Tradition and Innovation." *Mind, Culture & Activity* 6, no. 1 (1999): 3-33.

Leontiev, Dmitri A. "Znachenie I Lichnostnii Smisl: Dve Storoni Odnoi Medali" [The Meaning and Personal Concept: Two Sides of the Same Medal]. *Psihologicheskii Jurnal*, [Journal of Psychology], no. 5 (1996): 19-30.

Musin, Iliya A. *Vado Mecum.* Unpublished Manuscript and Abstracts of Musin's books: 1. *O Vospitanii Dirijera* [About Conductor's Development], 2. *Tehnika Dirijirovania* [Technique of Conducting], 3. *Uroki Jizni* [The Lessons of Life].

Tommasini, Anthony. "A Met Opera Guest Conductor Feels Overtones of Tension." *New York Times,* Arts Section (May 21, 2003): 1-3.

Niemi P., and Lehtonen, E. "Fore Period and Visual Stimulus Intensity: A Reappraisal." *Acta Psychology* 50 (1982): 73-82.

Nissen, M.-J. "Stimulus Intensity and Information Processing." *Perception and Psychophysiology* 2 (1977): 338-352.

INDEX

A

Active Relaxation 184, 228, 265, 273, 284, 317

Adler, Samuel 21, 26, 369

Advanced Techniques 110, 181, 188

Alcantara, Pedro de 49, 53, 78, 82, 83, 120, 155, 166, 167, 371

Alexander Technique 35, 49, 164, 371

Ancerl, Karl 146

Ancient Greece 15

Ancient Rome 15

Anokhin, Petr K. 53, 89, 118, 371

Ansermet, Ernest 4, 175

Anticipation 4, 30, 54, 77, 83-85, 88, 89, 107, 110, 114, 137, 138, 143, 168, 173, 174, 176, 177, 213, 214, 252, 326, 328, 329, 331-334, 357

    anticipatory beat 108

    anticipatory manner 30

    anticipatory mode 123, 353

anticipatory conceptual motion 92

communicative anticipatory technique 91

Appalachian Spring 250, 251

Apparatus (Conducting) vii, 70, 82, 115, 134, 159, 163, 197, 205, 222, 253, 329

    conductor's apparatus 56, 68, 84, 115, 118, 163, 192, 198, 215, 216, 223, 225, 294, 325, 343

    outer (physical) apparatus 134

    psycho-physical apparatus 61, 82

Applebaum, Samuel 48, 67, 370

Arm's Linear Position 193, 195, 197-199, 227, 234, 245, 262, 293

Audible Measuring 54, 173

Audible Time-beating 3, 17, 24, 138

B

Bach, Johann Sebastian 78, 79

Bandmaster 19, 76, 95

Barenboim, Daniel 34, 74, 372

Baroque Era 16

Baton 1, 2, 16, 24, 35, 54, 68, 74, 103, 108, 110, 124, 130, 147, 169, 192-194, 196, 343-347, 374, 375, 379, 382, 383

    baton as a time-giver 24

Battuta 38, 45, 54, 57, 61, 70, 95, 101, 175, 343

Beat 3-5, 16, 17, 28, 29, 38-40, 43-45, 49, 50, 54, 55, 65, 86, 99, 105, 106,

108, 114, 115, 126, 174, 175, 178-180, 188, 189, 192, 193, 195-198, 229, 234, 236-240, 242, 244, 245, 247-249, 252-254, 256-258, 260, 261, 263-265, 275, 277, 278, 281, 285-287, 296-299, 302, 303, 305

    beat subdivision 126, 249, 298, 299

    beating time 3, 16, 17, 19, 24, 25, 54, 56, 61, 66, 70, 77, 96, 99, 101, 138, 173

    beat-striking method 83, 84, 125, 353

    incomplete beat 296

    interactive modification of the beat 66, 173, 181, 253

    overcoming beat 40

Beethoven, Ludwig van 23, 78, 143, 154, 249, 261, 266, 296, 304, 308, 327, 334

Begging Gesture 127

Behavior 27, 44, 49, 53, 163, 206, 373, 378, 385

    human behavior 163, 165

Behavioral Science 85, 86, 206, 374

Benson, Herbert 7, 372

Benthall, Jonathan 104, 373

Berger, Nina Aleksandrovna 209, 372

Berlioz, Hector 25, 26, 31, 76, 78, 353

Bernstein, Leonard 117, 146

Bernstein, Nikolai 146, 176, 370, 383

Bichkov, Semyon Mayevich 86

Bilateral Symmetry 121

Biomechanics iii, 61, 145

    labor biomechanics 145

    social biomechanics 145

Bodegraven, Paul Van 196, 373

Bolshakov, V. Yu 206, 373

Bongaardt, Robert 385

Boston Symphony Orchestra 135

Brahms, Johannes 31, 114, 154, 189, 248, 261, 266, 304, 332

Brass Instruments 23, 24, 26, 43, 50, 62, 106, 107, 112, 183, 320, 323, 334

    trumpet 14, 16, 105, 106

    horn 14, 16, 105, 106

    trombone 21, 106

    tuba 22, 51, 106

Breath Control 184, 217, 219-221, 273, 312-315, 317-319, 321-323, 329

C

Celesta 182, 183

Chesterman, Robert 4, 62, 371

Chironomy 19

Choir 21, 26, 42, 106, 118, 183

Classical Period 16, 21

Cliché/Scheme 115, 133, 144, 157

Cliché/Symbol 132

Click 47, 51, 54-56, 86, 87, 115, 129, 180, 185, 244

Collective Performance 84, 156, 202, 203

Collective Self-organization 28, 84, 135, 137, 145

    collective internal leaders 137

Communication iv, xi, 3, 27, 51, 53-55, 68, 77, 85, 91, 96-100, 102, 103, 116, 117, 119-121, 129, 131, 138, 140, 143, 146, 150, 159-161, 173, 176, 191-195, 197, 199-201, 205-207, 274, 280, 343, 354-356, 374-377, 380, 385

    communicational channels 206

    communicational cycle 117, 166

    communicational method/tool x, 91, 181, 200

    communicational spot 103, 192-195, 336

    communicational transmitter 192

Concept Formation 7, 46, 47, 74, 88, 119-121, 128, 129, 138, 145, 274, 338

    composer's conjectural concept 80

    concept formative bonds 138

Conceptual technique 74, 84

    conceptual action 5, 87, 118, 140, 162, 201, 260, 265

    conceptual gesture 128, 149

    conceptual (informational) unit 91, 109, 145

    conceptual motion 11, 46, 47, 92, 141, 142, 145, 151, 168, 171, 176, 260, 294, 323, 326, 387 conceptual stimulus 90

conceptual upbeat 109, 171, 269

creative conceptual task 88, 125

Concertmaster 4, 24, 136, 137, 207

Conditioned Behavior 53

Conditioned Reflex 6, 36, 68

Conditioned Response 36, 37, 43, 57, 61, 65-67, 86, 89, 91, 92, 175

Conditioned Stimulus 57

Conducting

conducting apparatus xi, 70, 82, 115, 134, 160, 163, 191, 197, 205, 222, 341

conducting methodology 5, 69, 90, 95, 103, 129, 134, 156, 165, 176, 181, 192, 196, 214, 223, 236, 253

conducting on-the-beat 3, 4, 45, 54, 84, 86, 114, 173-175, 178, 181

conducting practical reflexes 33, 86, 165, 213, 240, 270, 273, 277, 322

conducting techniques ii, iii, v-vii, ix-xi, 1, 8, 9, 45, 84, 103, 106, 110, 132, 153, 159, 160, 163, 166, 171, 176-178, 181, 188, 191, 192, 196, 203, 205, 208, 209, 213-216, 222-224, 237, 244, 253, 260, 261, 265, 270, 275, 279, 296, 305, 312, 317, 325, 326, 331, 334, 338, 340, 343, 345, 353, 355-357, 361-368, 375, 376, 380, 386

Conductor's Action 3-5, 30, 41, 43, 44, 60, 84, 103, 107, 114, 116, 117, 122, 131, 135, 142, 170 177, 184, 216, 278, 331

conductor's artistic/creative intentions 56, 69, 82, 85, 116, 132, 133, 201, 235

conductor's inner impulse x, 87, 140, 142, 145, 146, 155-157, 178, 214, 236, 269, 326-330, 332 conductor's inner techniques 103, 131, 155, 201, 208, 325, 326, 333

conductor's motions iii, vii, 5, 45, 115, 123, 130, 223

conductor's space 192

conductor's toolkit ix, x, 216

Conductor's Apparatus 56, 68, 84, 108, 115, 117, 118, 163, 184, 190, 192, 198, 215-217, 223, 225, 294, 295, 312, 325, 343

Connington, Bill 35, 164, 170, 311, 378

Contour of Sound 64, 102-106, 108, 109, 112-118, 157, 170, 171, 180, 184, 185, 189, 191, 193, 194, 229, 248, 253, 260, 273-275, 294, 309, 317, 357

Coon, Dennis 30, 51, 373

Corsini, Raymond 46, 374

Coulston, Gillispie 374

Creative Will (Impulse) 142, 152, 153, 155, 201, 326

D

Decorous (Formal) Motion 129, 142

Del Mar, Norman 64, 183, 374

Descartes, Rene 6, 30

Dimensions of Conducting 93, 205, 208, 209, 242

> diagonal dimensions 121, 181, 245
>
> horizontal/linear dimensions 99, 121, 181, 184, 185, 205, 229
>
> multi-dimensional practical tool 63, 180, 181, 261, 294, 331
>
> psychological dimensions 191, 205, 208, 209

vertical dimensions 68, 180, 182-185, 209

Dotted Rhythm 241, 247, 297-299

Downbeat 174, 193, 196-198, 225-230, 232, 238, 240, 242, 247, 254, 262, 271, 278, 281, 283-285, 287, 289, 291, 292, 300, 306-308, 312, 314, 319, 346

    downbeat position 196, 225-230, 232, 247, 254, 262, 283, 284, 287, 291, 300, 306, 307, 312, 314, 319, 346

Dudarova, Veronika Borisovna 208

Dworetzky, John P. 374

Dynamic (Enforced) Practical Method 39, 56, 61, 70, 100, 118, 132, 134, 175, 180, 240, 281, 322, 355

Dynamics (in Medical Sciences) 36, 86

    dynamic muscular relaxation 169, 170, 172, 322

    dynamic reflexes/responses 38, 140

    dynamic stereotypes 36, 37, 56, 59, 61, 86, 175

Dynamics (in Music) 18, 21, 22, 29, 37, 55, 64, 75-77, 90, 112, 113, 118, 123, 127, 153, 154, 171, 173, 180, 187, 188, 237, 238, 281, 296, 297, 309, 328, 330, 333, 334, 340, 345

E

Earhart, Will 372

Elbow 193, 195-197, 225, 226-228, 245, 255, 262, 318

Ensembles 3, 5, 13-16, 18, 21, 24, 47, 67-69, 91, 104, 105, 109, 136, 142, 145, 149, 154, 180, 184, 200, 237, 294

Ernst, Roy 55, 76, 244, 377

Erzhemsky, George (Georgii) L'vovich ix, xi, xii, 2, 5, 7, 19, 27, 35, 36, 38, 45, 48, 54, 56-60, 69, 76, 77, 88, 89, 91, 95, 96, 99, 100, 122, 124, 126, 130-132, 134, 137-140, 143, 147-149, 155, 172, 176, 178-179, 208, 305, 343, 359, 375, 385

Eschenbach, Christoph 86

Ewen, David 375

Exposition 195, 304, 327, 333

External Apparatus ix, xi, 129, 184, 191, 192, 196, 198, 215, 216, 330, 331

External Conducting Techniques 6, 26, 84, 76, 97, 120, 129, 130, 131, 135, 138-140, 146, 166, 170, 176, 180, 184, 191, 192, 196, 203, 213-216, 305

External Symmetry 122

External Transmitter 120, 147, 148, 192, 216

F

Farberman, Harold 55, 56, 68, 75, 103, 136, 143, 150, 180, 192, 375

Figured Bass 17

Flesch, Carl 29

Flick 129, 180

Force-coming (Overcoming) Conducting 40, 56, 62, 70, 87, 89, 96, 100, 101, 108, 114, 115, 118, 129, 132, 140, 145, 170, 174-177, 179-181, 187, 193, 198, 203, 240, 243, 244, 253, 277, 278, 280, 286, 322, 354

    force-coming mannerism 47, 48, 62, 70, 101, 114, 125, 175, 178, 193, 195, 270, 322

Forearm 166, 188, 193, 198, 225, 226, 228-231, 233, 253-259, 312, 314,

332, 337

Freedman, Norbert 207, 374, 377

French Revolution 20

Freud, Sigmund 206

Furtwängler, Wilhelm 4, 30, 78, 85, 117, 124, 148, 149, 174, 175

G

Galamian, Ivan 78, 79, 376

Galkin, Elliot W. 14, 20, 56, 74, 98, 146, 376

Gamble, Michael 206, 376

Gamble, Teri Kwal 206, 376

Gergiev, Valerie Abisalovich 86

Gesture ii, x, 6, 8, 64, 65, 76, 90, 103, 119, 127-129, 140, 141, 144, 153, 154, 161, 162, 174, 179, 184, 185, 235, 239, 249, 250, 262, 280, 293, 330, 338, 339

    communicative modification of the gesture 184

    gesture-unit 109, 128, 296

    informational gesture 92, 146

    paroxysmal, seizure like gestures 165

Ginzburg, Leo Moritsevich 28, 274, 376

Glinka, Mikhail Ivanovich 248

Grand, Stanley 207, 374, 377

Grant, Joe, W. 76, 244, 378

Green, Elizabeth A. H. 56, 99, 103, 376

Grosbayne, Benjamin 103, 196, 376

Guitar 182, 183

Guyton, Arthur 376

H

Handel, George Friedrich 18

Harp 14, 16, 21, 26, 42, 105, 106, 182, 183

Harpsichord 16-19, 22

Harrison, F. L. 18, 373

Havemann, Ernest 51, 377

Haydn, Joseph Franz 18

Hindemith, Paul 31, 154

Holden, Raymond 27, 80, 88, 377

Holmes, Malcolm H. 375

Houston Symphony Orchestra 86

Hunsberger, Donald 55, 76, 244, 377

Hypothalamus 125

I

Ictus 3, 11, 47, 54-56, 129, 173, 185, 274, 280

Idiosyncrasy 44

Illustrative Conducting 8, 96, 123, 130, 132, 146, 269, 274, 276, 355

Imaginary Orchestra 83, 333, 334

Informational Principles in Development of Conductor's Apparatus 150

Informative Gestures/Motions 45, 96, 123, 296

Informative Impulse 135, 142, 145, 239, 278

Informative (Informational) Action 87, 135, 141, 146, 269, 323, 338

Informative Techniques 148, 190, 323

Inner (Conducting) Techniques 103, 209, 325, 326, 331-333

    inner apparatus 135, 153, 201, 208, 209, 323, 329, 356

    inner creative impulse/stimulus 77, 120, 140, 142, 145, 146, 149, 152, 153, 155-157, 178, 191, 209, 214-216, 236, 269, 326-330, 332

    inner creative intentions 77, 87, 123, 124, 138, 147

    inner modeling of ideal sound 143

Inner Will 87, 152, 158, 326

Instrumental in Music 14, 15, 34, 45, 57, 59, 63, 66, 67, 77, 86, 89, 101, 105, 175, 280, 333, 334, 357, 373

    instrumental ensembles 13-15, 21, 22, 67

    instrumental performance 14, 16, 34, 36, 40, 42 45, 46, 57, 59-61, 71, 86, 88, 90, 116, 169, 175, 280, 333, 334, 357, 373

    instrumental practical reflexes (responses) 33, 42, 45, 57, 59, 61, 62, 67, 70, 91, 169, 175, 177, 273

    instrumental psycho-physical mindset 57

    instrumental stereotypes 36, 38, 59, 86, 89, 175

    instrumental techniques 124, 185

Instrumental in Psychology and Physiology 33, 37

Instrumentation 16, 25, 31, 98

Interactive Techniques 284, 311, 317

    divided attention 83

    formation of concept of upcoming sound 47, 274

    interactive relaxation 184, 229, 265, 273, 284, 294, 311, 317

    pendulum 140, 242, 305-307, 309

    sling 305

    sound transferring 62, 253, 265

Intercommunication 38, 55, 74, 81, 87, 100, 116, 130, 145, 150, 356

    intercommunicative bridge 141, 208

    intercommunicative conducting 31, 45, 69, 97, 100, 103, 128, 129, 133, 135, 138, 174, 188, 192, 196, 198, 201, 213, 216, 229, 248, 275, 356

    human intercommunication 100, 115, 130, 356

Inviting Gesture 127

J

Jacob, Evelyn 384

Jansons, Mariss H. 86

Jordan, James 19, 375

Jung, Carl Gustav 206

K

Kahn, Emil 180, 193, 244, 378

Kahn-Speyer (Chan-Speyer), Rudolf 147

Kagan, Jerome 51, 377

Kant, Immanuel 2

Kapellmeister 19, 21, 27, 75, 76

Kazdin, Allan E. 119, 372

Keller, Charles M. 386

Keller, Janet Dixon 386

Kinesthetic (Kinesthesia) 150

Kinetics 145, 150

Kohut, Daniel, L. 76, 244, 378

Kondrashin, Kirill Petrovich 154, 378

Konzertmeister 18, 19, 21

Koussevitsky, Sergey Aleksandrovich 135

L

Laszlo, Judith I. 378

Lehtonen, P. 52, 387

Leibowitz, Judith 35, 164, 170, 311, 378

Leinsdorf, Erich 379

Leningrad Philharmonic Orchestra 85

Leningrad (St. Petersburg) Conservatory 1, 209, 372, 373

Leontiev, Alexei Alexeevich 53, 162, 359, 379

Leontiev, Dimitri Alexeevich 78, 82, 121, 360, 377, 386

Linguistic(s) 75, 96, 97, 116, 131, 134, 138, 150, 216, 239, 356 lingual unit 88

linguistic principles in development of conductor's apparatus 294

para-linguistic 138

pseudo-linguistic 134

quasi-linguistic 5, 46, 69, 83, 96, 100, 138, 180, 294

Liszt, Franz 27-29, 76, 96, 353

Losev, Alexei Fedorovich 60, 379

Lumley, John 55, 180, 193, 379

Lyadov (Liadov), Anatoly Konstantinovich 1

M

MacRae, Donald G. 104, 122

Madame Butterfly 154

Mahler, Gustav 29, 31, 76, 80, 88, 98, 145, 147, 148, 154, 189, 353

Malko, Nicolai Andreyevich vii, ix, 1, 2, 8, 9, 15, 30, 34, 35, 45, 74, 85, 103, 145, 147, 152, 153, 174, 377, 380

Mandolin 183

Mariinsky (Kirov) State Opera House 86

Medial Thalamus 125

Meier, Gustav 50, 76, 192, 380

Mental Action 53, 60, 90, 110, 142, 152, 169, 175, 176, 180, 200, 312, 356

Mental (Conducting) Techniques 117, 132, 134, 155, 166, 168, 208, 213, 214

mental anticipation 83-85, 90, 66, 110, 138, 168, 171, 173, 177, 213, 214, 326, 328, 329, 332, 357

mental (inner) apparatus 83, 130, 209

mental sensation of connection to the sound 166, 170

technique of constant psychological advancing 110, 117, 155, 181, 215, 333

Metrical Points 66, 100, 179, 180, 184, 188, 189, 197, 239, 253, 261, 274, 296

Metrical (Conducting) Schemes 46, 55, 66, 77, 98-100, 104, 117, 130, 137, 138, 140, 174, 178-181, 185, 189, 190, 192, 193, 197-199, 227, 229, 238, 252, 253, 258, 261, 263, 265, 267, 274, 280, 286, 287, 302, 322, 336

communicative modification of metrical schemes 180, 267

conventional metrical schemes 90, 97-100, 116, 128, 138, 180, 267, 276

metrical clichés 98

measuring of metrical schematic 54, 76, 173, 179, 224, 225, 278, 329, 336, 337

practical tool of signs/clichés 98

Meter 21, 31, 51, 55, 98, 113, 174, 187, 197, 198, 244, 249, 252, 260, 298, 301, 302, 305, 309, 337, 350

doubled meter 92, 237, 239, 240, 249, 250, 252, 298, 299

double-meter beat/motion 237, 239, 240-242, 244, 247, 248, 250, 252, 260, 301, 302

metrical unit (beat) 101, 187, 189, 275

one-pattern triple-meter metrical figure 243, 249, 296, 350

tripled meter 237, 239, 243, 245, 247-250, 252, 260, 299, 302

Modes of Upbeat 92, 127, 203, 270, 278, 280, 286, 293, 294, 305, 340, 343

    converted suspended upbeat 92, 123, 127, 171, 279, 286, 288-292, 294, 340

    converted upbeat 92, 107, 123, 233, 270, 279, 286-288

    incomplete preparatory upbeat 296, 297, 300-302

    intermediary upbeat 47, 236, 238, 252, 275, 294

    suspended upbeat 92, 107, 127, 171, 181, 188, 270, 279-282, 284-286, 288-294, 298, 299, 340

    triple-meter upbeat 92, 239, 244, 247, 299, 309

Morozov, Semen M. 121

Motion

    centrifugal motions 140, 305

    centripetal motions 140, 305

    circled motions 189, 200, 220, 247

    curved motions 126, 185

    elliptical motions 189, 260, 262

    force-coming motions 75, 89, 129, 179, 244

    innate meaning of the motion/upbeat 146, 236, 269, 293

    lowest (breaking) point of the motion 3, 65, 104, 105, 109, 169, 173, 174, 178, 229, 234, 277, 283, 300, 307, 318

    motion-image 145

    motion-impulse 46, 88, 91, 109, 142, 144, 145, 148, 149, 184, 189, 190, 192, 252, 269, 276, 278, 322, 323

    motion-transmitter 145

rounded motion 184-186, 188, 189, 243, 247-249, 254, 256, 258-260, 274, 175, 187, 299, 309, 316, 319, 337, 351

straight-lined motions 125

varied 'eights' motions189

Mottl, Felix 1

Mozart, Wolfgang Amadeus 18, 22, 23, 266, 304, 333

Mravinsky, Eugeny Aleksandrovich 85, 143

Muscular Relaxation 66, 162-173, 184, 228, 229, 265, 273, 283, 284, 311, 312, 317, 318, 357

active muscular relaxation 163, 167, 172, 184, 228, 229, 265, 273, 284, 311, 312, 317, 329, 357

dynamic muscular relaxation 169, 172

Muscular Tension 68, 85, 86, 90, 140, 161, 167, 175, 196, 217-219, 228, 232, 235, 294, 314, 316

excessive muscular tension 168, 196, 217, 228, 232, 235, 295, 322

inefficient muscular coordination 163

muscular contraction 34, 40, 45, 61, 62, 88, 90, 169

Muscular *Tonus* (*Tonicity*) 167, 317

Musical Conception 82, 156

Musical Instruments 13, 14, 33, 34, 36, 37, 61, 63, 68

Musicians Union 7, 101, 207

Musikdirektor 20, 21

Musin, Ilya Aleksandrovich i, vii, xi, xiii, 8, 9, 37, 45, 47, 56, 62-64, 66, 67, 75, 85, 89, 92, 98, 117, 120, 123, 125, 127, 139, 138, 141, 144, 154, 162, 174, 180, 185, 214, 216, 219, 222-225, 237, 238, 240, 243, 248, 250,

254, 279, 286, 287, 289, 293, 296, 303, 305, 338, 339, 344, 345, 361-370, 380, 386

Musin's circles 185

N

Napoleonic Wars 20

Neuhaus, Genrich Gustavovich 82, 164

Neurobiological 53

Neurology 52, 206, 383

Neuroscience vii

Neuro-physiology 51

neuromuscular responses 163

New York Metropolitan Opera 86, 130

New York Philharmonic 143

Niemi, P. 52, 385

Nietzsche, Friedrich 82

Nikish, Arthur 4, 29, 30, 145, 175, 353

Nissen, M.-J. 52, 387

Non-communicative Conducting 70, 87, 134

Non-dynamic Conducting Techniques 62, 87

non-dynamic informational action 83, 87, 89

Non-forcible Physical Action

non-forcible mannerism in conducting 43, 100

non-forcible (conducting) techniques 8, 132, 135, 140

Non-instrumental Physical Action 38, 45

Non-verbal Communication vii, 88, 121, 145

    non-verbal codes 134

O

Onno, Meijer G. 383

Operative Apparatus 128

    operational cliché 146

    operational tools 146

Orchestra

    Mannheim Orchestra 18, 22

    Orchestra Seating 24

    Nebuchadnezzar's Orchestra 14

Orchestral Conducting i, 1, 6, 14, 33, 103, 127, 150, 163, 358, 376

Orchestral Instruments 18, 22, 69, 70, 105, 106, 109, 181

Orchestration 16, 21, 25, 26, 31, 63, 98, 112, 171, 182, 189, 275, 309, 327, 328, 371, 381

Orchestre de Paris 86

Organ 16, 18, 42, 43, 68, 106, 182, 183

Outer Conducting Techniques 134, 163, 191

Overcoming Conducting Manner 40, 47, 114, 115, 170, 203

P

Pandora's Box 144

Para 138

Para-communication 139

Para-linguistic 138

Paris Opera 17

Pavlov, Ivan Petrovich 35, 36, 53, 380

    Pavlov's dogs 53

Pazovsky, Ariy Moiseyevich 147

Pendulum 140, 244, 305-307, 309

Percussion Instruments 15, 22, 106, 320

    bass drum 22

    cymbals 182

    idiophone 182

    membranophone 182

    side drum 22, 61, 64-66, 70

    timpani 16, 64, 66, 106

    triangle 22

Petrushka 250, 251

Philadelphia Symphony Orchestra 86

Phylogenesis 69

Physical Action 2, 38, 40, 86, 87, 133, 150, 169-171, 176, 312

Physical *Decoder* of Thoughts 161

Physical Energy 5, 87, 91

Physical Sensation of Connection to the Sound 166, 170

Physical Tension 36, 57, 68, 87, 140, 162, 164, 222

Piano (Pianoforte) 18, 22, 35, 66, 67, 76, 82, 106, 164, 177, 183, 284, 321, 331, 335

Piston, Walter 63, 182, 183, 379

Pitch Registration 150

Plane (Flatness) of Conducting 24, 27, 112, 229, 231, 233, 248, 240, 241, 245, 247, 252, 254, 259, 262, 263, 284, 287, 291, 337

Polhemus, Ted 104, 373

Prausnitz, Frederik 81, 136, 180, 193, 381

Preparatory Upbeat 47, 67, 153, 237-240, 243, 252, 297, 300, 301

Primary (Body) Posture 226, 312, 314, 316, 328, 339-341

Primary Downbeat Position 229, 319

    primary arm position 199, 223, 225

Principle of Dominant 125-6

Prokhorov, A. M. 379

Psychodynamics 86

Psychology x, 30, 37, 46, 48, 51, 52, 78, 82, 85, 88, 99, 119, 121, 122, 134, 160, 177, 206, 207, 358, 362, 371, 373-375, 377, 379, 384, 386, 387

    behavioral psychology 85

    psychology of conducting 48, 99

    psychological reaction on signal 89, 91

    psychological stereotype 206

Psycholinguistics vii, x, 85, 88, 131, 375

    psycholinguistic principles of conducting 45

Psycho-motor Skills 131

Psychophysiology iii, ix, x, 52, 387

    psycho-physical conducting techniques 63, 82, 171

    psycho/physical exercise in imagination and visualization 153

    psycho-physical functions of conducting ix, 69, 86, 89, 133, 155, 317

    psycho-physical (intercommunicative) action 2, 36, 38, 40, 42, 52, 53, 76, 87, 170, 175, 176, 202, 213

Puccini, Giacomo 154

Q

Quasi-linguistic 5, 69, 83, 96, 100, 138, 295

    quasi-lingual 46, 180

R

Reaction 5, 34, 41, 44, 46-49, 51-53, 57, 88-91, 104, 105, 116, 117, 120, 125-127, 135, 141-146, 148, 319-321

Rebound iii, 64, 103, 109, 114, 115, 177, 231, 240, 241, 244, 252, 281, 285, 286, 293, 296, 297, 298-302

    accentuated rhythmically-contingent rebound 297

    non- accentuated rhythmically-contingent rebound 297

    non-suspended rhythmically-contingent rebound 299

    non-suspended triple-meter rhythmically-contingent rebound 299 rhythmically-contingent rebound 107, 188, 297, 300-303

suspended rhythmically-contingent rebound 298, 299

suspended triple-meter rhythmically-contingent rebound 299

Reflex xi, 6, 33, 36, 37, 41, 43, 45, 57, 59, 61, 63, 68, 70, 86, 133, 140, 163, 165, 175, 213, 240, 270, 273, 277, 322

reflex action 6

Reiner, Fritz 58, 148

Rejection Gesture 127

Relaxation

interactive relaxation 284

primary relaxed physical mode 169

relaxation response 7, 370

technique of instant muscular relaxation 285, 292, 313, 314

Renaissance 15

Response 36, 37, 43, 57, 61, 65-67, 86, 89, 91, 175

involuntary response 6

repertoire of responses 35, 36

Reticular Formation 125

Rhoades, Rodney A. 217, 379

Richter, Karl 145

Rimsky-Korsakov, Nikolai Andreyevich 1, 209, 248, 304, 373

Robinson, Paul 381

Rolland, Romain 139, 148

Ropper, Allan H. 52, 383

Ross, Allan 180, 193

Rossini, Gioachino 296

Roth, Henry 48, 67, 372

Rounded Motion 184-186, 188, 189, 243, 247-249, 254, 256, 258-260, 274, 175, 187, 299, 309, 316, 319, 337, 346

>interactive modification of the rounded motion 186, 188, 274

Rudolf, Max 54, 76, 103, 105, 108, 180, 184, 193, 381

S

Sadie, Stanley 1, 9, 14, 15, 17, 18, 54, 380

Saito, Hideo 65, 382

Salomon, Johann Peter 18

Scherchen, Heinrich 74, 87

Schmid, Adolf 380

Schonberg, Arnold 31

Schonberg, Harold C. 24, 30, 124, 136, 382

Schuller, Gunther 58, 78, 80, 83, 137, 382

Scooping Gesture 120, 233-258, 260

Segalowitz, Sidney, J. 119, 378

Semantics 95, 96

>mono-semantic meanings 121, 138

>semantics of conducting 100, 116

>semantics of gesture 119, 145, 339

Serenade for Strings 248, 304

Serov, Aleksander Nikolaevich 123

Signal/Cliché 100

Sittard, Josef 88

Skinner, Jeffry 2, 375

Sling Gesture 305

Slonimsky, Nicolas 4, 78, 372

Solti, George 13, 74, 385

Spitzer, John 16, 22, 382

Spohr, Louis (Ludwig) 23-25

Spot of Communication 194

Springthorpe, Nigel 55, 180, 193, 379

Stamitz, Johann 18

Stanislavsky, Konstantin Sergeyevich 83, 164, 208, 380, 382

State (Psychological and Physical) 41, 50, 52, 327

    emotional state 48, 52, 327

Status 50, 52

Stern, Issac 48, 67

Stimulus 5, 6, 34, 46, 51, 52, 57, 66, 87, 88, 104, 126, 127, 156, 157, 167, 387

    audible stimulus 5, 51, 52, 85

    stimulus conditioned 57

    stimulus visual 5, 51, 52, 85, 87, 104, 105, 127, 387

Stoddard, Hope 383

Stoessel, Albert 196, 383

St. Petersburg (Leningrad) Conservatory 1, 209, 370

St. Petersburg Philharmonic Symphony Orchestra 85

Strauss, Johannes Jr. 309

Strauss, Richard 31, 139, 147, 148, 189

Stravinsky, Igor Fyodorovich 31, 250

Strike 3, 4, 17, 33, 47, 54, 66, 87, 95, 106, 125, 129, 140, 169, 175, 179, 180, 187, 189, 197, 198, 231, 232, 234, 240, 253, 275, 279, 289, 308

    beat-strike 3, 5, 38, 39, 44, 48, 54, 106, 173

    force-coming (striking) mannerism 129, 280

    inaudible strike 101

    interactive modification of the strike 187, 253

    on-the-strike 3

    striking stroke 129

    visual strike 173, 178, 274

    wrist strike 54, 188, 231, 232, 244, 257, 262

String Ensemble 16

String Instruments 15, 16, 23, 42, 49, 57, 62, 63, 68, 105, 106, 112, 116, 182, 320, 328, 332, 334

    violin 17-19, 22, 23, 35, 49, 62, 63, 70, 79, 106, 376

    viola 22, 70

    cello 62

    double bass 42, 49, 106, 135

Subthalamus 125

Symphonic Conducting 1

Syntax 96, 97

Syntax of Conducting 95, 97, 102, 116

T

Tanner, George A. 78, 217, 381

Tchaikovsky, Pyotr Ilyich 113, 248, 304, 308, 327, 328, 339

Tcherepnin, Nikolai Nikolayevich 1

Techne 82

Temirkanov, Yuri Khatuevich 86, 123

Temporal 89, 91, 106, 237, 281, 289, 292, 296

    temporal delay 42, 43, 106, 107, 183, 297

    temporal interval 3, 5, 6, 44, 104

    temporal lag 106, 107

    temporal marks 79

    time-gap 43, 104

Time-lag 3, 5, 41-46, 69, 106, 107-110, 113, 176, 183, 184, 193, 323

Tommasini, Anthony 386

Tonicity 167

Touché 89

Tourte, Francois Xavier 22

    Tourte-style bow 22

Traffic-control Type of Conducting vii, x, 124, 235

U

Unconditioned response/reflex 36, 89, 91, 163

Underground Conductors 137

Upbeat 42, 45, 47, 67, 68, 77, 92, 109, 118, 123, 136, 143, 146, 151, 153, 154, 171, 179, 188, 235-245, 247-250, 252, 254, 260, 261, 265, 267, 269, 270, 273-282, 285-290, 292-297, 299-302, 305, 309, 320, 322, 323, 326, 327, 329, 330, 340

    incomplete upbeat 92, 297, 301, 302

    incomplete preparatory upbeat 92, 296, 300

    interactive modification of the upbeat 188, 270

Upbeat-Impulse 109, 237, 238, 269, 327

V

Verbal Apparatus 161

Verbal Communication 120, 121

Vicinity of Sound 63, 103, 106, 112, 115, 117, 228, 229, 248, 260, 270, 274, 341

Victor, Maurice 52, 381

Viennese Classical School 97

Viotti, Giovanni Battista 22

Visual Impulse 54, 185, 274, 280

Vygotsky, Lev Semyonovich 88, 100, 119, 131, 134, 383, 386

W

Wagner, Richard 25-27, 29, 31, 76, 81, 153, 154, 355, 377, 384

Walter, Bruno 8, 62, 63, 74, 79, 80, 381, 384

Waltzes 309, 350

Waxman, Maron L. 379

Weber, Carl Maria von 24

Weingartner, Felix 27, 78, 153, 154, 384

Westrup, Jack 14, 15, 17, 18, 373

Wiener, Norbert xi, 150, 384, 385

Wilson, Conrad 373

Wilson, Robert Harry 196, 373

Wolman, Benjamin B. 206, 374

Woodwind Instruments 23, 24, 43, 50, 62, 106, 112, 320, 334

    piccolo 21, 50

    flute 16, 22, 50, 304

    oboe 16, 22, 50, 105, 332

    English horn 21, 50

    clarinet 16, 18, 22, 50, 332

    bass clarinet 50

    bassoon 16, 21 22, 50

    contrabassoon 21, 50

Wrist 54, 56, 188, 193-195, 198, 226, 227, 229-234. 244, 253-257, 259, 262, 265, 266, 271, 283, 312, 314, 317, 318, 332, 337, 344, 347, 349-351

modification of the wrist strike 232, 257, 262

wrist rounded motion 254-256, 259, 265, 266

wrist strike 54, 188, 231, 232, 244, 257, 262

Wundt, Wilhelm 30

Y

Younghusband, Jan 13, 14, 19, 20, 22-24, 26, 385

Z

Zaslaw, Neal 14, 16, 22, 382

Ziloti, Alexander Ilyich 28, 385

Oleg Proskurnya

Dr. Oleg Proskurnya is an Assistant Professor of Music and the Director of Orchestras at Beloit College in Beloit, Wisconsin. Dr. Proskurnya holds a Doctor of Musical Arts degree in Orchestral Conducting from the University of South Carolina. He founded the International Academy of Advanced Conducting in 1997.